ISBN 978-1-333-08324-3
PIBN 10277385

This book is a reproduction of an important historical work. Forgotten Books uses state-of-the-art technology to digitally reconstruct the work, preserving the original format whilst repairing imperfections present in the aged copy. In rare cases, an imperfection in the original, such as a blemish or missing page, may be replicated in our edition. We do, however, repair the vast majority of imperfections successfully; any imperfections that remain are intentionally left to preserve the state of such historical works.

1 MONTH OF
FREE
READING

at

www.ForgottenBooks.com

By purchasing this book you are eligible for one month membership to ForgottenBooks.com, giving you unlimited access to our entire collection of over 1,000,000 titles via our web site and mobile apps.

To claim your free month visit:

www.forgottenbooks.com/free277385

HIGHLANDS OF
ASIATIC TURKEY

HIGHLANDS OF
ASIATIC TURKEY

BY

EARL PERCY, M.P.

ILLUSTRATED

LONDON

EDWARD ARNOLD

Publisher to H.M. India Office

1901

TO

MY TURKISH FRIENDS

AND

THE FRIENDS

OF

TURKEY

CONTENTS

LIST OF ILLUSTRATIONS

* *These illustrations are from photographs taken by* A. HEBER PERCY, Esq.

HIGHLANDS OF
ASIATIC TURKEY

HIGHLANDS OF ASIATIC TURKEY

CHAPTER I

EASTWARD HO!

" *Ashiga Bagdad uzak deyl dir.*" "To the lover it is no far cry to Bagdad." So runs the Turkish proverb, and it was partly the peculiar fascination which Asiatic Turkey exercises over all who know it well, that drew me in the summer of 1899 to embark upon my third expedition into the interior.

I had on previous occasions already traversed the wooded highlands and bleak steppes that lie between Lake Van and the Black Sea, and the wild mountainous district of Hakkiari that forms the watershed of the Upper Zab, the Bohtan, and other affluents of the Tigris. I had crossed from the Mesopotamian Valley to the Mediterranean by the stony and forbidding track which, following the course of the Lower Euphrates from Hit to Deir, diverges through the Palmyra oasis to Damascus; and by the more interesting highroad that connects the crowded cities of Mosul, Diarbekr, and Urfa with the Upper Euphrates at Biredjik, and restores the traveller to civilisation at Aleppo. But as yet I knew nothing of those mighty ranges of the west, the Anti-Taurus and the Taurus, through whose gorges the "great river" forces its way

A

on that long and devious pilgrimage from its cradle in the uplands of Erzerum to the desert confines of Syria and the marshy plains of Chaldea.

With the general characteristics of much of this part of the country every one is of course familiar who has read that most fascinating of all recent books of travel, "The Wandering Scholar in the Levant," and the interesting address delivered by Mr. Vincent Yorke at a meeting of the Royal Geographical Society in 1895. But the road followed by these two authors lay northward through Erzingian to Trebizond, whereas the one which I wished to pursue is that which runs in an easterly direction, for the most part along the bed of the river, from Malatia through Kharput, Palu, and Mush—probably the least well-known of all the great caravan routes to the Persian frontier.

Scarcely any one ever travels in these regions for pleasure, and those whose official duties or commercial interests compel them to visit such centres as Kharput or Van, naturally select the easier and more direct roads through Samsun and Sivas, or through Trebizond and Bitlis. Whatever information one may wish to procure with regard to the more circuitous and difficult routes must be obtained either from missionaries, few of whom have lived for many years in the country, or else from Consuls, who, during their brief residence in the remoter provinces, have been able to devote some of their leisure time to exploration, and have, it may be, buried their experiences in the pages of a Parliamentary Blue Book, from which they can only be disinterred at the cost of an abnormal expenditure of time and trouble.

Never have I experienced such acute discomfort, even among the tribal settlements and camps of the

Arabs and Kurds, as I was forced to put up with in many of the squalid hovels which afford the only available night's shelter on this "main" road. It would be affectation to pretend that experiences of that kind enhance the pleasure of travel, and yet I firmly believe that they contribute materially, even if they are not actually indispensable, to the profit to be derived from it. The more one sees of Oriental countries, the more strong becomes one's conviction that, without associating with the people, and living to some extent, at all events, the same life as theirs, one can practically learn little or nothing about them. The traveller on the Nile who threads the half-modernised bazaars of Cairo, or chaffers for *anticas* with the itinerant dealers of Assuan or Luxor, leaves Egypt almost as ignorant of the habits and modes of thought of the fellaheen as if he had never been there. Anglo-Indians who have spent the best years of their life in the most untutored of the native States, are the first to admit how little they know of the feelings and ideas of that vast congeries of race and religion whose interests are confided to their charge, but with whose daily routine and domestic society they are absolutely and necessarily out of touch. It is the main reason which, to my mind, robs a journey in the interior of Morocco of half the interest it would otherwise possess, that the condition of that country, and the native dislike for the foreigner, precludes him from the possibility of intimate intercourse with its people. He cannot, without grave risk, diverge from the recognised routes for which the Government provides him with an escort, and when, each night, he pitches his camp within the enclosure of prickly pear and aloe that surrounds the Moorish village, he lives in his own tent, and not in the huts or tents of the natives. Those who, like Mr. Harris, have been long enough in the country to acquire an intimate acquaintance with its language, form, no doubt, a conspicuous exception to the rule; but the average visitor does not and cannot see more than the mere externals of the daily life of a people whose natural antipathy to Europeans is probably only excelled by that of the Chinese.

In Asiatic Turkey the conditions are altogether different. I know of no Mussulman country in which hospitality is so cordially and lavishly extended to the stranger by men of every class, race, and creed, or in which less hesitation is displayed in admitting him to the society of the domestic circle. Over and over again I have seen a Turkish or Armenian peasant, acting under no compulsion whatever, evict from his house his own women and children in order to make room for visitors, when there is no recognised *odagh* or guest-house provided for their accommodation; and that not merely in the settled districts that lie along the great arteries of communication, but even in the wildest haunts of the untamed nomads of Kurdistan. True, it is a hospitality which has its inconveniences in the insatiable though unwittingly impertinent curiosity of your hosts, and the indescribable filth and squalor of its surroundings. You will pass many a sleepless night, and ride off in desperation before the first streak of daylight to escape from the swarming legions that issue from roof and walls to greet the unfortunate intruder. Even when convinced by ocular demonstration of the presence of these noisome tenants, which at first is always strenuously denied, an eloquent shrug of the shoulders will testify to the inability of your entertainers to comprehend the acute annoyance that it causes. You may protect yourself by sleeping in your tent, and in some villages the cabins are so airless, so heavy with the reek of cattle and the smoke of *tezek* (dung) fires, that no averagely constituted European could endure them for more than an hour or two. But it is precisely in these places that the erection of separate quarters for yourself is often attended with the greatest risk and difficulty. The snow is perhaps lying several inches deep on the ground, or the only level spot available is a pool of standing water. During the late autumn the thunder-storms often burst with such terrific violence, and are accompanied with such a deluge of rain, that even if you succeed in pitching your tent before the storm breaks, you will assuredly wake after a brief and troubled slumber to find yourself without a stitch of canvas overhead and your baggage drenched through. Indeed, you may think yourself fortunate if the baggage is there at all, for the natives are proficient thieves, and unless a very strict watch is kept by the zaptiehs and muleteers, they will find an opportunity for pilfering, more especially if they know that a rifle, a gun, or even a pistol, may be the reward of their dexterity.

So long as you put up in a native house, and it will generally be that of the village headman, you may feel tolerably secure against attempts of the kind, since your host will regard himself as morally, if not legally, responsible for your safety. In the whole course of my experience, I have never once had to complain of theft while under a native roof, except among the Kurds of Mount Ararat, who are, of course, under Russian, not Turkish jurisdiction. But when camping out, I have often found it necessary to rely on my own vigilance, owing to the impossibility of trusting either the muleteers or the zaptiehs. It may happen that you have no discretion in the choice of the former, and however much you may dislike the appearance of a "katirgi," you must take him or remain where you are. He will look after his animals, provided that you have made it clear that you accept no responsibility for them, and travellers in Asiatic Turkey cannot be too strongly warned against buying their own animals from a mistaken motive of economy. But he will look after nothing in which he has not a personal interest. Unlike the Moor, he is the laziest and most intractable of servants, and when the weather is cold or inclement, he will always seek refuge, if he can, in some neighbouring hovel, and leave a solitary " gendarme " to maintain guard over the camp.

As a class, and a much-maligned one, I have a great admiration for these "zaptiehs." Badly clothed and worse paid, continually on the road in all weathers, and subsisting for days together on a few crusts of bread and a little rice, their spirits seem never to flag, and, as I have had cause to know, they are ready to prove their fidelity even at the cost of their lives.[1] They have been abused for their insolence and brutality to the peasants and their rapacity in collecting the taxes, and that there is some ground for the accusation I do not deny. Considering the class from which they are selected, the utter lack of all humanising elements in their surroundings, and their absolute dependence on the will of their superiors, it would be surprising if such were not the case. But put any body of European soldiers in their place, place them under the same conditions, give them the same schooling and the same opportunities of tyranny and oppression, and the Turkish zaptieh would, in comparison, appear a paragon of moderation and discipline.

[1] " Notes from a Diary in Asiatic Turkey," p. 181.

Certainly I have never seen any evidence of the universal detestation of these men which some writers have asserted to exist among the villagers of the interior. Isolated instances of bullying, of blackguardism and extortion, and a general assumption of superiority is, I believe, all that can honestly be charged against them. I have seen them sitting over their evening meal joking and chaffing in the most friendly way with the peasants, Moslem and Christian alike. I have joined in the conversation, and heard them corroborate the grievances of those whom they are supposed to browbeat and oppress, and endorse their complaints of the rapacity of governors and the lawlessness of neighbouring tribes. I have known them disregard the orders of their superiors and risk their displeasure rather than expose me to danger or annoyance, and on several occasions I have heard the villagers inform them that unless they asked politely for what they wanted, they might go elsewhere and forage for us and for themselves as best they could. That is by no means an uncommon experience among some of the hill-folk, who resent the intrusion of these men, not because of their character, but because of their uniform, and the claim which it implies of an authority over their country on the part of the Government which they are exceedingly reluctant to admit. I once travelled for many miles with a zaptieh who, having at the outset discarded both his uniform and his rifle, plainly regarded himself as little more than an apologetic testimonial to my own good character and peaceable intentions. Under such circumstances the gendarme is of little use except in so far as the fact of his presence enables one to hold the Government responsible for any loss or damage one may sustain on the journey—a responsibility which they

would otherwise consider themselves justified in re-
pudiating.

For these reasons it is always safer, and certainly
more interesting, to put up in the native houses wherever the conditions are tolerable, for it is only by so
doing that you gain the opportunity of seeing the
people at their ease and of eliciting information in
the ordinary course of conversation without increasing
their natural reserve by conveying to them the impression that they are being subjected to a cross-
examination. To propound leading questions, suggested
by the preconceived ideas of yourself or others, is of
course perfectly futile, for, like the Irishman, they will
always give the answer which they imagine you prefer,
and will cheerfully follow up the information by statements on the same subject which no human ingenuity
could reconcile. The only way is to let them talk,
and throw in a word now and then which may turn
the conversation in the direction you desire. All
Orientals are children, and the average native of
Anatolia and Kurdistan is not only a child, but one
of very limited intellectual capacity. His deficiencies
in this respect are the results, not so much of a limited
education, as of low mental calibre, and many of the
traits that are commonly attributed to obstinacy among
the upper classes, or to apathy and fatalism among the
lower, arise in fact from a constitutional inability on
the part of both to understand the ideas which are
almost self-evident to ourselves. Even the better informed among them often impress one as being quite
incapable of deducing the most obvious conclusions
from admitted premises, or of forming approximately
coherent opinions of their own.

For anything which requires a talent for organisation, whether in the sphere of the public service or of

private enterprise, the Turk is generally incompetent, and therefore obliged to fall back on the sharper and more adaptable faculties of the Greek and Armenian. And it is this superiority of intellect—not any educational advantage or inferiority of physical condition, that makes the Armenian peasant more keenly sensitive to the evils of his situation than his Mussulman fellow-subject and neighbour. The one is not only conscious of, but is apt to overrate his own abilities, and cousequently, even when not subjected to actual oppression, resents, no less in Russia than in Turkey, any conditions which impede their free exercise. The other, unconscious of any such endowment in himself, and partly denying, partly despising its existence in his more pushing rival, remains equally indifferent to all misgovernment which does not assume the tangible form of personal ill-treatment and spoliation. Even in that case his resentment is mitigated by his conviction that it is, after all, a necessary part of the system which has existed for centuries, which seems to him a law of nature, and from which he, in his measure, may reap some benefit. Set up an incorruptible judiciary, devise an equitable basis of assessment, and enforce impartiality in the collection of the taxes, and the first feeling of the peasants themselves would be that you were attempting to defraud them of the opportunities which they now enjoy of making advantageous bargains with the tax-farmer and the judge.

People at home who cry out in righteous indignation when a good governor is reported to have been removed from a province in which he has, at great personal sacrifice to himself, done his best to reform the administration, are perhaps too apt to forget that it is precisely against men of that character that the greatest number of petitions are forwarded to Constantinople from the locality demanding their recall. There is no desire for reform, in the sense in which we understand the word, among the masses of the population. They are not heavily taxed, and they occasionally succeed in compounding with the collectors for a smaller sum than they ought to pay. If unable to defend themselves against the raids of a robber tribe or to retaliate with advantage, they would of course like to see their tormentors suppressed. But they know from experience that this operation will entail the quartering of the soldiery upon themselves, and on the whole they prefer to wait until some rival tribe has asserted its superiority over their enemies, or until both have been so weakened by their mutual feuds that they become equally innocuous to others.

On the other hand, there is a general and a growing feeling among them that their condition is steadily altering for the worse. They are undeniably poorer than they were, their taxation has not been lightened, and they are aware, and impatient, of the constantly increasing demands made from Constantinople for large drafts of money from the local exchequers, while little or nothing is expended upon the development of the provinces. That is a feeling which, if it is allowed to grow, will eventually undermine, although it may never lead to an open repudiation of, the Sultan's authority. It must be remembered that one of the inevitable and most irreparable consequences of the attacks directed five years ago against the life and property of the Armenians has been to impoverish, and well-nigh to exhaust, one of the richest sources of revenue which the Eastern provinces possessed. The Armenians were the wealthiest and most industrious class of the population, the greater part of the business of commerce and exchange was in their hands, and the proceeds of the annual war-tax levied upon their men in lieu of military service amounted in the aggregate to a very considerable sum. It is impossible to form any accurate estimate of the number of those who perished in the massacres, who fled to Russian territory, or who have since emigrated to America and other countries of the West. But that it was sufficiently large to inflict a grave pecuniary loss on Turkey is certain, and if that loss is to be made up, it can only be by the imposition of new taxation, which the Mussulmans and the poorer Armenians are unable to bear, or else by a very substantial reduction of expenditure. Half measures are no longer possible if the Turkish Empire is to retain more than the shadow of its independence, and there is no symptom so ominous at the present moment as the widespread apprehension which exists among every class of the inhabitants that nothing can now avert or arrest that decline in their material prosperity of which they are becoming more keenly sensible every day.

In selecting the route which I have described, my ultimate object was to make a more systematic and detailed exploration than I had hitherto been able to do of the little known country of the Nestorian Christians, which is bounded on the west, from Bitlis to Mosul, by the river Tigris, and on the east by the frontier line of Persia, between the latitudes of Lake Urmí and Kermanshah. The conditions of life in that region, among what may be regarded as the last of the independent clans, are as unique in their character and interest as the political problems to which they give rise ; and recent developments, of which I had received accounts from time to time since my last visit, made me no less anxious to renew my acquaintance with the principal actors in the drama, now apparently approaching its climax, than to add something, if possible, to the rather scanty geographical knowledge which we at present possess of the remoter and less accessible districts. Before my departure from England I had received, through Her Majesty's Ambassador at Constantinople and his Excellency the Turkish Ambassador in London, the honour of a cordial invitation from His Majesty the Sultan to pay a visit to Yildiz on my way; and it was with little suspicion of the impending war with the Transvaal, of the outbreak of which I remained in absolute ignorance until some months afterwards, that I set out with my cousin, Mr. Algernon Heber Percy, in the third week of August, for that most beautiful of all the cities of the world, the Gate of East and West.

CHAPTER II

WE reached Costanza, the Roumanian seaport, after midnight, and went on board at once. It was a pretty glimpse, a line of twinkling lights fringing the low promontory, a crowd of ships and fishing craft in harbour, and eastward the placid stretch of waters sleeping in the "long glories" of the moon.

To any one who is already familiar with the magnificent route through the Balkans, the Vienna-Costanza line offers two distinct advantages. You save a night in the train (and two are quite enough in the dust and heat of midsummer), and you also feel that you are entering Constantinople by the front door instead of being smuggled in at the back. But the features of the country between the Austrian capital and the coast, dreary interminable flats, often submerged for miles, and wayside stations decorously and hideously Europeanised, are not calculated, it must be confessed, to interest or enliven the traveller.

The Black Sea crossing occupies a little over twelve hours, the steamer just touching at the Asian shore of the Bosphorus to put down the Roumanian mails before she drops anchor in the Golden Horn. I stayed but a short time in the town, in order to complete the necessary outfit for the journey and to visit the collections in the Museum at Stamboul, which, admirably arranged under the direction of Hamdi Bey, have recently acquired fresh interest by the addition of the most remarkable finds from the American excavations at Niffur. The interior of St. Sophia was being repaired at considerable expense, and, owing largely to the Sultan's liberality, the bazaars had recovered something of that stately magnificence which they wore before the earthquake a few years ago. The only other noticeable change was the attempt for the first time to introduce the electric light into Pera, an attempt which, if current gossip is to be believed, required some ingenuity as well as patience on the part of the promoters. When the original dynamo was ordered, the authorities, it is said, took fright at a word so suggestive of explosives, and the infernal machine was only smuggled in eventually by sending it through the custom-house in separate and unsuspicious-looking pieces.

My audience with His Majesty was to take place after the Selamlik on the following Friday, and Sir Nicholas O'Conor, having business to transact in the city, had asked me to meet him at the Porte, where I hoped to have the pleasure of meeting the Grand Vizier and H.E. Tewfik Pasha, the Foreign Minister. The latter, however, was detained at the palace, but Rifat Pasha, a striking personality with his white beard, slim figure, and old-fashioned courtly demeanour, received me most civilly, and asked many questions about my experiences in the country south of Erzerum and Baiburt, where some of the early years of his life had been spent.

Having taken our leave, we threaded the long bare passages of the building, which swarmed with a motley throng of secretaries lounging about and talking—in strange contrast to the formality and decorum of an office at Whitehall—and drove down to the quay at Topkhane, where the Embassy launch was waiting to convey us to Therapia. On our way up the Bosphorus we stopped to make a brief call on Mr. Strauss, the able and genial representative of the United States, at the pretty house which stands low down by the water's edge, and completed a delightful day by a brief stroll in the evening towards the village of Buyukdere.

Over the northern sky hung a sheet of livid blue thunder-clouds, seamed in every direction by quick forks and splutters of rose-coloured lightning, which, long after night had fallen, shone with an almost noon-day brilliancy on the rising waters of the narrow strait. The morning of the 25th, however, broke in cloudless sunshine, the air as mild and balmy as on a spring day in England, and the beautiful terraced gardens of the Embassy were fragrant with the mingled scent of the fir-woods and flowers, among which fluttered a host of huge red-winged privet moths, purple empe-rors and white admirals. Going on board the launch soon after eleven, we dropped down a short distance to the Yeui Keui pier, and drove between a double line of regiments to the house overlooking the mosque, where rooms are reserved for the Ambassadors and any of their friends who may wish to watch the weekly pageant of the royal procession. Soon after we had taken our seats the master of the ceremonies, a short-bearded Afghan, came up to present the Sultan's com-pliments, and the troops being by this time ranged in position below, the ceremony began.

On the side of the street leading from the palace were placed the ordinary regiments of the line, two men being posted at intervals by the side of each tree, lest the wooden palisades surrounding the trunks might afford a hiding-place for would-be disturbers of the peace. Opposite them were stationed the Arab troops from the Hedjaz in their gorgeous blue and red striped uniforms, with scarlet turbans on their heads circled by broad green twisted cords. To the right, in the direction of Constantinople, where, just outside the mosque enclosure, the common people assemble, sat the mounted lifeguards with the red pennons fluttering from their lance-heads, and beyond the dazzling white of the tapering minarets lay soft and hazy the sail-flecked, violet-tinted sea and the faint grey-blue lines of the Asian shore and the island of Prinkipo.

Presently the ladies of the harem drove up at a foot's pace in closed carriages, while behind them walked a group of the royal princes, followed at a short interval by Edhem Pasha, the late commander in Thessaly, a stout brown-bearded man of middle age, and the other officers of the staff. Standing conspicuously together a little in front of the troops, and also on foot, were the Sultan's favourite son, his tutor, and two small play-fellows. The prince, who held his sword drawn, is young and pleasant-looking, and bears a marked resemblance to his father. His chances of occupying the throne are at present remote, for by the Turkish custom, which vests the succession in the eldest male branch of the reigning family, the next heir is his uncle, the Sultan's brother, and after him the descendants of Abdul Aziz, the murdered predecessor of Murad, whose madness keeps him a prisoner still in one of the palaces of the Bosphorus. This fact, it may be remarked in passing, is in itself a sufficient refutation of the assertion which has been made in some quarters that Murad owes his life to the Sultan's fear of similar reprisals against his own son.

Scarcely had the ladies of the court and the generals taken their places, when the voice of the Muezzin was heard calling to prayer from the gallery of the minaret, the troops presented arms, and the short sharp howl, which is the Turkish mode of cheering, went up three times in rapid succession as the Padishah's carriage turned the corner, preceded by several riderless horses of the purest Arab breed. The forward seat was occupied by the Sultan himself, a short, rather stooping figure, with a dark pointed beard, fine, close-set, rather furtive-looking eyes, and a long hooked nose ; touching his fez repeatedly, as he turned from side to side in acknowledgment of the salute of his troops. Frouting him sat the late Osman Pasha, the grizzled and hoary veteran of Plevna, the idol of the army, and the constant and sole companion of his master on all public occasions, except the annual feast of Bairam, when His Majesty used to take his youngest son with him to the mosque in Constantinople, where the time-honoured ceremony is performed of kissing the mantle of the Prophet. He glanced up and bowed as he passed the windows of the Ambassadors' room, and then driving straight to the doorstep of the mosque, alighted and entered the building. Half-an-hour elapsed before he reappeared, accompanied by the Sheikh-el-Islam, tall and conspicuous in his long flowing robe of green. The regiments had in the meantime been disbanded, and His Majesty returned to the palace at a slow trot, holding the reins himself, while an emulous crowd ran and pushed the carriage from behind.

Sir N. O'Conor, Mr. Melanitch, the Embassy dragoman, and myself, then proceeded up the hill, a five-minutes' walk, to the Yildiz kiosque. It is a new building, with an unpretentious exterior, and badly lighted inside. Ushered through two antechambers into a room hung with large maps, we were furnished with refreshment in the shape of coffee and cigarettes, and found H. E. M. Constans, the French Ambassador, also awaiting an audience. Twenty minutes elapsed before Munir Pasha, the Sultan's interpreter (who died a few months ago), came to invite Sir N. O'Conor to the royal presence, and, after another quarter of an hour, I was summoned to join him.

His Majesty walked to the door as I entered, shook my hand, and graciously expressed his pleasure at seeing me in Constantinople. He then took his seat on a low ottoman not far from the door with his back to the window, motioned us to be seated, and half rising again, offered us a light for our cigarettes. The conversation was conducted through Munir Pasha, a fat man, with a puffy face, big expressionless and nervous eyes, and a terribly asthmatic wheeze, which sometimes rendered it difficult to catch what he said. Not that it mattered very much, for I was generally able to understand His Majesty's remarks, in spite of his rather rapid habit of utterance, before they were translated into French; and I found it difficult to remember the etiquette which demands that you should hear the same observation or question repeated twice over before you are permitted to reply. It struck me that the Sultan was looking very much worn and overworked. The perpetual shifting of his position, the extreme pallor of the countenance, and the weary restless appearance of the keen dark eyes, all seemed to tell of the strain which must result from that incessant and close attention which he bestows, with the insatiable appetite of Frederick the Great, upon the minutest details of administration; and the recently established and most inconvenient custom of holding the reception for all the Foreign Ambassadors on Friday, naturally makes that day an almost intolerably heavy and fatiguing one.

He questioned me about my previous travels in Anatolia and Kurdistan, expressed his interest in my intended journey, and his hope that I should find harmonious relations existing between all sections of his subjects in the interior. Referring to the difficulties of provincial administration, he remarked that everything depended on the individual character and energy of governors, and that much remained to be done in the way of developing the internal resources of the country. In particular, he alluded to the important scheme now under consideration for bringing water from the Beyshehr lake to irrigate the vast plains of the salt desert in the neighbourhood of Konia. I ventured to express my hope that the same beneficent policy might, in the course of time, be extended to other parts of the Empire, and notably to the vilayets of Mosul and Baghdad, where a soil of marvellous fertility would, with proper drainage and irrigation, quickly yield a return quite as great or greater than that of the Nile valley. To this view he readily assented, but pointed out that the main obstacle to carrying out works of improvement on a large scale was the difficulty of finding sufficient funds to meet the initial outlay.

It is indeed the cardinal difficulty which lies at the root of the Turkish problem, and which must be met before any substantial advance can be made in the direction of removing administrative abuses and bettering the condition of the people. Unfortunately it is one which can only be removed by great sacrifices on the part of Turkey herself, and a cordial and frank understanding with those Powers who are honestly anxious to promote her progress on the path of material and moral prosperity. These, it is clear, can only advance her a loan on conditions which will safe-

guard their own interests, on the one hand, by an
adequate guarantee for the security of their money,
and the interests of Turkey herself, on the other, by a
pledge that the present useless and extravagant expenditure on official sinecures shall be ruthlessly cut
down, and that the sums which are advanced shall be
economically and profitably spent on undertakings of
a sound and remunerative character. If, rather than
submit to conditions of this kind, Turkey seeks relief
from her financial embarrassment by applying for a
loan from Powers whose designs are political, and who
will therefore be amply satisfied by any arrangement
that consolidates their own influence and hold over the
country, while at the same time it increases the weakness and dependence of their client, she will be doing
more to abrogate her own freedom and autonomy
than any submission to partial and temporary control
on the part of a friendly ally would have entailed. It
is to be hoped that she will realise this fact before it
is too late, and her well-wishers in England will meanwhile rejoice at the more cordial relations and the
better understanding which already exists between the
two countries. The policy of "nagging" has done
no good, as might have been foreseen, and as Germany
had the sense to perceive long ago. It is on the lines
upon which she is working, and upon which it was,
and perhaps is still, in our power to co-operate with
her, that the hopes of ultimate salvation for Turkey
rest; and at the close of my interview with His Majesty
he expressed his pleasure in knowing that among the
supporters of Lord Salisbury's Government there still
prevailed the friendly and sympathetic sentiments towards his country which are among the oldest of the
political traditions of the Conservative party. Again
shaking my hand, he wished me a cordial *bon voyage,*

and returning in the launch to Therapia, I bade farewell to my kind and delightful hosts, Sir N. and Lady O'Conor, and went back to the town to make my final arrangements for the start.

The most perplexing problem was, as usual, the engagement of a capable and trustworthy servant. If you are to converse with the governors and higher officials in the interior, it is almost a *sine quâ non* that you should have some one capable of supplementing the cursory knowledge of the language which is all that most people can hope to acquire without a long residence in the country. Turkish is an easy language to learn superficially, but a very difficult one to talk well, and unfortunately the stock of polyglot servants is a small one. Most of them are Armenians and Greeks, neither as a rule satisfactory, and the higher class of dragoman will not stand the rough work, the hard riding, and poor fare which one has to put up with in out-of-the-way districts. Turks, on the other hand, who are almost always conspicuously honest and faithful, rarely speak any language but their own, and if they do, it is generally because at some period or other they have acted as kavasses at the various consulates, and in that capacity have acquired habits of comparative luxury and indolence which render them indisposed to undergo the hardships and fatigue of travel.

After many futile inquiries, I engaged at the last moment a stalwart Montenegrin from Cattaro, who had roamed over most of the provinces of Turkey in Europe, although he had never penetrated beyond the coast-line of Asia Minor. His account of himself was promising and concise. He spoke French (of a dialect, I imagine, peculiar to Montenegro); he had, "thank God," never had an illness in his life, and he was prepared, in the event of any accident to myself, to prove his fidelity by promptly committing suicide on my corpse. "Nous sommes tous comme cela, vous savez, nous Montenegrins," he wound up with an apologetic grin as if he were describing the effects of some peculiar and unaccountable disease. I may add that his subsequent conduct entirely bore out the ·character he gave of himself, though whenever we entered any of the more turbulent districts on the frontier, he invariably employed every artifice he could think of to dissuade us from exposing him to the danger of having to fulfil his pledge of self-immolation, and an unhappy experience in the past of the modest waters of the Jordan had given him an almost hysterical detestation of rivers in general. Poor man! he suffered many things in the course of the next few months! He nearly always tumbled off a horse in mid-stream, and for more than a week on the Lower Zab and the Tigris he spent sleepless nights, imagining every moment that the raft-skins were on the point of collapsing, and that he would find himself battling for life in the fierce swirl of the rapids. But with the natives he got on very well, and created a great impression by his magnificent appearance and superb attire. On his head he wore a forage cap of black cloth braided with gold lace; his upper garment was a long and full white frock with petticoats reaching below the knee, worn over a waistcoat of crimson braided with black; while his dark blue knickerbockers with red knee edges and white stockings were confined at the waist by a voluminous sash of striped yellow and green silk. The only serious fault he had was an extremely quick temper, which led him to pull out his pistol on the slightest provocation, and we never felt quite certain that we could trust him to obey our strict injunctions that he was never to fire it unless we told him to do so. He had an undisguised contempt for the manners and customs of the natives, which he took care to express on all occasions with the most unflattering candour, and he frequently assured us with transparent veracity that he would never have set foot in the country at all if he had had an inkling of the worry and annoyance he would have to undergo.

At last everything was ready, and at daybreak on the 27th August we found ourselves on board the little ferry-steamer bound for Haidar Pasha. Nothing could be lovelier than the view looking up the Golden Horn in the first flush of the summer morning, the domes and minarets of St. Sophia and the great mosque of Sultan Ahmed gleaming high over the level wreaths of mist, with a red glint as of fire flashing from every window, and the tall masts and rigging of a large Brazilian armoured cruiser glistening like gold in the sunrise. An hour later we were safely ensconced in the train and steaming along the cypress-dotted shores of the Bay of Marmora.

As far as Eskishehr the country was already familiar, as I had traversed the same line on my way through Angora to Samsun. Beautiful glimpses of the sea and its transparent creeks seen between orchards of pear, apple, and fig, and vineyards laden with fruit, give place to finer effects as the train enters the hills, where trim villages of clean wattled houses with red-tiled roofs lie clustered along the foot of ravines or perched upon slopes, every inch of which is cultivated wherever the ground is not too stony. These in their turn are succeeded by the naked grandeur of a long and narrow limestone gorge, whose precipitous sides, covered in places with slender creepers, and the brawling torrent below bordered with acacias and willows, remind one forcibly of the scenery in some of the lower passes of the Balkans.   Lastly, beyond Eskishehr the vast and dreary plateau is reached which extends with unvarying monotony from Angora southward to Konia and eastward right up to the foot of the Bulgar Dagh.

One of the loveliest parts of the line is that which passes the reedy fringes of the Isnik Geul (lake), its calm surface broken by the frequent rises of some apparently large species of trout.   A thriving trade must be carried on in walnuts, to judge from the extraordinary number of these trees, many of them splendid specimens, which one sees from the windows of the train.   On the whole, the company's service is not bad, so far as the comfort of the passenger is concerned, though some idea of the rate of speed may be gathered from the fact that a big and famished pariah dog, which we enticed with bread, cantered easily alongside for more than half a mile until his hunger was assuaged.   The employees are mostly French-speaking natives, and the notices at the stations are written in the same language, instead of in German, as one might expect.

At Eskishehr the accommodation is of the most scanty and unenticing description, and the train starts again for Konia at 4.30 A.M., to allow for the fourteen hours which are required to accomplish the intervening distance of 200 miles.   The branch line to Konia passes through a more diversified part of the plateau than that which runs to Angora, for the interminable stretch of level plain, dotted with poor-looking crops of corn or coarse yellow grass, yields at intervals to woods of stone-pine and Scotch fir, while the bare hills are in places covered with patches of a richer red-coloured soil.   The houses, built for the most part of stone with red-tiled roofs, are here and there crowded together under the overhanging crest of limestone cliffs that crop out of the soil in isolated groups. Considering the comparative scarcity of water, there is an astonishing quantity of birds of various kinds —partridges, pelicans, hoopoes, goatsuckers, magpies, bitterns, great bustards, white eagles, and "blue crows," with wings of lustrous azure edged with black, and ruddy brown bodies. The white pulverised limestone which covers everything causes a glare of painful intensity, and it is a welcome relief to come occasionally upon broad acres of wild-flowers, blue vetch, lavender, and white convolvulus. A few windmills and a large number of brickkilns dot the landscape in the neighbourhood of Afium Kara Hissar, where the train stops to allow twenty minutes for lunch. It is a fair-sized town, straggling along the base of a lofty cliff of reddish trachyte, crowned with the ruins of an old castle, and derives its modern name [1] from the cultivation of the opium, which forms the staple of its produce.

It was close on eight o'clock before we arrived at Konia, and were met by a messenger from Ferit Pasha, the Vali, who had been informed from Constantinople of our intended visit, and had sent to offer us his compliments, expressing a hope that he might have the pleasure of seeing us next day. Mr. Keun, the British Consul, who was unfortunately laid up with an attack of malaria, had kindly lent us the assistance of his kavass, and we took up our quarters for the night in a Greek inn near the station, which, although bare, was at least tolerably clean.

[1] Black Opium Castle. The old name, according to Professor Ramsay, was Akroenos, and it was here that the Byzantine army in 740 inflicted their crushing blow on the forces of Seidi Ghazi, the Saracen commander.

CHAPTER III

SELJUKS AND GERMANS

THE town of Konia[1] lies on a dead flat, broken only by a low range of hills, of which the most striking and prominent feature is a curious volcanic cone, over-. looking the little village of Sarai Keui, and variously known as Kara Bourja or St. Pierre (Agios Philippos), from the small basin of water on its summit, which is said to remain always at the same level, and is regarded with veneration as a place of pilgrimage by the Greeks, and by the rest of the community as a pleasant resort in the hot weather.

Of the old walls of the Seljuk epoch, faced with large stone blocks and adorned at intervals with square towers, little remains to-day but the mud core. As usual in the East, the solid material has been used for other buildings, and the Greek inscriptions, chiefly of a funerary character, which are frequently disinterred from the foundations, were in all probability themselves transported originally from the site of the old Greek walls which ran at some distance from the modern town, near the suburbs of Meram. In the courtyard of a school which the present Vali is building for the Mussulmans, I found several blocks carved and inscribed, which have been discovered for the most part in the surrounding villages, and are eventually to be properly housed in a museum. None of them

---

[1] The Turkish equivalent of το Κονιον, the Greek rendering of Iconium (Professor Ramsay).

appeared to be of a very early date, except a small one without any inscription, which bore a grotesque but graphic representation of a man ploughing with two oxen, and which, like the mutilated lions scattered about the town, seems to have the same characteristics of Phrygian art as the similar specimens at Angora. The others were apparently all intended as records of the munificence of some public benefactor.[1]

A few fragments of this kind are practically all that are now left to remind one of the old Roman capital of Lycaonia, the colony of Hadrian and the theatre of St. Paul's missionary efforts. Whatever archæological interest or architectural beauty the town possesses is centred in the numerous monuments of that brief but brilliant period of little more than 130 years, during which the royal master-builders, the descendants of Alp Arslan, rivalled in the heart of Asia Minor the activity and public spirit of a Periclean age. But even these have suffered much from the ravages of time and the vandalism of succeeding generations. The old castle of Uch Kaleh is a mere wreck, and the palace of the Sultans is represented by a dilapidated brick edifice, which is fast crumbling to dust on the heap of accu-

---

[1] One of these sculptures represents a tall figure clothed in a tunic or kilt reaching to the knee, and holding the right hand of a similarly clad but smaller figure. The latter clasps in his left hand a book, while a female figure on his other side extends a circular wreath over his head. The inscription seems to be—

TYMΦOPLLYMΦOPOY
ANECTHCENEAYTON
KAITHNYYN.

Another, obviously the upper part of a drinking trough, represents two warriors charging each other on horseback, while a small male figure stands between the combatants. Above is a bull's head between heavy wreaths, and a short mutilated inscription—

ANECHCENEAYTOY
EYNOIACXAPIN.

mulated rubbish upon which it stands. The wall is of great thickness, and the upper storey, which apparently rested on two projecting brackets, is perforated by a fine arch, round the top of which runs a sadly injured but beautiful band of glazed and lettered tilework. The lower portion of the building is decorated only by the rude representation of an heraldic lion carved in stone.

The mosques, on the other hand, of which there are an incredible number, have preserved much of their original beauty intact. That which bears the name of its founder, Alaeddin, the last of the Seljuk kings, who held under his sway the whole of the present Asiatic dominions of Turkey, with the exception of Armenia and Mesopotamia and the Greek empires of Nicæa and Trebizond, and who gathered to his court at Konia the flower of the intellectual and artistic life of his day, stands on the crest of the hill above the palace. It is of great size, oblong in shape, and commands a magnificent panorama of the town. The interior is curious, the spacious hall containing about sixty marble columns of a greyish-blue colour, some of them plain, and some fluted or decorated with the love-knot pattern so familiar in the Armenian churches of Ani. One has a long inscription in the Greek character near the base, and there are traces of the obliteration of a similar record on another. The *mimber*, or pulpit, is of wood, exquisitely carved, and the fine Mihrab[1] is adorned with Persian tiles, or with paintings ingeniously designed to conceal the fact that many of the plaques have been picked out and sold, a fate which has also befallen some of the carpets, of which there was formerly a large and valuable collection in the mosque. The same artifice, instances of which may also be seen at

---

[1] The niche facing in the direction of the Kiblah (Meccah).

Constantinople, has been employed on the walls, and
at a little distance it is difficult to detect the fraud.
In a small chamber opening on the right aisle are
a row of seven or eight catafalques of the Sultans
covered with green cloth. On the whole, the character of the building is plain and severe, and in point
of beauty and interest it cannot compare with the
Tekke or mosque of the Mevlevi dervishes, and the
adjacent Turbe or mausoleum of their founder, Hazret
Meviana.

The two form a single building, the entrance of
which lies through a pretty little courtyard containing
in the centre a marble-canopied fountain for ablutions,
surrounded by apricot trees, marigolds, and sunflowers.
Finely carved doors lead into the interior, which is
unequally bisected by two huge squared pillars. Both
sections are covered with domed roofs, and the first,
which constitutes the mosque proper, where the prayers
are said, is of about equal length and breadth. The
second, the floor of which is boarded like that of a
ball-room, is reserved for the dances of the dervishes,
a platform on two sides being railed off for the accommodation of the musicians, who keep time to the dancing
with an accompaniment of large hide drums. Along
the right of the building runs an uninterrupted aisle,
subdivided into small chapels resembling those of a
Roman Catholic Church, in which are ranged side by
side the coffins of the founder of the order and his
successors. These are covered with gorgeous trap-
pings, and at the head of each is placed the long linen
turban of the deceased, wound into a coil resembling
a gigantic plume. In front of the principal tomb hang
a number of fine china candelabra and huge wax
candles, while the walls are decorated with text inscriptions from the Koran let into the surface, and the

names of Allah and the Prophet lettered on coloured tiles.

The exterior of the building is remarkable chiefly for its tall conical steeple of dazzling bluish-green faience, which rises above the Turbe, and may be seen from most parts of the town.

Close by is another fine mosque, the Azizieh, with slender tapering minarets, and in the street below the old palace a tiny Medresseh or college, which originally served as a mosque. It consists of a roomy hall, roofed with a tiled dome, and containing a large bath in the centre, while in a smaller room beyond it stands a single catafalque like those in the Alaeddin mosque, similarly covered with green cloth, and a head-dress of coiled linen.

The bazaars are uninteresting, and the number of decayed and crumbling houses which have been left untouched when their owners removed to a more attractive quarter, gives to the western portion of the town a melancholy and disordered appearance. The few poplars scattered about the streets form a grateful contrast to the general air of dust and squalor, and nowhere, except in Cairo, have I seen such a quantity of fine sepulchral monuments. Many of these, indeed, remind one forcibly of the tombs of the Mamelukes, and are often profusely decorated with arabesque carving and tracery. I noticed in particular an elegant little building, said to have been at one time a Christian church, but now used as a depository for petroleum, an octagonal-domed structure on a square base pierced with round windows or holes on each side.

The population of Konia is estimated at about 18,000, of which little more than a third are Armenians and orthodox Greeks. The larger portion of the Greek community have their headquarters in the neighbouring village of Zilleh, and Hamilton, describing his visit in 1842, asserts that they are the descendants of those who were driven from the city by the invaders, and that "they still enjoy great independence, and are not subject to the Turks." There are no Jews, but the Tartars have a quarter to themselves as at Angora, and practically monopolise the trade of *araba* (cart) drivers. The Turkomans are seldom found in the vilayet, the nomad element being supplied by Yuruks, a sect who profess Mahommedanism, but have no mosques of their own, while the Kurds are confined principally to the neighbourhood of Kochhissar. Ill-feeling between the Mussulmans and Christians may be said to be almost non-existent, and at the time of the massacres any danger of disturbance at Konia was anticipated by the exertions of Kiamil Pasha, who was then Vali, and Chelebi, the head of the college of dervishes.

The members of this remarkable brotherhood, whose characteristic dress is a black tunic and an enormously tall hat of buff-coloured felt, have been long distinguished for their tolerant and even friendly attitude towards the Christians. Griffiths,[1] who traversed the country in the early years of the nineteenth century, specially alludes to this trait, which is the more curious considering the missionary zeal of the order, and adds several interesting particulars with regard to the ceremony of initiation. The novice has to submit during a continuous period of a thousand and one days to the most menial offices and drudgery of the kitchen, the omission of a single day entailing the renewal of his entire period of probation. He is then presented by the " Chief of the Kitchen " to the Sheikh, who, suspending his bonnet between his finger and thumb over

---

[1] "Europe, Asia Minor, and Arabia," by J. Griffiths, M.D., 1805.

the head of the candidate, repeats the following Persian verses composed by the founder, Jelaluddin, the poet and friend of the Sultan Alaeddin :—

" It is true greatness and real felicity to shut the heart against all human passions. To renounce this world is the happy effect of that virtue which the grace of our Holy Prophet inspires."

He then covers the head of the new dervish with his bonnet, and turning to the Chief of the Kitchen, addresses him in these words :—

" May the services of this dervish thy brother be acceptable at the throne of the Eternal and in the eye of our Founder. May his satisfaction, his happiness, and his glory increase in this nest of the humble, in this cell of the poor." " Let us exclaim Hoo in honour of our Founder."

Upon this all the assembly cry " Hoo!" and the Superior concludes with a few paternal exhortations upon the duties of the office and an invitation to the whole assembly to embrace and acknowledge the brother.

I was told that celibacy is not a rule of membership, and the morality of the Order is not commonly held to be above suspicion. The Chief is the supreme head of an organisation which extends throughout the Turkish Empire, and numbers about 160 colleges, and the office is hereditary, passing from the father to the eldest son.

I drove over one afternoon, at the special request of the Vali, to the village of Meram, where the wealthier Moslems and Chelebi himself have their summer villa residences. It is a pretty place bowered in orchards of apricot trees, which are cultivated for the sake of the kernel oil, the price of which has of late years risen considerably, while the value of the opium crop has greatly decreased, and is now chiefly exported by way of Smyrna to Egypt. Unfortunately the Sheikh was not at home, and his younger son, with one of the dervishes, was left to perform the duties of hospitality. Conducting us through a garden gay with scarlet runners and large rose-petalled guimauves (marsh-mallow), the yellow centre of which, when dried, supplies the well-known medicine for coughs, they ushered us into a large cool room with a fountain of running water in the centre, and regaled us during our brief conversation with coffee, cigarettes, and a somewhat unpalatable decoction of flowers and *eau-sucré*. The older man was reserved and the boy too shy to be talkative, so, after waiting half-an-hour on the chance of Chelebi's return, we were obliged to give up the hope of making his acquaintance and returned to the town.

Among the pleasantest of my reminiscences of Konia are the interviews which I had with the Vali, Ferit Pasha. A man still in the prime of life, with a clever and vivacious expression of countenance and the most courteous of manners, I have met few of his countrymen who gave me a stronger impression both of zeal and capacity. Keenly alive to the backward condition of the country as a whole, and of his own vilayet in particular, he launched out at once into an enthusiastic description of the new project, of which the Sultan had already spoken to me, for the irrigation of the Konia plain. The engineers commissioned to look into the details of the scheme had already made their report, and estimated the cost of its execution at about £250,000. The water is to be brought from the two lakes of Karaviran and Beyshehr, which are situated at a distance of some fifty miles from the town, and connected with each other by a small stream ; and if the initial expense does not prove a prohibitive one in the present embarrassed state of the Turkish finances, the ultimate success of the undertaking is assured.

Unlike many of the central and southern provinces, which have been almost depleted of their inhabitants, the district of Konia contains a large and industrious population, eager to undertake the reclamation and cultivation of the soil, while the completion of the Anatolian railway affords an impetus to trade and agriculture which is lacking in the more fertile tracts between Angora and the Black Sea. Already large annual crops of cereals and flax are raised, but in many parts of the vilayet water can only be procured with immense difficulty and trouble, and Hamilton mentions instances in which the wells have to be sunk to a depth of from twenty-five to thirty fathoms. In addition to the potential capabilities of the soil, the district possesses great mineral resources, which only require the application of capital in order to be profitably exploited, and claims have, I believe, already been made for concessions to work coal or lignite in the mountains near Karaman, as soon as the prolongation of the railway in that direction enables a reduction in the present cost of carriage to be made. There are other minerals in the region round Adaya, and saltpetre is found in considerable quantities at Eregli and transported to Konia, where, after being passed through a cauldron to boil, it undergoes three successive washings in large tanks.

Another flourishing industry which has been recently started is the manufacture of carpets, in which Mr. Keun, the British Vice-Consul, has taken a great interest. There are three firms in the neighbourhood, one at Avshehr, another at the Christian village of Silleh, and a third at Konia, where a workshop has

been set up on the premises of the Consulate. After
the preliminary cleansing and preparation, the wool is
dyed in big reservoirs, and stretched upon a frame
hanging from a thick beam that runs the whole length
of the shed. The employées, Armenian and Greek
girls, sit in a row along the foot of this frame, and
work with amazing rapidity, inserting between each
thread the coloured piece which is required, and which
is then pushed to the bottom and snipped off with a
large pair of scissors. The patterns, supplied from
Constantinople, are framed and hung up in front of
them, and the carpets are said to be superior to those
of Smyrna, besides being more moderate in price,
though at present they are less widely known. The
principal difficulty in carrying on the business is one
not unknown in Europe, but less common in Turkey,
the liability of the workpeople to go on strike !

For many reasons the larger share of the trade of
Konia is in the hands of Germany, and unless English
merchants bestir themselves the balance is likely to
be increasingly in her favour wherever the railway
goes. Her interest in the line gives her of course a
special advantage, which is increased by the willingness of her traders to study the conditions of the
market, and to make special efforts to create and meet
the demand for their goods. They find it profitable
to employ commercial agents at a higher rate of pay
than English houses are willing to give, and a well-
known Austrian firm has commissioned a lady to
teach the use of their sewing-machines to the fair
occupants of the harems. We may legitimately congratulate ourselves on the superior quality of our
manufactures, but it is a question whether our competitors are not wiser in recognising that, owing to
the poverty of their customers, considerations of price

must necessarily exercise with them a more determining influence than those of quality, and that custom once secured is not likely to be alienated. Their readiness to take small orders, and to supply catalogues of their goods with price lists calculated in terms of the native currency, are also important factors in securing their predominance in a growing market, the loss of which may one day be a matter of serious regret to ourselves.

The subject of the commercial future of Asiatic Turkey has acquired fresh interest and importance by the recent concession to the Anatolian Railway Company for the construction of a line to the Persian Gulf. This concession, which has already excited the apprehensions of Russia and led to similar demands on the part of France in Syria, has been represented in some quarters as a diplomatic victory for Germany. If so, it is one upon which we at least may heartily congratulate her, since whatever interests, commercial or political, we have in the country will be alike promoted by the opening up of its communications. The policy, selfish and immoral in itself, of retarding the development of the Ottoman Empire, and thereby weakening its pecuniary and military resources, is one with which we can have no sympathy on grounds either of principle or of expediency. Time was when we might have occupied the position and undertaken the work which has now fallen to Germany to perform, but we allowed the opportunity to slip. Foreign companies have taken over all the lines which were originally under English management, except that which connects Smyrna with Aidin and Dineir. For this result the responsibility does not rest wholly with the British Government. It is no doubt true that foreign States are ready to extend both moral and financial support to commercial enterprises on the part of their subjects which may lead to the extension of political influence, whereas our statesmen entertain more doubt as to the existence of any necessary connection between the two, and will under no circumstances render substantial assistance except in the form of diplomatic pressure. The British promoter is, therefore, necessarily handicapped at the outset in the race for concessions, and investors at home are not inclined to put their money into schemes which do not at the same time offer reasonable security and a fair prospect of immediate return.

The worst consequence of this position of affairs is not so much the forfeiture of valuable opportunities, as the suspicion and distrust excited in the minds of the Turks by the numerous schemes which have from time to time been pressed upon them for their acceptance. Of *bona fide* offers from British sources I believe the number had been exceedingly small, and this may, in some measure, account for the preference shown by the Sultan for schemes submitted by the German syndicate. It must be remembered that the Anatolian Company has so far scrupulously fulfilled its engagements, that it has done more than any other to open the interior to traffic, and that it has earned the gratitude of the Government by the facilities which it afforded for the rapid conveyance of the Asiatic troops to the front during the recent war in Thessaly.[1] Con-

---

[1] The Haidar Pasha - Ismid line was originally run by a Franco-Belgian Company, and was bought by a group of German capitalists, headed by the Deutsche Bank, shortly after the Russo-Turkish war of 1877–78. A concession to extend the line to Angora and Cæsarea was soon after obtained, and the new section as far as Angora was opened to traffic in 1887. This was followed in 1893 by a further concession for the branch from Eskishehr to Konia, and the shares being concentrated in the hands of the Bank, the railway is now virtually the property of the German

siderations of a different character might naturally have inclined the Sultan to place in other hands the execution of the new project for a further extension. It is scarcely possible that a mind so acute as his can have failed to realise the advantage which would accrue to Turkey could she free herself from the burdensome liability at present imposed upon her by the guarantee system. Not only does it involve an actual pecuniary loss to the Treasury, but, as I have elsewhere [1] explained, it operates as an automatic check on the expansion of trade by withdrawing all incentive to balance expenditure by receipts.

That railways in Asia Minor can be made to pay without any artificial stimulus of the kind has been demonstrated in the case of the Smyrna-Aidin railway, which still continues under British management, and is, I believe, a conspicuous financial success. Under the terms of the original concession, the Anatolian Railway Company has not merely the right, but is under an obligation to extend the Angora branch *viâ* Sivas to Diarbekr and Bagdad, whenever the receipts from the lines already constructed suffice to free the Government from their existing liability. They have therefore already a prior claim to the construction of a through line to the south, although, of course, complementary schemes have been at various times suggested, which by the adoption of a less circuitous route might seriously prejudice its prospects. Without entering at length into the details of these schemes, it may be observed that they fall naturally under two heads, those which, following the line of the southern or northern

Empire. The locomotives, the rolling stock, and the rails were imported from Germany, and it has been calculated that of the total cost of the Anatolian system at present existing 70 per cent. has gone into German pockets.

[1] See "Notes from a Diary in Asiatic Turkey," pp. 18-19.

Taurus and the Upper Euphrates, would cross to Diar-bekr and descend the Tigris Valley, and those which, starting from the terminus at Konia or Damascus, would pass through Aleppo to the Euphrates at Deir-el-Zor and follow the lower course of that river to Hit and Bagdad.

Now in comparing the respective merits of these projects, it must be remembered that, from the Turkish point of view, the objects to be aimed at, although not incompatible with one another, are entirely distinct in character. On the one hand, there is the commercial consideration, which appeals perhaps less forcibly to the Government than to the concessionaires, because while the financial risk which it incurs on account of the guarantee is tangible, certain, and immediate, the resultant profits are at best problematical. On the other, there is the military consideration, which is felt to be an urgent one, owing to the vast increase of Russian armaments along the eastern frontier, and the impossibility, under present conditions, of a rapid mobilisation of the forces of defence.

In the event of a sudden outbreak of war, the Turks would have to rely mainly on the garrisons stationed at Erzerum, Bayezid, and Van, and the troops belonging to the fourth army corps, which are quartered at Erzingian. The regulars and reserves drawn from other parts of the interior would be obliged to march long distances over difficult and often mountainous country, where there are no good roads and but little fodder for horses, while the nearer avenues from Samsun and Trebizond would be closed to troopships from Europe by the command which the Russian navy would have in the Black Sea. The advantages which modern warfare gives to the defending over the attacking force would be almost neutralised in the case of Turkey by her lack of efficient artillery and the inadequate training of her men ; and it may reasonably be doubted whether the invading army would experience any great difficulty in capturing within a few weeks of the commencement of hostilities the principal fortresses along the border. The possession of Van would enable it to strike at once on Bitlis, and secure the only practicable approach to the fertile plains of the south, so that by the time that reinforcements had arrived, all the most important positions would be already in the hands of the enemy.

It is, therefore, from the strategic point of view, a matter of the first importance that means of rapid communication should be established as soon as possible between the coast of the Mediterranean and the western shores of Lake Van. For this purpose the Aleppo-Deir-Bagdad line would of course be utterly useless, whereas a prolongation either by way of Kaisariyeh Malatia and Kharput or *viâ* Konia Marash and Urfa to Diarbekr could be easily linked up with Bitlis, and might possibly prove besides, from a commercial standpoint, an equally, if not more, valuable speculation.

Personally, although conscious of the little weight that attaches to any but the opinion of experts in such a matter, I have my doubts whether any through line in the immediate future will turn out to be a profitable investment. For one thing, it must traverse extensive tracts which are but very sparsely populated, and which for many years to come will hardly repay cultivation. The passenger traffic is likely to be small, because few people who are not pressed for time will care to face the additional fatigue and discomfort of the overland journey, especially during the hot season ; and unless the service is a faster one than any which at present exists on the western lines, and is supplemented by improved arrangements on the part of the British India Steamship Company in the Gulf, the saving of time as compared with the Suez Canal route will be almost insignificant. The necessity of a double transhipment will render the cost of forwarding goods to India by this road a very heavy one, and when we recollect that it now pays better to take them all the way by sea to Calcutta than to unload at Bombay, in spite of the comparatively low freight charges on the Indian lines, it is difficult to believe that the expense of putting them ashore at Haidar Pasha or Smyrna and re-embarking them at Basrah will be compensated by the gain of little more than a week in transit.

But whatever validity there may be in such objections applies with tenfold force in the case of the Aleppo-Bagdad project. The northern line would at all events pass through several cities of considerable size and population, whereas the southern one, after reaching the Euphrates at Deir, would run through a region of more than 300 miles in extent in which a few scattered villages and an occasional plantation of date trees by the side of the stream alone break the hideous monotony of the limestone desert. If the information which I received is correct, the Company have stipulated for a Government guarantee of 15,000 francs per kilometre, and as the distance is roughly 2000 kilometres, the total liability of the Exchequer would amount to the enormous sum of 30 million francs. From this must be deducted the estimated profits of 3000 francs per kilometre, making an aggregate of six millions, so that the actual loss to the State on the construction of the line would be 24 million francs.

It is, I think, much to be regretted that before

granting the concession the Porte did not insist on some mutual compromise between the existing companies. An offer was apparently made by the Anatolian group to the Smyrna-Aidin Company for a fusion of interests, but it fell through owing to the unwillingness of the English company to be absorbed, and the promoters then turned with greater success to the French, who hold the concession for a branch from Smyrna to the junction with the Eskishehr-Konia line at Kassaba. For reasons which I have stated above, I do not believe that a concession to run from Dineir *via* Karaman and Aleppo to the south (which is the only one on a large scale that the English company could hope to secure) would be a remunerative one, and if that route was to be selected, the construction would naturally be entrusted to the Germans, whose line is already further advanced, and whose receipts would probably be diminished by the competition of a rival line passing through Karaman. On the other hand, an amalgamation of the German and English companies, if it could have been arranged, would have rendered easier the speedy completion of any new undertaking and avoided many of the difficulties which now surround it. The necessity of a guarantee might have been obviated by the greater facilities for raising a loan in the London than in the Berlin market, and a general understanding arrived at which would have averted the possibility of international misunderstandings, such as might arise in regard to any eventual prolongation of the line from Basrah to Koweit, where the interests of Great Britain and India are intimately and directly concerned.

The distribution of the various lines among the concessionnaires belonging to different Powers is only too likely to result, as in China, in provoking claims to separate spheres of interest, and may increase the reluctance of the Government to encourage schemes for developing the country which they believe to be a covert menace to its independence. The policy of "a fair field and no favour" is the only one which can reconcile the true interests of Europe and Turkey, and restore to the impoverished and long-suffering inhabitants of Anatolia a measure of prosperity to which they have long been strangers.

CHAPTER IV

THROUGH CAPPADOCIA

THE track from Konia to Eregli runs over a bare expanse dotted with tufts of spinifex and lavender, and swept by frequent dust-storms. In the winter season, lasting usually for seven months, during which severe frost and snow are not uncommon, the wheeled traffic must be subject to great difficulties, for the plain is often flooded with water, and in many places the ground is banked up to preserve the road from inundation. A wretched little guardhouse, stationed at a distance of about thirteen hours from the town and occupied by a single zaptieh, affords shelter to travellers for the first night, and on the evening of the next day, after passing Karabunar, where there is a small khan and a not very interesting mosque of Sultan Selim with a leaded dome, the headquarters of the Kaimakamlik are reached.

The modern Heraclea—the Cybistra of the Cappadocian kings—lies, half-concealed by poplars, in the centre of a fertile oasis of cornland, watered by the little Ivriz stream, that rises about eight miles to the south. The value of the crops raised in the district is shown by the fact that although last year's harvest was not a particularly good one, the tithes were sold for 60,000 Turkish lira, an advance of more than half on the receipts of the preceding year. The tithes, in fact, constitute the main bulk of the revenue, for there is no land-tax, and oxen and camels are exempted from the tax imposed upon sheep.

We had already deposited our baggage in the inn when the Kaimakam, Ismail Haki, came in, accompanied by Mr. Prodomos Poritides, an agent of the Anatolian Railway Company, and insisted that we should take up our quarters in his own house, where he provided us with a clean and comfortable room and a most excellent but oily dinner, consisting of the usual meat-kebabs and egg-plant stewed in butter and oil, with honey and delicious cool syrup made from the cherries grown in the neighbourhood.

The chief attraction of Eregli to the traveller and antiquarian is its proximity to the marvellous Hittite rock sculpture at Ivriz. Winding out of the town, past the fine Seljuk minaret of the mosque of Sultan Alauddin and the military depot built at the same period, the road crosses a broad stretch of plain between luxuriant fields of barley and maize, brilliant with blue cornflowers, vetch, and mallow. The small Ivriz stream, threading its rapid and meandering course between grassy banks overhung with willows, has to be forded repeatedly, as there are no bridges. The water is extraordinarily clear and icy cold, but the natives of Eregli prefer for drinking purposes the water of another small stream which they have brought from the hills close by.

Half-an-hour's canter brings the rider to a pretty glade of walnut, hazel, and poplar, fringed with dense thickets of blackberry and gay with the ripe scarlet fruit of the Cape gooseberry. Here we came upon a party of Ivriz peasants picking hazel-nuts, with which they filled our holsters, and, rounding a fine group of naked cliffs, found ourselves unexpectedly in face of the famous rock-carving. It stands on the outskirts of the little village, lying in a lovely hollow of the lowest range of the Bulgar Dagh, and scarcely visible for the mass of trees by which it is surrounded. Right above the cluster of houses rises a narrow gorge, closed by tremendous walls of limestone, and from the tumbled boulders at its foot bubbles up the water, which has probably run for some distance underground, and in the course of a few hundred yards is swollen by tributary springs to a considerable torrent. Close to the source from which Ivriz takes its name,[1] its worn base washed by the swirling brook, the graven rock towers to a height of some thirty or forty feet. A tiny path runs round it, sloping downward in a tangle of mossy stone and creepers to a lower channel, where the burn plunges in foaming cascades beneath the shades of spreading walnut and willow. The upper rivulet being half empty, we were able to distinguish and photograph some lines of hieroglyphs traced on the rock a few feet below the sculpture, which during a rise are entirely submerged. Another inscription is cut above the figures, which have been generally taken to represent a Hittite king adoring a gigantic divinity about four times his own size. The latter wears a horned cap and huge buskins with upturned shoe points, while a smile of fatuous benignity illumines his countenance from one enormous ear to the other. The hair and beard are curled, the right hand holds a bunch of grapes, the left a massive ear of corn, and between the legs projects a part of some instrument not unlike the toe of a ploughshare. It is possible that there were originally other sculptures which have been purposely destroyed, and there is a decided resemblance between the line of detached cliffs on the

---

[1] The Greek Βρυσή, a "running spring," as opposed to a fountain jet (πηγή).

HITTITE SCULPTURE, IVRIZ

higher slope of the hill and the celebrated rock galleries of Yasili Kaya, near Boghaz Keui. On the other hand, the remaining sculpture at Ivriz has more of an Assyrian character than the designs north of the Halys, and may for that reason be not improbably assigned to a later epoch of Hittite history.

On our return to Eregli, the Kaimakam proposed that we should attend the evening festivities organised to celebrate the twenty-sixth anniversary of the Sultan's accession. The discordant strains of a band of three musicians playing respectively the spinet, the violin, and the flageolet, made all conversation during dinner impossible, and having finished our coffee, we issued from the house in state, preceded by the orchestra, two little boys carrying staves, and a heterogeneous mob of ragamuffins with torches. Along every window sill of the house was ranged a row of guttering candles, fixed in position by means of their own melted tallow, and over the door swayed a few miserable lanterns which every gust of wind threatened to extinguish. The band struck up an uncertain imitation of Osman Pasha's March, but ceased playing suddenly as we crossed the cemetery, a proceeding which aroused the melancholy humour of the president of the Belidieh,[1] who had just joined the procession, and remarked that he did not suppose the dead would object to the music being continued. I confess that I thought the feelings of the living equally entitled to consideration, but did not say so, and indeed my attention was now distracted by fears for my personal safety. At every ten paces a playful youth in the van let off a rocket into the air, or sent it whizzing from side to side of the road, so that one had to execute a series of agile leaps to avoid being burnt. The preservation of any

[1] Municipality.

semblance of dignity was out of the question, but no
protest was made, and at length we arrived in disorder
at the Konak.   Stumbling up a rickety flight of stairs,
we were ushered into a mean-looking apartment overlooking the street, where an enthusiastic crowd amused
themselves by heaping fuel on two flaming braziers
and tossing squibs among each others' toes.   The
notables of the village sat in a circle round the room
and talked of nothing in particular for some five
minutes, after which we descended again into the
street, and resumed our comic-opera march to the new
municipal buildings.   These were still unfurnished,
but at the head of the staircase a temporary platform
had been erected on the landing, for all the world like
a village school-room got up for a political meeting.
Here for the second time we sat in solemn and aim-
less session, while a tumultuous rabble thronged the
vacant space in front, and the Kaimakam's little boy,
aged three, with a particularly big head, was accom-
modated with a chair at our side.   Presently a few
officers made their appearance belonging to the corps
of Redifs,[1] of which there are about twenty-five in the
barracks, and progress being reported, we continued
our pilgrimage till we arrived at length at our
destination in the big square of the depôt.   A line of
chairs had been set out in the open for the officials,
the military and ourselves, facing the enclosure, which
was filled to overflowing, and divided from the crowd
by a couple of small bonfires.   Over our heads was
suspended a wooden box decorated with Turkish
flags, and no sooner had we seated ourselves than it
caught fire from the swinging lamps beside it, and
the national emblems were reduced to ashes before
they could be cut down with the aid of my knife,

[1] The reserves.

and the box itself hauled up to the roof to extinguish the blaze.

As soon as the excitement had subsided, the staff-major politely offered to show us a Circassian dance, but unfortunately the only two Circassians present refused to perform, as the only instrument capable of working them up to the requisite pitch of enthusiasm was a flute, and no flute could be found. A juggler, however, was prevailed on to dance to the accompaniment of a pair of castanets, and was joined by a common soldier in a burlesque imitation of his performance.

I was particularly struck throughout the evening with the ease and familiarity with which even the smartest of the young officers, newly arrived from the military college at Constantinople, mixed with the lowest of the crowd and squatted beside them on the ground.

The violinist was next requisitioned, for his accomplishment was a rare one, and had been acquired at Konia, where he had also picked up a little English. Finally, when all other resources had been exhausted, the spinet-player brought his instrument to me and begged that I would play an English tune. A grim and awful silence of expectancy fell upon the whole crowd as I picked out with one finger the strains of the National Anthem and an air of Gilbert and Sullivan's. Some of the officers assured me that they recognised the originals, but I doubted it; and as the morning air was decidedly chilly and the entertainment appeared to be pretty well at an end, we took our leave and returned home with the Kaimakam.

On leaving Eregli the salt desert is re-entered, and the only features that redeem the tameness and solitude of the landscape are low ranges trending in a south-westerly direction from the Hassan to the Karaja Dagh

D

on the left, and the ridges of the Taurus to the right. Occasionally one passes a camp of nomad Turkomans, their circular-shaped tents made of bent basket-work and covered over with loose white felt mats. The surface of the ground is perforated with an amazing number of little lemming burrows, which apparently do not go deep or communicate with one another, for their occupants can be easily flooded out by a bucket-

TURKOMAN TENTS

ful of water. Storks also are very numerous, and were earlier visitors than usual, since, two years ago, when I visited Angora more than a week later, they had not yet arrived. We put up for the night in an *odagh* at the village of Klisse Hissar, which stands on a low mound at about half-an-hour's distance from Bor. The name—wrongly rendered by Hamilton as Kiz Hissar, and by Murray as Kizli Hissar—is derived from the two Turkish words *kilisse* (church) and *hissar* (castle), and may indicate the previous existence of a Christian church on the spot; for the ancient Tyana, dating from Assyrian times, was in the later days of the Roman Empire the see of a Metropolitan.

The discovery here of the famous Hittite "Bor stone," described by Mr. Hogarth and Mr. Ramsay, renders it probable that similar inscriptions lie concealed under the soil or hidden in native houses; but although the villagers displayed great interest in the subject of "written stones," and volunteered to show us several, we found nothing of any importance. A white marble slab let into a mud wall and bearing the heraldic device of a nondescript animal, half-dog, half-griffin; a few scattered capitals of the Corinthian order, ornamented with bulls' heads and wreaths; and a big basaltic block, originally circular in form, with lines of Greek inscription running round it, but now almost obliterated and broken into several fragments, were all that we saw. The ground is littered with ancient ruins, of which scarcely more than the foundations are now visible; but one fine Doric column of marble still stands erect, and a row of massive limestone arches that once supported an aqueduct by means of which water was brought to the town from the western slopes of the Taurus, bears unmistakable evidence of the Roman occupation.

The modern village of Bor, which lies due west, is separated from Klisse Hissar by a low ridge of limestone. Local Greek tradition, of doubtful value, derives the name variously from the root of the verbs πορίζεσθαι, signifying a place for provisioning troops, and πορεύεσθαι, in allusion to its position, as the pass where the Bulgar and Hassan Dagh come nearest together. It is a quaint little mud-village, ringed round by gardens and vineyards, the vines trailing over the walls and hanging in festoons from the trellis work that is stretched across many of the narrow streets.   Here also, as in Konia, a flourishing carpet industry has been started, and the three hundred looms at work afford employment to a large number of children at the liberal wage of four piastres per head per day.   Many of them were quite tiny, wielding scissors a third of their own size, and passing the wool in and out with marvellous precision and rapidity. The facial type in these parts is often very fair, and I noticed one girl of extraordinary beauty, her delicate white face peering out of masses of ruddy auburn hair that escaped in a multitude of small plaits from beneath a thin braid hung with gold coins.

From Bor it is an easy drive to Nigdeh,[1] a fair-sized town, built in two separate quarters on low sandhills, with a narrow bit of ground between.   In the intervening space is the Mussulman burying-ground, well worth a visit for the sake of the beautiful tomb of Havanda, which in its way is one of the most perfect specimens of Seljuk architecture to be found anywhere. The ground plan of the building is hexagonal, but the upper portion is sixteen-sided, and covered with x-quisite carving, twisted tracery, and heraldic figures. A low conical dome tops the edifice, and over the sculptured lintel of the door is the date 1344, and the words " Allah kerim," God the merciful.   Not being able to decipher the inscription myself, I had to trust to the interpretation of the Mutessarif, but his assertion that the sentence following read " Havanda, wife of Alauddin," compelled me either to doubt his literary

---

[1] *Nigdeh.* Various and conflicting accounts are given of the derivation of the word.   One derives it from the Greek Νικη, "victory;" another from *nig*, which I understand to be an Arabic term for "good;" and a third from *nik*, the Persian equivalent for "bad."

acquirements (since the lady in question must have died nearly a hundred years earlier) or else to conclude that the work was not completed until long after her husband's decease.

Many other inscriptions of Seljuk date cover the marble headstones in the cemetery, and it is much to be regretted that no competent scholar has yet visited the districts comprised in this the old empire of the Sultans of Rum, in order to compile a thorough and careful record of their architectural and archæological treasures. At Konia, Kaisariyeh, Divrigi, Nigdeh, Karaman, Sivas, and even as far east as Erzerum, there are innumerable mosques, caravanserais, and tombs, which would repay the closest study, and might yield the most valuable historical information. Much of the annals of that little-known period which intervened between the collapse of the Roman power in 1071 at the battle of Melasgerd and the first victory of the Mongols in 1243 [1] may rest undeciphered in these inscriptions, which are gradually crumbling away or suffering mutilation at the hands of those who are unable to understand their interest. The ordinary traveller cannot afford the time and labour of copying them, and even if he could, he would be wasting a great deal of energy to no purpose in transcribing many which have no significance whatever. Photography is of little use, for the inscription is often placed in an inaccessible position round the dome or door of a mosque; but the task of any competent scholar would be easier now than it has been for many years past, owing to the perceptible decrease of ignorant fanaticism among the population, and their grow-

---

[1] The Emirate of Karamania retained a partial independence up to 1472.

ing familiarity with the strange tastes and oddities of Europeans.

The western quarter of the town is thickly planted with poplars, and occupied entirely by Christians, most of whom are Greeks. The older quarter, with its narrow winding lanes, stands on a spur of soft volcanic rock, and contains the mosque of Alaeddin, a handsome Medresseh with a roofed entrance of heavy stalactite design, and the old castle built in the fifteenth century. This is now used principally as an armoury for rifles belonging to the local corps. The Martinis are being gradually discarded for Mausers, but many of the men are still armed with the inferior weapons captured during the Greek war.

The Mutessarif of Nigdeh was an interesting and well-informed man, who had been recently transferred from the Kastamouni vilayet on the shores of the Black Sea. He told me that province drew a revenue of more than £16,000 per annum from the magnificent forests on the mountains along the coast, the wood being stored for six months before it is used for building purposes, or seasoned artificially by heating in ovens for a few hours. Our host was a Greek director of the tobacco *regie*, and a Greek doctor who spoke French usually acted as interpreter. These doctors, almost always belonging to the same nationality, go through a preliminary course of training in the Medical College at Constantinople, and are then attached to the various municipalities, drawing monthly salaries at the rate of 300 piastres (about £3) in a kaza, 500 in a sandjak, and 800 in a vilayet. In some of the more unhealthy districts, like Bagdad, the salary is slightly higher. They are, of course, allowed to take fees in addition from their patients, but the peasants have long been accustomed to expect treatment gratis, and therefore add very little to the official pay. Vaccination, like primary education, is compulsory and free of charge, but there is still a certain feeling of prejudice against it. Diphtheria, which has been epidemic for some time in the vilayet, has been successfully treated with antitoxin, but the difficulty and delay in procuring fresh supplies from Constantinople have been the cause of many deaths. The climate is severe, considering the comparatively low altitude—not 4000 feet above sea-level—and during the winter months, when the snow lies in heavy drifts, the wolves of the Taurus, which are said to cross with the ordinary pariah dogs, become so bold that they frequently enter the streets of the villages. Wild sheep are almost the only large species of game to be found in the vicinity.

The direct road to Nevsheher crosses the plain without touching a single village till it reaches Geuljik, the ancient Limnæ, mentioned in the writings of St. Gregory of Nazianzen, and still tenanted by a number of Greeks. The only vestiges of old times are a broken shaft or two of white marble columns lying on the surface of a small mound. Everywhere the peasants were winnowing the corn, and from time to time wreaths of fine sand, whirled high in the air by a passing breeze, floated like fleecy clouds across the level expanse towards the jagged line of the Soghanli Dere on the northern horizon. The khan at Melegop affords a convenient halting-place, and many of the houses, as in other villages in the district, are either built entirely underground, or have a subterranean storey with deep wells closed by blocks of stones. The water is pumped out by means of wheels into large oblong tanks of black basalt, from which it passes through taps into similarly hewn troughs below. The

old mediæval church, dating from the reign of the
Byzantine Emperor Zimisces, himself a native of
Cappadocia (969–976 A.D.), is also built below the
surface, from which a flight of steps leads down into
the nave, partitioned off from the baptistery on the
left by a low wooden screen. Two gigantic stone
pillars support the roof, the centre of one, which is
crooked and hardly shaped at all, being perforated by
a winding staircase, giving access to the wooden pulpit
box suspended at a height of about twelve feet from
the floor. Silver ikons or representations of saints,
modern work dated 1826, lie on a table by one of
the pillars, or are hung on the wall to the right of the
pulpit. These are kissed by the congregation as they
enter the church. and in front of them stand several
huge wax candles. A few coins were shown to us,
most of them belonging to the Byzantine period, and
a curious iron hoop-ring engraved with the figure of a
boy dressed in a short tunic, and apparently absorbed
in the adoration of a cock perched on a tripod.

From Melegop the road continues over the plain to
the Greek village of Iuegi and the curious hovels of
Kuvenjalik, nestling at the foot of a naked cliff, the
surface of which is pierced by hundreds of artificial
caves. Beyond, the bare sandhills close in, forming a
grim and desolate-looking pass, to the left of which
rises a barrier of precipitous walls along the sky-line.
Under their frowning rocks, capped with basaltic lava,
lies the straggling village of Goreh, and, with scarcely a
break between, the large town of Nevsheher, like the
tiers of an amphitheatre, covers the whole hillside,
sweeping from the castle-crowned summit over the
Mussulman quarter down to the level plain of the
Halys river. The road below becomes impassable for
carriages at this point, as it is flooded with the water

used for irrigating the luxuriant gardens in the valley; but on our arrival we found the Kaimakam, a Greek doctor, and the chief notables of Nevsheher awaiting our appearance, with two superb Tripoli horses to take us up the steep slope. The houses are all built of stone, and there is a large Greek church, Nevsheher being an important diocese of Kaisariyeh. The priest in charge paid us a visit, accompanied by several representatives of the Christian community and two diminutive girls, who presented us with bouquets of wild-flowers and recited an elaborate address of welcome, in which they had been evidently, but unsuccessfully, coached beforehand.

The streets are rough and unpaved, and there are no buildings of any antiquity, for the castle, like the rest of the town, was built by Ibrahim Pasha about 180 years ago.

Before proceeding to Kaisariyeh, we made a short excursion to the village of Aravisson,[1] near the banks of the Halys. The general aspect of the country is depressing in the extreme, the road scarcely more than a track worn in the volcanic tufa and pumice, and bordered by vineyards, from which any passer-by can gather as much fruit as he pleases. Were the soil properly watered, the grape cultivation ought to be a very profitable industry, but the rains are uncertain, and consequently the price of the produce fluctuates enormously from year to year. Birds of various kinds appeared to be plentiful, magnificent white eagles with black tips to their wings, hoopoes, stonechats, and a species like woodpeckers, with brilliant green backs and bellies, throats of a light yellow tint, ruddy-brown capped heads, and black beaks. Two villages only, Nar and Chat, did we pass as we drove over the glaring

---

[1] Sometimes called Yarapsun.

white and arid downs, broken by deep ravines, and presenting a most uncanny appearance owing to the multitude of natural cones of every shape and size which spring on all sides from the slopes of the hills. It looks like a survival from some prehistoric age, a wilderness of miniature and extinct volcanoes stretching as far as the eye can see, here an isolated peak towering to the height of several hundred feet,

EARTH-CONES NEAR NEVSHEHER

and there a cluster of small ones packed so close together that there is scarcely room to pass between. But, as a matter of fact, their origin is due to the same action of the elements that has cleft the deep gullies, and, penetrating between the interstices of the harder volcanic rock on the surface, has worn a passage through the underlying strata of sand and ashes, forming a rounded pyramid that slopes from its rocky apex to a broad and crumbling base. Many of them have been excavated by human industry and pierced with doors and windows, while near Yarapsun the cliffs themselves have been hollowed out into dwellings of one or more storeys in height, rooms containing huge grinding stones and wells, and decorated with coarse red frescoes, which rains and weather have well-nigh effaced. The seemingly religious character of some justifies the conjecture that these caverns may have been used by the eremites of the desert in the early days of Christianity, but local tradition assigns them to the times of the Mongol invasions and the reign of Saper II.

Yarapsun itself lies at the foot of a big naked spur jutting out above the river. There is a small khan, provided with a vine-trellised arbour and garden, and a fine konak in course of construction. The governor, who has only the rank of mudir, paid us a short visit, but conversation was impeded by the presence of a garrulous official, who was a stark-staring lunatic, but fortunately harmless.

It is said that a large Hittite stone was discovered here not long ago, and has since been transported to Constantinople, but the only antiquities brought to us were coins of the later Roman and Byzantine epoch.

After returning to Nevsheher we took the direct route northward by Ujissa, where the cones again crop out in thousands, many of them tenanted by innumerable rock pigeons, and at sunset reached Injesu, the headquarters of a sandjak, at the edge of the Argæus plain. From this point the first full view is gained of the great mountain, rearing its stately snow-streaked summit and thirteen thousand feet of rock against the eastern sky, while below it rise the straggling minarets and domes of the historic city of Kaisariyeh.

CHAPTER V

KAISARIYEH

THE modern town covers but a portion of the site occupied by the old city, the walls of which were rebuilt by Justinian, and included part of the original but now ruined settlement known as Eskishehr. Their area was still further reduced by the Sultan Alaeddin, their present form dating from a later restoration in 1577. The successive ravages of the Seljuks and Mongols and the repeated earthquake shocks, one of which occurred as late as 1840, just before Hamilton's visit, have destroyed all but a few of the larger public buildings, and the houses and bazaars are entirely modern.[1] The castle, with its two massive towers and crenellated battlements, built about 600 years ago, is in a very dilapidated condition, and the courtyard is choked with a crumbling mass of mud houses, but its walls are worth climbing for the sake of the magnificent view of Mount Argæus, with its twin peaks and long undulating slope, stretching away to the south.

The Mutessarif, Deman Pasha, like most of the wealthier inhabitants, had left Kaisariyeh for his summer villa on the lower slopes of the mountain, and only came into the city for a few hours to transact business at the konak. He had two years before been governor of Mersina, at the time of the arrest of an agent of the Austrian Lloyd Company, who in-

---

[1] The bazaars are fine, and entirely roofed over. They are said to contain more than 1050 shops.

curred the suspicion of the authorities that he was engaged in the distribution of relief to the Armenians. Since taking over his new appointment he has displayed his interest in the locality by adding a tea-garden to the konak and commencing the construction of a girls' school for the daughters of the richer Mussulmans. During our interview, at which he was attended by a colonel of the Redifs entrusted with the supervision of the large saltpetre works near the town, he ordered a number of carpets of local manufacture to be brought in for our inspection. The industry was started after the massacres as a means of relief for the people, and the pieces are all worked by hand, both in wool and silk, in the various houses. Judging by the specimens shown us, I should say that these carpets are of finer make than those of Bor, and in point of texture and colour the silk ones approach more nearly to the quality of the old Persian than any I have seen. Unfortunately the demand has not kept pace with the supply, and has already sunk so low that the finest are being actually sold for less than the cost price.

From the konak the governor invited us to accompany him to the mosque of Houvant, the most celebrated in the place, and went in without either taking off his own shoes or asking us to do so. The interior contains nothing of interest, but to the left of the entrance is an exceptionally fine Seljuk tomb of the thirteenth century, octagonal in shape, and adorned with elaborate arabesques, and a frieze of intertwined inscription running round the base of the dome.

The American missions are situated in the Armenian village of Talas, lying at the edge of a gully under the round hill of Ali Dagh, or the "Two Brothers," on the summit of which stands the venerated church of St. Basil, bishop of Cæsarea. There

are besides a hospital for seven patients, two schools
for boys and girls, to which the children of Greeks are
also admitted, and often prove themselves quicker and
more manageable than the Armenians. The latter
are a numerous body, especially in the outlying villages, and several of their monasteries are of great
antiquity. From one of these—the monastery of Surp
Garabed—I was told that the Russian Government
had not long ago purchased an ancient and valuable
manuscript of the Gospels. The villagers, although
reluctant to part with it, at last consented under pressure from the Porte, and received in return a small
annual endowment of £60.

Like most of the western towns, Kaisariyeh
suffered but little during the period of the disturbances, and although the revolutionary committees had
displayed great activity at Yuzgat and Marsovan in
the north-west (a cause to which the Vizier attributed
the outbreak at Talori in 1893),[1] they do not seem to
have extended their operations to Kaisariyeh, where
the commandant of the troops used his best efforts to
allay the excitement. But the town has not escaped
that most disguised and expensive of blessings vouch-
safed by the Porte, out of consideration for the feelings of the Powers, the Commission of Inquiry presided over by Shakir Pasha,[2] who is said to have drawn
more than £1000 from the local treasury, in addition
to his salary of £500 per month. The resources of
the Angora vilayet are large, but a considerable proportion goes every year into the exchequer at Constantinople, and the salaries of the provincial officials,

[1] Consular Reports, Turkey, 1894, C. 7894.

[2] This Commission was the outcome of a long series of negotiations
between the Porte and the Embassies, but Great Britain disclaimed all
responsibility for the appointment of the Mufettish or president, Shakir
Pasha.

perhaps because irregularly paid, are fixed on a somewhat high scale. A vali receives, I believe, about £250 a month; a mutessarif £60, and a moavin (the assistant and representative of the higher and subordinate governors), who is generally a Christian,[1] only £25.

The judiciary is in as bad or even worse a plight. There can be little doubt that the introduction of the Code Napoleon was a mistake. It is not suited to local conditions, and the intricacies and difficulties which it involves afford endless opportunities for miscarriage of justice. In the old days, when the governor, with two or three associates, sat to adjudicate upon every case himself, and disposed of it summarily, justice, albeit of a rude kind, was much oftener secured, and without the endless delay and expense involved by the present system. The judges are now three in number, one Greek, one Armenian, and one Turk, selected nominally by the people, but in effect

[1] One of the reforms upon which special emphasis was laid by the Ambassadors in drawing up this scheme of reform. Where a governor, vali, mutessarif, or mudir was of one religion, his assistant was to be of the other. This was in principle accepted as an alternative to European control over the appointment of the higher officials, upon which Great Britain alone was anxious to insist, but which, as Russia pointed out, would have made the Powers responsible for the actions of men of whose character they were unable to judge, and whose subsequent conduct they would have found it difficult to criticise. The Turkish Government naturally viewed such an innovation as imperilling its authority over its own subjects, besides detracting from its independence and prestige. While, therefore, reserving its right to appoint Mussulmans as governors of the vilayets and sandjaks, it consented to accept the rule that their assistants should be of the opposite faith. And this has been pretty widely, if not universally, put into practice. As might have been expected, however, the Christian moavin has no practical authority, and, like his coreligionists on the Medjliss (Council), almost always defers to the wishes of the Mussulman members. Where race feeling has not been embittered, as at Mardin, Angora, and many other places, the adherents of the two religions work harmoniously together, and the Christian has the authority and influence which his business capacity and intellectual talents have always gained for him before any reform scheme was promulgated.

by prominent individuals of the community at the dictation or advice of the governor, and holding their appointments for a term of three years. By way of ensuring the impartiality and incorruptibility of these men, a salary of £2 10s. per month is assigned to each, and must be set against a sum, often amounting to as much as £100, which he has had to expend in bribes in order to obtain the appointment. At the head of the bench is a president nominated from headquarters, and the interests of justice are finally secured by the periodical visits of a judicial inspector similarly appointed. This gentleman makes an occasional tour, staying about ten days in the chief centres, and during his visit the officials vie with each other in at once rendering his stay agreeable and engrossing his time by hospitable invitations to entertainments in the outlying villages. Thus it happens that when the hour for his departure arrives, he finds himself in a thoroughly cheerful and lenient frame of mind, and makes no difficulty about attaching his signature to any document or report which is presented to him. There is also a financial inspector, who is bound to certify the accuracy of the provincial accounts, but, as the treasurer would probably forfeit his place if he failed to conceal irregularities on the part of the governor, some method of compromise is generally arrived at which reconciles the interests of all parties, even if it involves the sacrifice of strict financial probity.

Such, at all events, is the opinion widely held of the results of the present system by the ordinary natives, and in discussing these matters I carefully refrain from quoting the views of missionaries, because from the Turkish standpoint they might not be regarded as entirely impartial witnesses. The Government is at least entitled to the credit of having

deferred, though involuntarily, to the wishes of Europe
on the question of judicial reform, and of having put
into active operation the remedy which they proposed.
In point of fact, it was no remedy at all. It rested on
the erroneous assumption, which pervaded every clause
of the reform scheme, that the admission of Christians
to posts in the judiciary, the police, and the civil administration would serve as a check upon the most
flagrant abuses. But these abuses arise not from the
nature of the system or the religious persuasions of
those entrusted with its working, but from the inadequacy of their salaries and the almost universal and
ingrained habit of corruption. The only guarantee
for the independence of the judiciary in England, as
for the purity of our Parliamentary system, rests, as
history proves, not on any natural superiority in the
national character, but on the action of an enlightened
and educated public opinion, which assumes that men
who accept certain posts have sufficient means to enable them to resist the temptation to corruption. The
absence of any corresponding public opinion in Turkey
is due to the manifest impossibility of entertaining such
an assumption. To disregard this fact, and to propose
a remedy of a kind that calls up recollections of School
Board controversies in the House of Commons, is merely
to intensify the evil, and still further compromise the
chances of judicial impartiality by introducing into the
administration of the law the disastrous elements of
religious strife.

But do not let us throw all the blame on the
Turkish Government for a failure which we ought to
have foreseen and for which we are mainly responsible.
The Consular Reports testify to temporary and local
improvements, but they are not the result of the
panacea which we put forward. If several of the

E

judicial staff have been dismissed by the Vali at Erze-rum,[1] yet little has been effected by the judicial inspec-tors, and financial reform must precede the reorgani-sation of the various departments.   At Kharput the inspectors have taken up office, and committees of preliminary inquiry, duly composed of Christians and Mussulmans, have been established.   Yet the official comment is, "The new arrangements must prove an additional burden on the Christian taxpayers, as the cost is to be defrayed from the proceeds of the vilayet." The admission that some good has been done by the new inspectors at Van must be set against the report from Diarbekr that the only possible improvement lies, not in the multiplication of officials, which only in-creases the expenses of administration and widens the area of corruption, but in the appointment of a better class of men and the conferment upon the Valis and Mutessarifs of powers of summary jurisdiction, as the judges are not trustworthy!   The same testimony is given in regard to the enrolment of Christians as moavins and subordinate governors, or as members of the police force.   At Van the order of the Vali that no taxes were to be taken from families owning less than four measures per head was disregarded by the zap-tiehs because they had themselves received no salaries. At Erzerum eighteen Christians had been added to the police force, making a total of fifty-one out of 218; but the Armenians would have nothing to say to Shakir's Commission, those who wished to join the police force being in many cases deterred from doing so by the menaces of their co-religionists, and con-sequently declining to enlist, although a bounty of £10 was offered to every tradesman for each Armenian recruit he could produce.[2]

[1] Raouf Pasha.   Turkey, No. 7, 1897, *passim*.   [2] Turkey, No. 1, 1896.

An interesting light, it may be added, is thrown on this information by the subsequent comment of the Consul that the police had done good service in tracking the revolutionaries.[1] " Zaptiehs cannot live if their exactions from the villages are stopped," is the declaration of Mr. Monahan at Bitlis; and the Christian who accepts unpaid service under the Government must either be disloyal to his superiors or earn the hatred and contempt of those whose religion he professes, but with whose nationalist aims he has no sympathy.

These results were foreseen by Sir Philip Currie[2] himself, who remarked in one of his despatches that " the appointment of Christian officials might do more harm than good," and that " only a strong European control on the spot could secure equal liberties." They were realised by Russia[3] when she refused to insist on the appointment of a mixed gendarmerie, which, in her opinion, could but make matters worse ; and no doubt the true explanation of the action of the Powers was the desire at all hazards to satisfy the public conscience of Europe by deluding it into the comfortable idea that it had done something tangible to fulfil its responsibilities. The root of the evil was clearly discerned, but the only remedy for it was dismissed as impracticable, for, as the British Ambassador declared, " it was impossible in the existing state of the finances to demand that the cost of administration should be a first charge on the revenues of the vilayet."

[1] Turkey, No. 7, 1897.

[2] Now Lord Currie. History fully corroborates his view. When the Morea was still part of the Turkish Empire, its inhabitants were not made more contented and loyal because their taxes were assessed and collected by the Proestoi whom they elected, or because they were represented by their own Primates on the Pasha's council at Tripolitza. No officials of the Porte were ever so detested as the Greek Phanariots in Roumania.

[3] Turkey, No. 1, 1896.

It would have been far better not to touch the subject at all, for we cannot now disguise from ourselves the truth, to which universal testimony has been borne by those present on the spot, that by increasing the charge on provincial administration we have actually intensified the financial pressure which it should have been our first object to relieve. Either on her own initiative or with the assistance of friendly Powers, Turkey must sooner or later cut down the expenditure upon superfluous officials, which is mainly responsible for crippling her resources, and regulate the extent to which the local exchequers can be drained by demands from the capital. The next step is the full and punctual payment of adequate salaries to the judges and officials, and, in my opinion, this should be accompanied by a change, at all events temporarily until public opinion has been brought into a healthier state, in the direction, not of greater decentralisation, but of a more rigid control from headquarters. The principal members of the local Medjliss, *e.g.* the Defterdar, as well as the governor and judges, should derive their appointments directly from the capital, and their salaries should be a primary and fixed charge on the provincial revenues. The temptation to local corruption, perhaps the worst because the most widely distributed, and therefore the most uncertain, would be enormously lessened, and although the competition for appointments might still involve the bribery of high-placed officials at Constantinople, it would be subject to two valuable checks. On the one hand the sums offered for posts would tend to approximate to a definite proportion in relation to a fixed and calculable salary, and on the other hand the Government would have every inducement to discourage irregularity and peculation subsequent to acceptance of office, which would diminish the surplus available for Imperial purposes after the charge for local services had been met.

At present it is the province which suffers from the corruption of officials, while the central Government reaps the primary, and perhaps the whole, advantage accruing from any economy or improvement which may be effected. It is a curious fact that the systems established by the Abbaside Khalifs, under which the prosperity of the Empire was raised to the highest pitch it has ever attained, was also the perfection of the principle of paternal, autocratic, and centralised rule. Under the early republican rule of the Hashimides and Ommeiades, the Ameers and Valis, selected exclusively from the Arabs of Syria, were allowed a latitude which is said to have resulted in misgovernment, although even during this period the successors of the Prophet reserved to themselves the right of appointing the civil judges with fixed salaries, who were independent of the governors. Each province was assessed, but it was allowed to levy its own taxation, and the national exchequer received nothing but the balance which remained over after the cost of the civil administration and of the military establishment had been defrayed. Growing dissensions among the claimants to the Caliphate led to increasing favouritism in the assignment of posts, and governors were allowed to rule their provinces for longer periods through deputies over whom they exercised but little supervision. The rise of the Abbaside power in the eighth century was marked by a more liberal exercise of patronage, which was thenceforth bestowed upon others than the Arab caste, and also by a curtailment of the tenure of office. Governors were transferred at frequent intervals from one province to another, and elaborate safeguards were introduced against an abuse of their authority. Military officers were associated with them in the capacity of advisers, and representatives of the Government of Bagdad were stationed at their courts to keep a careful watch over their conduct and report to the central authorities. The towns were allowed a considerable latitude in the management of their own affairs, provided that the taxes were punctually paid, but audit offices were established in all the larger centres, and careful registers of provincial accounts were deposited in the Central Bureau of Taxation. Finally, a Board of Inspection, presided over by the Chief Minister or by the Caliph in person, was instituted for the special purpose of investigating complaints and grievances and enforcing the attendance of governors.

A comparison of this system with the existing one suggests reflections by no means favourable to the extension of representative and decentralised institutions in the East.

Absolutism is capable of great good as well as of great evil, and it is the only form of government which appears to be possible in Oriental countries. But it is not easily reconcilable with the democratic principle, which also forms a prominent feature in Turkish institutions, and which has received a sanction and extension under the rule of the Osmanlis to which may be attributed many of the worst evils that afflict the Empire. Between the throne and the people there stands no aristocracy of birth, and, in the strict sense of the word, no middle class. The humblest peasant, be he Christian or Mussulman, may, and often does, attain to the highest offices in the State, and the provinces are ruled by men who have in many cases received little education, and whose training has been the usufruct of successive posts which afford them many opportunities of enriching themselves, but few, if any, of bettering the condition of those entrusted to their care. They possess neither the means nor the liberty to initiate improvements without sanction from the capital, and their actions are jealously scrutinised and reported upon by irresponsible intriguers and spies, who find it easy to impose upon Ministers naturally suspicious and generally ignorant of local conditions. The absolute seclusion imposed upon those in the direct line of succession to the throne renders it in the highest degree improbable that any Sultan will have the force of character or the experience which would enable him to make a clean sweep of the bureaucratic clique in whose hands rests the practical control of affairs, or to select men in their place in whose capacity and integrity he could confide. He may be, and probably is, perfectly conscious of the character of many of those who surround him. Baker Pasha once said that he had been told by the Sultan himself that he knew his own Minister of Justice would take a medjidieh (four shillings) for a bribe. His difficulty lies in forming an estimate of the capacities of untrained men to take their place, and the consequence, as I have been myself assured by several governors who talked to me on the subject, is that however upright their intentions, however sincere their desire to do their duty may be, they find themselves continually at the mercy of men whose one occupation in life is to traduce and misrepresent their motives, and whose efforts are seconded by every blackguard in the place who has discovered that his liberty of plunder or oppression has been curtailed.

Appoint good men, pay them well, give them reasonable security of tenure for a definite period with the prospect of reappointment, and punish them severely and for reasons publicly stated when they do wrong, and you will have an administration at least as good, and probably better, than any which exists in those recently emancipated States with which comparisons unfavourable to Turkey are perpetually, and in some respects unjustly, drawn.

The problem is by no means so hopeless as it appears. There is no lack of good men, even among the present occupants of the higher provincial posts. What is wanted is the compilation of an official list, recording the names and past services of every candidate, and a method of selection which, without derogating in the slightest degree from the discretion of the Sultan, will afford him better means of judging of qualifications, and greater security against the exertion of undue influence upon his advisers. The easiest method of arriving at this result is the adoption of the principle that in the multitude of counsellors there is safety. You may bribe one or two men, but unless you are a millionaire you cannot easily bribe a whole board. The constitution of an advisory council, composed of a fairly large number of judges or Ministers, and entrusted with the duty of submitting to the Sultan names for appointment or promotion, would also provide a convenient and competent body which might be charged with the further duty of investigating and reporting to His Majesty on any complaints or petitions formulated against a governor during the course of his tenure of office. It might be understood that no complaints would be entitled to a hearing unless they were duly transmitted and their *bonâ fides* attested by prominent and representative persons in the vilayet (*e.g.* the heads of the Moslem community and of the various Christian millets), who would thus become responsible for statements that might subsequently prove to have been unfounded in fact or vexatious in their character. The spy system would thus be deprived of its *raison d'être*, and while full liberty of choice and action would be reserved to the Sultan, who could disregard the advice and findings of the Board were he so inclined, he would at all events be supplied with the material for an unbiassed decision, and enabled to demonstrate to his own subjects his readiness to investigate their legitimate grievances.

The principle of combining the Christian and Mussulman elements in the civil administration has been also introduced in connection with the collection of taxes. In the Kaisariyeh vilayet the sheep-tax as well as the tithe is farmed, and the imposts, in accordance with the provisions of the reform scheme, are collected by men chosen from and by the members of the various religious communities, the Gregorians, the Protestants, and the Catholics. They are accompanied on their rounds by the zaptiehs, who are not supposed to be invested with any authority such as formerly enabled them to extort for their own advantage a higher amount than was actually due. It has already been explained that a strict enforcement of this theory, in the absence of regular and sufficient pay—now frequently twelve months or more in arrear—is practically impossible, and the same holds good with regard to the army, from the ranks of which many of the gendarmerie are selected.[1] Instead of being a primary or even a

---

[1] The zaptiehs are as a rule time-expired men, commanded by the Alai Bey, generally a colonel transferred from the *nizam* (regulars). In some cases a conscript is passed straight into the gendarmerie, and once enrolled he would not be called out again to serve with the regulars. The zaptieh is distinct from the police force, carrying arms and wearing a green tunic with orange braiding instead of a dark blue one trimmed with green. The police are a civil force under the control of a Chief Commissioner in

secondary charge upon the provincial revenue, the pay of the soldiery depends on the temporary condition of the local exchequer, and if the cash in hand is insufficient, money has to be forwarded from the capital to make up the deficiency.   In practice the monthly sum of twenty piastres is issued to the men only at Ramazan and the two Bairam feasts.   Consequently, when the time of their discharge arrives, they have large arrears owing to them, for which they obtain an order upon the treasury of the vilayet in which they intend to reside.   The presentation of these orders is often met by counter-claims for arrears of taxation, and the net result is that the unfortunate applicant receives nothing at all, or finds himself actually out of pocket after a number of years spent in the service of the State.

An evil which is much felt and complained of by the merchants at Kaisariyeh is the insecurity of the roads.   In Hamilton's day the mountains to the east were still infested by robber bands of Avshars and Kurds, and in the south he mentions the devastation and ruin which had been occasioned by the forays of a notorious freebooter, Choppan Oghlu.   The condition of the country has no doubt improved since then, but peaceable travellers are still molested and robbed on their way from the town to the villages, little more than two miles distant, and bales of merchandise are constantly intercepted and pillaged when passing Circassian settlements on the road between Konia and Kaisariyeh.   The apathy of the authorities of the

the towns, who is directly responsible to the Governor, and whose duty is to submit every day a "Journal" reporting the arrival, movements, and antecedents of all strangers.   They are employed with the foot zaptiehs for purposes of arrest, while the mounted gendarmes are chiefly used as escorts or guards to the tax-collectors.

district lays them under the not unnatural, if unfounded, suspicion of being actuated by hostility to
the Christians. The Greeks and Armenians together
constitute nearly one-half of the total population of
the town, and practically the whole of the export trade
is in their hands, for the small Mussulman shopkeepers and retail dealers confine themselves to
the supply of local wants.[1] It is obvious that a
determined effort would very soon put down highway robbery in the immediate neighbourhood, and
that if a signal example was made in the case of one
Circassian village, caravans would in future be freed
from molestation. The plea, which may legitimately
be advanced in the case of less civilised districts to
the east, that marauding bands of nomads can always
take refuge from the zaptiehs in mountainous and inaccessible tracts, is clearly not applicable where the
offence complained of is committed by the inhabitants
of a settled village.[2] The fact that the Circassians
are a class of aliens and recent immigrants from the
Caucasus, and that for nearly forty years they have
enjoyed not only the protection but the liberality of
the Government, which assigned special districts for
their occupation, constitutes an additional reason for

[1] The majority of the merchants of Kaisariyeh are middlemen engaged
in the distributing trade ; and with the exception of the manufacture of
saltpetre and carpets, already alluded to, the principal industries are
fruit-growing and the supply of articles of consumption. Melons recently
imported have been found to thrive well, and quantities of dried raisins
and wine are made from the produce of the vineyards which flourish on
the volcanic slopes of Argæus. The celebrated *pastirma* or jerked beef
is supplied by the large herds of cattle which are imported annually from
Erzerum.

[2] In another vilayet where similar depredations are common after dark,
the Governor is said to meet all complaints with the reply, "Sensible
persons like myself stay at home at night. If you were sensible you
would do the same !"

prompt and severe punishment of all delinquencies on their part. The duties of the gendarmerie are not heavy, and they ought to be more constantly employed in patrolling the roads; but the best hope for the future of this part of the vilayet lies in the prolongation of the railway from Angora, which should certainly not be delayed or abandoned owing to the adoption of other schemes in the south.

CHAPTER VI

THE ANTI-TAURUS

BETWEEN Kaisariyeh and the Euphrates, along the banks of which our eastward journey lay, runs the great range of the Anti-Taurus, breaking away from the Taurus at the Cilician gates south-east of Eregli, and having as its two outposts Mount Argæus on the west and Ararat on the boundary line that divides the Empires of Russia, Turkey, and Persia.

Though not uniformly the loftiest, it is the most continuous of all the ranges that traverse the continent of Lesser Asia, except the southern barrier of the Black Sea coast, which extends with scarcely a break from the main ridges of the Caucasus to the shores of the Ægean. The Taurus chain, composed of a number of separate links, sometimes divided by considerable intervals, sometimes crossing each other at right angles, terminates at Kharput in two divergent arms, which touch the frontier at Kotur and Rowanduz respectively, and are connected by the transverse ranges of Hakkiari and Tiari. No great waters, other than those of the Tigris, take their rise from the barren gorges of the Taurus, whereas the slopes of the Anti-Taurus, which in the west are clothed with dense forest, are the source of almost every important river that irrigates the plains of the interior. Both of the tributary streams, which unite below Egin to form the headlong torrent of the Euphrates, spring, like the Russian Aras, from its eastern highlands in the neighbourhood of Erzerum and Bayazid, while the western provinces of Sivas and Angora owe their amazing fertility to the currents of the Yeshil Irmak and the Halys, which flow down from the ridges north of Kaisariyeh.

The district is traversed by a network of roads which, radiating from the uplands of the Uzun Yaila south of Sivas, connect with Marash by the valleys of the Upper Saris to the west and of the Zamanti Zu to the east. Between these stretch the two main forks of the Anti-Taurus, running south and south-west, the former known as the Bimboa Dagh, and the latter by the names of the various passes which afford communication with the Argæus plain. Of these the shortest and most difficult leads through Tomarze over the Dede Bel, but, as I wished to visit the Hittite monument at Ferakdin, I chose the more circuitous route which traverses the Gez Bel and, making a détour to the north-east, rejoins the highroad at Shahr.

We left Kaisariyeh at daybreak, accompanied by our servant, a single zaptieh, and a portentously fat but ever-cheerful katirji, who was perpetually falling asleep and tumbling off his horse. In spite of his protestations he proved absolutely ignorant of the road ; and the monotony of marching at caravan pace being too much for our patience, we decided to face the inconvenience and risk of leaving our baggage unprotected, and for the next two days to shift for ourselves with the help of our solitary escort.

Riding by Talas and Zingir–dere, another Armenian village one hour beyond, we climbed a steep stony slope beneath the eastern face of Argæus, the red crags on its summit towering grandly above us into the deep blue of a cloudless sky. Descending from the crest of the plateau (6300 feet), and diverging from the Tomarze road near the small hamlet of Chormekji on the southern side, we cantered across a wide expanse of rolling downs sparsely dotted with cultivated fields and villages. The only one which we actually passed through was the Armenian village of Jujun, and a miserable cluster of mud hovels near the ravine of the Zamanti Su. As there was no path to guide us, and the zaptieh had never even heard of Ferakdin,[1] we wandered about for more than an hour under the broiling sun before we struck the right cart track and reached our destination late in the afternoon. Most of the villagers seemed as ignorant as our companion of the existence of any sculptured rock in the neighbourhood, and it was only after persistent efforts and minute descriptions that we at length succeeded in awakening the torpid memory of the headman, and inducing him to show us the spot, just half an hour's walk from his own house !

The rock is one of a line of low perpendicular cliffs which skirt the side of a ravine, and until you come close up to it, there are no visible signs of any sculpture. Almost overhanging a tiny stream, the subject of the panel, a libation scene, has an obvious and appropriate reference to the situation, which resembles that of Ivriz, whereas the rock-carvings of Boghaz Keui, placed on the tops of the surrounding hills, seem to have more connection with the worship of the heavenly bodies than with that of the forces of nature. On the other hand, the design of the Ferakdin figures, almost identical in point of costume and attitude with that of the Boghaz Keui reliefs, belongs probably to an earlier period than the sculpture at Ivriz.

[1] Mr. Le Chantre identifies it with the Dashtarkon ("the pass of Argæus") mentioned by Strabo. " Mission en Cappadoce," 1893-94.

Some modern writers, it is true, have been disposed to assign all the Hittite texts and sculptures to the period between 2500 and 2000 B.C. During the greater part of this period the kindred race inhabiting the lowlands of the Tigris were ruled by the *patesis*, or priest-kings of Kish, the successors of Dungi, King of Ur, whose Empire extended—as the excavations of M. de Sarzec at Telloh have proved—to the shores of the Mediterranean, and carried on a lucrative trade in cedar-wood, gold dust, diorite, lapis-lazuli, and bitumen with Syria, Upper Egypt, Phœnicia, Sinai, and Media. The invasion of Kudur Nakhundi in 2290 B.C., which transferred the nominal sovereignty to Elam, probably introduced little real change in the conquered territories, for the native dynasties continued to govern as vicegerents of the foreigner, and scarcely more than a century had elapsed before Babylon, under the rule of the Kassite Hammurabi, again succeeded in asserting its independence.

The Hittites of the west, meanwhile, continued to recognise the suzerainty of the parent stock, and Carchemish appears in 2200 B.C. as one of the various tributaries of Babylon. The next five centuries, however, witnessed the re-establishment and consolidation of the Elamite power in the south, and the rise of an independent Assyrian kingdom in the north. Egypt too began to stretch out her hands towards the coastlands of Asia Minor. The Syrian seaboard was invaded in the sixteenth century by the armies of Aahmes and Thothmes III., and when, after a brief interlude, the Mongol dynasty of the Hyksos had been expelled from the Nile valley, the rulers of the eighteenth dynasty again turned their attention in the same direction. The friendship and alliance of Rimmonnirari of Assyria, Burnaburiash of Babylon, and Dusratta, the Vannic king of the Minni, were in turn solicited by the Thothmes and Amenhoteps, who viewed with jealousy or alarm the growing independence of the Hittites of Pteria, Carchemish, and Marash. To this period, in all probability, belong the cuneiform tablets, written in the same style as those of Tel el Amarna, which are frequently unearthed in the walled citadel of the Hittite capital at Boghaz Keui.

But Assyria, however eager she might be to curtail the power of the confederacy beyond the Euphrates, was in no way desirous of furthering thereby the ambitions of the Pharaohs. Single-handed they could do nothing, and the occasional conflicts between the Judges of Israel and the Hittite clans of Syria must have inflicted almost as much or as little damage and annoyance on the northern empire as the fruitless victory of Rameses at Kadesh in 1330 B.C. The staff upon which Egypt had leant was to pierce her own hand. In the ninth century she fell a victim herself to the same power which, led by Shalmanezer II. in 832, swept the Hittites from the Amanns to the Taurus, and in 717 placed the victorious standard of Sargon on the walls of their last stronghold at Carchemish.

If the commonly accepted chronology be even approximately correct, it is evident that the period to which the various Hittite monuments might conceivably be ascribed covers a space of at least 1500 years. The language represented by the hieroglyphic texts may no longer have been in general use between the first and second millennium before Christ, yet it by no means necessarily follows that the sculptures upon which they are found belong to an anterior date. Cuneiform may have become the ordinary medium of oral and written communication in the Hittite, the Vannic, and the Chaldæan Empires, while the ancient

symbols were still intelligible, at least to the educated
classes, and employed, as we employ Latin to this day,
in commemorating religious traditions or historical
events.   Not only have the excavations at Boghaz
Keui, Euyuk, and Carchemish (Jerablus) failed as yet
to bring to light a single bilingual inscription, but even
on the curious Hittite *stele*—covered with hieroglyphs
—which Dr. Kolewey had just discovered among the
ruins of Babylon when I revisited them last year,
there are no cuneiform characters to guide us in the
task of interpretation.   It is scarcely reasonable to
suppose that a religious monument of this kind, set
up in the heart of a foreign capital, was a mere trophy
of war, unintelligible to the inhabitants.   More probably the dwellers by the Euphrates recognised in the
gods and language of the Hittites the deities that
were worshipped, the tongue that was spoken by their
Accadian ancestors, before the marsh lands were re-
claimed or the walls of Babylon built.   To them
the decipherment of the hieroglyphics presented no
greater difficulties than we find in the transliteration
of classical abbreviations, which have long ago been
incorporated in the literature of our own country.

But if the form of language employed affords no
certain clue to the date of the numerous sculptures
scattered over Anatolia, from the Halys and the Taurus
to the Euphrates and the Mediterranean, some light at
all events may be thrown on the problem by a study of
the varying character of their art.   Coming originally
from a land in which stone was scarce, and rock-
sculpture consequently unknown, it may well be that
the Hittites of the west never thought of perpetuating
their legends and history in this form at all, until after
the language in which they had been handed down
had ceased to be the language of their everyday life,

though it still retained its place in the worship of their
gods.   The unmistakable influence of Egypt, which
appears in the Hathor-headed bulls or the half-human,
half-animal figures of Euyuk, would naturally lead one
to infer that they belong to the period from 1650 to
1500 B.C., during which the most intimate political
connections existed between the two Empires.   On the
other hand the influence of Assyria, which is scarcely,
if at all, noticeable in the sculptures of Ferakdin, but
is strongly marked in the panel of Ivriz, and still more
so in the lion-guarded gates and storeyed galleries of
Boghaz Keui, suggest an origin of later date (*circa*
1400–1000 B.C.), when the Hittite tribes, having congregated in large cities and acquired the science of
elaborate fortification, turned for the refinements of
their art and civilisation to the people whom they had
not yet been taught to regard as their most inveterate
foes.

The Ferakdin panel is a small one, and is divided
into two sections.   On the extreme left stands a tall
man, wearing a high conical hat, shoes with upturned
points, and greaved leggings, while on one shoulder
he carries a curved wand.   He may not unreasonably
be conjectured to represent the Great God of the
Hittites.   Facing him is a cone-shaped altar, supporting the seated figure of a child.[1]   The head has been
sadly mutilated, and this may account for the peculiar
sharpness of the features, which recalls the appearance
of the ibis-headed gods of Egypt.   On either side of
the child are hieroglyphic signs, and behind him, facing
in the same direction, is a smaller-sized man, dressed
like the god, and pouring water from a vase upon the
ground.   The second section is a repetition of the first,

[1] Or, as some archæologists have conjectured, an eagle.   I am unable
to recognise the slightest resemblance.

except that the actors are women instead of men.   On
the left, facing the altar and child, whose features in
this case are more distinguishable because less damaged, is a lady of gigantic proportions, probably the
Great Mother Goddess, seated upon a throne and wear-

HITTITE SCULPTURE—FERAKDIN

ing a long robe and low rounded cap.   On the right,
behind the child, stands another woman, the Hittite
Queen, of smaller stature, and girt with a close-fitting
tunic, who performs the same act of libation as her
consort.   Beyond the panel runs a straggling line of

hieroglyphs, and one of the signs is a rough delineation of the human hand, the outstretched finger pointing to the adjacent sculpture.

Pursuing our way up the gorge of the Zamanti, narrowing in some places to the smallest dimensions, where the swirling water rims the base of beetling crags and seems literally alive with trout, we reached in three hours the village of Chatar Oghlu, in a grassy meadow under the lower spurs of the mountains, and were promptly assailed by a pack of magnificent wolf-dogs. Here began the sharp ascent of the stony hillside, a ribbon of green marking the course of a tiny rivulet down the hollow, by the side of which large herds of cattle were grazing. In order to strike the Tomarze road it was necessary, after reaching the top, to mount at a transverse angle to the ridges, climbing and descending the steep shaly declivities on foot, and watering the horses at the narrow trickles of water that thread the bottom.

The scenery is pretty but not striking, and after regaining the road we wound our way up the Gez Bel (6800 feet), among massive boulders of rock, where the air was fragrant with the sweet scent of the pines that cover the slopes, many of them standing like gaunt and naked skeletons, or lying strewn in every direction and blackened by fire to the colour of ebony.

Debouching from the higher passes, the road now enters a vast and cultivated plain, at the farther limit of which stands the Circassian village of Akbunar. Here we put up for the night in the principal house, and were provided by our hosts with big bowls of clotted cream and curdled milk. The inhabitants were perfectly friendly and cordial, nor did I notice the least signs of antipathy between them and our Turkish zaptieh. Professor Ramsay in his interesting book, "Impressions of Turkey," after remarking that "the broad distinction of Christian and Moslem is wholly insufficient and even misleading," goes on to say: "The Turkish peasants entertain a stronger hatred towards the Circassian, rigid and pious Moslem as he is, than towards the Greek or Armenian Christian. You often meet a Greek in a Turkish village, but you rarely see a Circassian in a Turkish village, or, if you do, he glares about, feeling himself an enemy among enemies." I am rather inclined to describe the sentiment of the ordinary Turk towards the Circassian as one of contempt for his manners, mingled with a respectful awe of his predatory instincts. In some respects the Circassians are not unlike the Kurds. They are rather vain of their personal appearance, generally going about in the large towns in their old national garb, a close tunic stuffed with cartridges, and their "glare" is as characteristic an expression on the features of their fellow-countrymen in the Caucasus to-day as it is on the face of the exiles in Anatolia. They may feel themselves enemies among enemies, but the feeling is not sufficiently strong to deter them from venturing into the large towns, where, like the Kurds, they swagger about with conscious superiority, the authorities, as a rule, allowing them to do much as they please. A quaint feature of their villages is the number of wooden platforms which are erected on forked tree-stems to hold the barley straw.

A ride over the rich uplands, thickly sown with corn, and across a small ridge of hills, brings you down upon the Saris Su, which rolls its limpid stream over a gravelly bottom among copses of willow, oak, and berberis from the Armenian village of Shahr.

The modern settlement, built on both sides of the

river, occupies the site of the old Comana, the head-quarters, as its name implies,[1] of the worship of the great Earth Goddess Ma. Whatever the date of its foundation as a centre of that Mongolian cult, which, emanating in all probability from the aboriginal settlements in Chaldee, overspread in varying forms the greater part of the country between the Black Sea and the Mediterranean, it survived by more than a thousand years the overthrow of the kindred city shrines of the Hittites at Boghaz Keui and Carchemish. Even after Pompey's conquest in 65 B.C., the native ruler of Cappadocia, which was not deprived of its independence until the reign of Tiberius, still stood in wholesome awe of his formidable rival, the high priest of Comana. "A terrible war would break out if the high priest—young as he is, and well equipped with horse, foot, and supplies—were minded, as men thought, to take up arms in his own defence." So wrote Cicero in one of his Letters,[2] and the cursory allusion is amplified and illustrated by the brief but graphic narrative of Strabo. The Cataonians, a nation of ecstatics, may be, he tells us, the subjects of a king (*subditi regi*), but it is to the sovereign pontiff that they render obedience. Royal honours and priestly dignities are showered upon the members of his family. He commands a vast revenue from the broad acres assigned to the Temple of Bellona, and directs the ministrations of the six thousand priests and priestesses, the prototypes of the Amazons of Greek legend, who serve within the sacred precincts.

[1] "The place of Ma." *Cf.* Mazaca, "the shrine of Ma," the ancient name of Cæsarea. Strabo mentions the absurd derivation from the "mourning locks" (*coma lugubris*) deposited here by Orestes and his sister Iphigenia, who were supposed to have brought the worship of Diana from Tauric Scythia.

[2] Lib. xv. Ep. iv.

Yet of all this regal state and gorgeous ceremonial no visible memorial survives.   Clear-cut inscriptions, delicate carvings there are, but their language and art are the language and art of the Roman Hieropolis, not of Cappadocian Comana.   On the left bank lies a mass of shapeless ruin and the auditorium of an ancient amphitheatre, now almost entirely covered by a land-slip from the steep hill that rises behind it.   On the

TEMPLE AT COMANA

right stands a solitary relic of what was probably in former times a temple, a noble archway on a smaller scale, but otherwise not ·unlike that of the famous Temple of Augustus at Angora, decorated with Corin-thian mouldings and figures of the "leaf and egg" pattern.   About a quarter of a mile from the village, in a bleak and shadeless glen dotted with low scrub, are the more perfect remains of a small temple, of which the *cella* has been scarcely injured, although

much of the roofing has collapsed. The entrance
to the lower storey, the floor of which is below ground-
level, has been partially blocked with fallen stones, and
can only be passed on all-fours. The interior consists
of an oblong chamber, perforated on two sides by long
recesses like *loculi* for the reception of the dead,
and at the far end there is a larger aperture, which
apparently gave access to a staircase communicating
with the upper storey, now closed by impenetrable
masses of masonry of extraordinary size and thickness.
The chapel above, a bare space without any trace of
columns, enclosed by solid walls of squared stone, is
covered by a roof, of which the remaining portion,
overlapping the side looking towards the valley, is tri-
angular in shape, and has a slightly projecting cornice.
Below, in a line with the apex of the triangle, is a
large window with a rounded arch, between two
smaller ones of the same design. Behind the temple
stands a solitary column, and near it the fragments of
two others bearing a Greek inscription, which begins
with the word " Heliodorus." The only other relic of
interest is a fine but rather coarse mosaic, that forms
the flooring of one of the hovels in the town, a bold
design of birds and flowers worked in black upon a
white ground. There is, I believe, another of the same
period close by, but it reposes at present under the
ruins of a house which has recently fallen in.

Continuing southward from the left bank of the
Saris over a high crest (5800 feet) and crossing a rolling plateau, the track passes the village of Yalak and
others, tenanted by Avshars. This curious people, of
whom very little is known, seem to have come from
the Persian province of Azerbaijan, and to have been
driven into the hills by the Circassian immigration from
the plateau which they originally occupied south of

Sivas. Their religion is said to be the same as that of
the Kizilbash or Redheads, a mixture of Shiite Moham-
medanism, Christianity, and Paganism ; but the Turks
deny that they have any at all, and I have never been
able to induce them to discuss the subject. They do
not seem to resent inquiry, but the question appears
neither to interest them nor to convey much significance to their minds, and I suspect that the majority
of them have merely adopted the superstitions of
their neighbours without accepting the dogmas of
the Sunni faith or retaining any definite ones of their
own. No doubt their transition from the nomad
state has modified their original peculiarities, and
although I cannot assert that they now intermarry
with the other races of the interior, it is very difficult
to trace any marked difference between them and the
Kurds.

The latter have several villages close by, and at
Keklik Oghlu we stayed in one of their houses. These
Kurds have adopted a pastoral life, and although the
climate must be trying during a cold season in the
Anti-Taurus, they no longer shift their tents, as the
roving bands of the Diarbekr and Dersim highlands do,
between the *kishlak*, or winter camping-grounds, in
the plain, and the *yaila*, or summer quarters, in the
hills. They are handsome, well-built men, with complexions of an unusually dark olive tint, and coal-black
eyes and hair ; and whereas the eastern Kurds almost
invariably wear moustaches only and trim them carefully, these generally wear long and unkempt beards.
They are also far less jealous of the appearance of their
women in public, and our host actually allowed his
wife to assist in the cooking of our dinner. But the
appalling filth of the room in which we slept, or tried
to sleep, and the vigour of its animal life, drove us in

desperation to saddle our horses before sunrise and
continue our march to Geoksun.

Built on a high mound above the river of the same
name, it contains a few well-built houses, in one of
which we accepted the hospitality of a Kurd, once a
celebrated robber of Marash.   Except as a convenient
halting-place, the town offers no inducement to the

KURD OF THE ANTI-TAURUS

traveller to stop, but I was interested to observe the
enlightened efforts which had been made to improve
its sanitation.   No one attempts such a thing in most
towns in Asiatic Turkey, which are built on the dungheaps of centuries, but here some thought had been
obviously given to the matter, with the result that all
the drainage was carefully conducted into the little

rivulet that trickled through the street and provided the population with its supply of drinking water!

A school inspector paid us a visit during our stay. He told us that French was a compulsory subject in the Turkish schools, but added, "Of course we look upon England as our friend. Why is England so unfriendly to us? Can we do anything to regain her good-will?" I explained to him that our feelings had been a little shocked by occurrences of a kind to which we were not accustomed at home, and which seemed to indicate a regretable want of appreciation of the rights of person and property. "Yes," he admitted, "those events were much to be deplored ; but you do not know how seditious the Armenians are, and how the missionaries undermine their respect for our authority by the teaching in their schools. How easy it would be for us if we could deal with them as Russia does in the Caucasus! But we know very well that if we were to follow her example and shut up these schools, the European nations would at once interfere and protest against our action."

A mile to the south rises the Ayer Bel to a height of 6300 feet. The northern slopes are quite bare, but from the top, looking in the direction of Marash, the scenic effect almost equals that of the Zigana near Trebizond, range on range of densely wooded hills glimmering with every gradation of blue beneath the rays of the rising sun. All day long we rode under the shade of spreading planes, with gleaming white stems, stone and Austrian pines, juniper, rowan, oak, willow, fir, and *tespi* trees covered with small, apricot-flavoured fruit, the dark brown kernels of which the natives thread into necklaces and rosaries.

This part of the country seems entirely depopulated. Tekir Yazi, once an Armenian village, is now deserted, and the only vestiges of human habitation are a few Kurdish huts or covered gipsy-like waggons. The road drops over three thousand feet to the level of a stream, and following the banks for about ten miles, climbs almost perpendicularly through vineyards and gardens belonging to Kurds to the Armenian hamlet of Furnus. Here are some three hundred houses, one of which is occupied by an aged Armenian priest, a

THE AYER BEL

venerable old patriarch with a flowing snow-white beard, whom we found reclining on a bench in the verandah beneath the branches of an overhanging plane, grasping a long staff in one hand and petting with the other a little white prick-eared spaniel from Adana that lay on the mattress beside him. He is known to the Turks by the name of the "mad bishop," in his earlier days a very active champion of the Church

militant, who, having headed or promoted several
local risings against the Government, was for some
time exiled to Constantinople. The Armenians in
this district recognise the authority of the Catholicos
of Sis, who still looks upon himself as the equal of
the Catholicos of Echmiadzin, although his influence,
like that of the third Catholicos of Akhtamar near
Van, has been gradually reduced within comparatively
modest limits. The people are more independent in
character than their co-religionists of Kurdistan, and
the national spirit is probably stronger in these parts
owing to the survival of an independent kingdom in
the west for more than two hundred years after the
cession of Ani to the Byzantines [1] and its subsequent
ruin by the Seljuks.

From Furnus the sandy track strewn with boulders
pursues an erratic course through the pine glades,
affording lovely glimpses, now and then, of the
forested outlines on the eastern horizon, and the castle-
like crags that rise abruptly from the folds in the valley
beneath. Large chameleons and lizards darted among
the stones or lay basking in the sunlight, and the dead
leaves and thistles rustled weirdly as they fluttered
down the passes on the breeze. Crossing the Furnusi
stream, where the pines along the banks have been
burnt to clear a space for gardens, you come suddenly
on a piece of old road with diamond-shaped paving,
the work of Murad Pasha two centuries ago, and from
the top of another steep ascent look down on the desolate valley of the Jihun. The river, rolling in a
broad channel, is spanned by a magnificent bridge of
three arches, also built under his auspices, and on the
farther bank is a small guardhouse where travellers are

---

[1] 1046 A.D. The principality of Lesser Armenia lasted from 1180 to
1374, when Sis was captured and destroyed by the Sultan of Egypt.

provided with coffee in an arbour roofed with dead
leaves and twigs of sycamore and plane.

A few more miles of bleak stony ground have still
to be covered before Marash is reached, a by no means
imposing-looking town, built in straggling lines along
a spur, the crest of which is crowned with the scanty
remains of an old castle. Fair accommodation can be
obtained in a house belonging to the agents of the
tobacco *regie*, but many of the better class of houses
belonging to the wealthier Armenians were destroyed
during the riots which occurred at the time of the
insurrectionary movement in the neighbouring town of
Zeitun. This was the only instance in which the
Armenians made a determined effort at resistance,
and ultimately succeeded in obtaining terms from the
Turks. The inhabitants of Zeitun had been known
for long as a turbulent and intractable race; no
traveller or caravan could feel safe within reach of
their marauding bands,[1] and the small detachments of
troops despatched against them by the Government
from time to time proved hopelessly inadequate to
restore order in the district or to impose upon the
rebels the authority of the Sultan. Since the last
outbreak, however, ten years ago, there had been no
open rupture, and when the rising eventually took
place in 1896 it was in all probability due to a
misunderstanding.

A body of some 300 Zeitunlis, hearing or pretend-
ing to have heard of a plot to massacre the inhabitants,
marched down from the hills and surprised a company
of Turkish troops which was being sent up from
Marash. Having succeeded in this unexpected on-
slaught, they fell back upon Zeitun, and attacked the

---

[1] I was told by a governor in the west that he had been himself plundered by these Zeitunlis within the last few years.

Turkish garrison in the fort which the Government had built in 1878, at a distance of about a mile from the town. The besieged, although they were provided with several pieces of heavy ordnance besides a considerable quantity of rifles and ammunition, surrendered after a brief resistance and were sent down as prisoners to Zeitun. Meanwhile the insurgents set to work to make preparations for the defence of the fort against the Turkish reinforcements which were being hurried up from the south. By this time (it was winter and the state of the roads rendered the movement of troops difficult) a force of 30,000 men had been collected at Marash, while others were marching upon Zeitun through the south-western passes of the Anti-Taurus, sweeping Puruns and the Armenian villages on their way. A large number of refugees, thinking to escape the force which was being moved up under the command of Ali Pasha from Adana, had congregated at Furnus, where they were overtaken and massacred to a man, the soldiers setting fire to a monastery erected by the bishop, who was absent at the moment, and when he realised his loss nearly died of a broken heart.

Warned by this example, the Armenians, concluding that no abstention on their part would acquit them of the suspicion of connivance with the movement, flocked in hundreds from the surrounding districts into the city, thereby of course greatly increasing the difficulty of provisioning the defenders. Before leaving Marash the soldiers, roused by this time to a pitch of fury which Ferit Pasha, the commandant of the troops, did nothing to allay, looted the bazaars, burnt part of the town and the theological college belonging to the American Mission, and massacred between seven and eight hundred of the Armenians, although they were careful to spare the women. The Mutessarif, who refused a guard for the Mission, was believed to have not merely acquiesced in the outbreak, but to have actively incited the riot by spreading false reports to the effect that the Zeitunlis had killed many of the Mussulman peasants, assaulting and mutilating their women. Even before the rising, the suspicions of the population in Marash had been wantonly excited by the folly of the Armenian residents, who for some years past had been accumulating and concealing fire-arms in their houses, despite the earnest and repeated warnings of the missionaries. The contagion of fanaticism spread as far as Aintab, seventy miles to the south, but with less disastrous results, for the bazaars, unlike those of Marash, were divided into separate quarters for the Mussulmans and Armenians, and the Christians were consequently able to barricade the street and defend themselves by firing on their assailants from the roofs.

Having wreaked their vengeance and completed the work of destruction at Marash, the army set out for Zeitun, and, under cover of a dense fog which lasted for three days, crept up unperceived to the foot of the fortress. Thereupon the defenders, despairing of their chances of effective resistance, knocked a hole through the wall close to the ground, and, setting fire to the building, stole away unperceived and shut themselves up in the city. Completely beleaguered, and suffering severely from the ravages of famine and disease, they yet succeeded in repelling every assault for more than a month, when the Powers intervened, and the Consuls were sent to arrange terms of peace, on the basis of an indemnity on the one hand, and on the other a concession to the Zeitunlis that, for the future, they should have a Christian governor of their own.

G

However culpable their action, which entailed wide-spread misery on those of their compatriots who had no part in the plot, it is impossible to withhold our admiration for the gallantry and pluck which they displayed, and which are the qualities least common in the Armenian character. It is to be hoped that they will now settle down as quiet and peaceable citizens, and that the Turks will recognise that it is to their own interest to enlist the loyalty of such men rather than to crush their manliness of spirit and reduce them to the position of discontented serfs. Time will no doubt be needed to efface the memories of the past; but the Armenian, whatever his many faults may be, is marvellously little prone to resentment, and the town of Zeitun has already recovered a certain degree of prosperity. An industry has been started for the manufacture of coloured cotton for women's dresses, and the money invested in it brings in a very considerable return.

The present Mutessarif of Marash, the third since the date of the disturbances, was formerly governor of Bayezid, and seems to take a real interest in the development of the sandjak. He was endeavouring to make a good *chaussée* to Aintab, and had commenced the construction of a bridge over the Erkenez Su; but found himself much hampered by the lack of revenue available for further works in the Aleppo vilayet and the high price of labour, which amounted to an average of three piastres (about 8d.) per man per day. The advent of the railway would, as he pointed out, give an impetus not only to the cultivation of a soil of great natural fertility, but also to the exploitation of the copious mineral and other resources of the district. Rice, pulse, and cotton are already grown in large quantities near Marash, and wild tea at Albistan, on the direct route through Gurun to Sivas, while a variety of timber abounds on the sides of the Anti-Taurus and the cedar-clad slopes of Amanns to the south. A glance at the map reveals the existence of mines in every part of the mountain ranges,[1] from Sivas and Konia in the west to Diarbekr in the east. Silver is found at a village six hours from Marash, splendid iron at Zeitun, coal, lead, and mineral springs near Albistan, while petroleum is washed down from the highlands of Kaisariyeh by the waters of the Jihun. With the establishment of proper means of communication it should not be difficult to attract capital to these parts, and the consequent influx of labour from other districts would reduce the price of working and provide a fruitful source of revenue to replenish the exhausted coffers of the Treasury.

[1] Bulgar Maden (Taurus silver mines) and Bereketli Maden (abundant mines), near Eregli ; Keban Maden, near Kharput ; Arghana Maden, near Diarbekr ; and Maden Shehr (town mine) on the Kara Dagh, near Karaman, &c. Near Erzerum there is a coal-mine ; but it is not exploited, and the *tezek* or dung fuel is supplemented by firewood which has to be brought from a great distance.

CHAPTER VII

THE TAURUS

THE route which runs from Marash through Besne and Kiakhta over the Taurus is not the most direct to Malatia, but it derives a special interest from the fact that it probably follows the line of the old Roman road between Samsat on the Euphrates and Malatia, the ancient military posts of Samosata and Melitene. An able summary of the arguments in favour of this supposition is given in Mr. Yorke's paper, to which allusion has already been made, and it had been suggested to me that it might be worth while to make the attempt (which I was, however, obliged subsequently to abandon) to cross the mountains from Kiakhta to Gerger, and to follow by land the bend of the river through the gorges which Von Moltke descended by raft.

The first part of the journey, after crossing the Erkenez Su and the spurs of the Kapuchin Dagh, lies over undulating country, covered with dwarf cut-leaved oak, to the Kurdish settlement of Bazarjik (3000 feet), on the farther side of the Ak Su or White River. All the houses are surrounded with wooden palisades, inside which the cattle are herded for the night, and the natives subsist chiefly on buffalo milk and rancid cheese. A rough track continues due east through the oak woods past the villages of Girit—a corruption of the word Crete—in which the Mussulman refugees from the island, since its occupation by Greece, have been settled—and Jenjere, a collection of dismal hovels in a stony wilderness, where the traveller finds it easier to procure goat's milk than drinkable water. From this point onward the road becomes an artificial stair-case, paved with huge round pebbles, and, surmounting the ridge that overlooks the valley of the Owdere Su, enters Besne, a village of some 1500 houses. The desert gorge in which it stands is so narrow that many of the houses appear at first sight to form part of the hillside, and the only prominent features of the place are a superfluous number of rather ugly minarets. As the spot has the reputation of being very feverish, the Kaimakam considerately assigned to our use a house standing by itself more than a mile to the north, where, on our arrival, we found a dozen men performing their devotions upon the carpeted roof. Their protracted orisons completed, they showed us into a large and comfortable room, and invited us to share their evening meal of stewed gelatinous *bania* and sweet potatoes.

The next day was spent in crossing the two valleys of the Owdere Su, a mere trickle of water at this time of the year, and the Geok Su, over downs dotted with vineyards and a few small and dilapidated villages. The thermometer ranged from 100° in the shade during the daytime to 80° at night, and the rapid changes of temperature before sunrise, as one rode up and down the nullahs, produced very much the same feeling experienced in swimming through cross-currents of water. The only large town, Adiaman, is built on slightly rising ground near the foot of the Taurus, and surrounded by gardens. Large quantities of Roman coins are dug up in the neighbourhood, and a little to the eastward, at Perre, are the remains of a fine

three-arched aqueduct and rock-tombs of the same
period. The latter are square shaped, with four side
niches, and over the entrance of one of them is a
woman's bust, rudely sculptured and much defaced.
The Roman military road, which is clearly visible
alongside of the aqueduct, near a beautiful spring of
clear cold water fringed with thickets of blackberry,
disappears again almost immediately, and no traces of
it are discernible again even in the vicinity of the
great bridge over the Bolam Su.

A short ride along the base of the mountains to
the north-east brings you to the banks of this river
flowing beneath the peak of the Nimrud Dagh, a
mountain which, viewed without its snow covering,
hardly, I think, deserves the encomiums which some
travellers have lavished upon it. Wild figs grow
luxuriantly along the banks of the stream, inter-
spersed with the inevitable dwarf oak and masses of
terebinth trees hung with pink clusters of berries; and
about a mile from the point where it debouches upon
the plain, the channel is spanned by that most splendid and impressive monument of Rome's architectural
genius, the bridge of Vespasian and Severus.

Its wonderful state of preservation, the enormous
span of its arch,[1] and the noble simplicity of the whole
structure appeal the more forcibly to the imagination
from the apparent incongruity and purposelessness of
its situation. Were it, as it seems, the approach to
some great capital strewn with the crumbling evidences
of departed grandeur, we could understand the reasons
for what must have been a prodigious expenditure of
labour, time, and money in this wild and remote region,
on the far verge of the Empire. But not only is there
no sign of a city; the very lie of the ground seems to

---

[1] 112 feet. The height is 56 feet.

ROMAN BR DGE, K AKHTA.

disprove the previous existence of any road by which an army could have marched up through the main passes. There is the bridge and nothing more. Slabs bearing inscriptions of the two emperors who erected and restored it are built into the solid masonry below the battlemented coping, and on either bank stand two sentinel columns[1] without a trace of ornament or carving; but the ground falls in stony hummocks to the river-bed, as though neither pickaxe nor spade had ever disturbed their rugged outlines. Behind the cliffs, springing abruptly from the water's edge, narrow as if they would meet across the chasm, while their walls, falling inwards toward the base, form a vault of inky blackness, against which the massive fabric stands out clear and distinct like an arch of the purest white marble.

Not far off is the little village of Kiakhta, clustering round the foot of a precipitous limestone crag which overhangs the gorge of the Kiakhta Su, its summit outlined by the mouldering walls of an old castle. The central keep, which has a more modern appearance than the rest of the building, and is constructed of smaller stones, commands a striking view down the ravine of the hills to the south, and the great columns of the so-called monument of Karakush, standing out against the horizon. On the inner wall of a semicircular room built into the exterior line of fortifications overlooking the western valley is an inscription which the Kaimakam informed me bears the name of "Malik Mansur," the second son of Saladin, and the reported founder of the castle. Local tradition, however, is associated only with the period of its occupation by the Kurds, before the Government asserted their authority over the nomad tribes of the Taurus, and, long

---

[1] A column on the left bank is the only one destroyed.

since deserted, the whole structure is now rapidly crumbling to pieces.

With a view to carrying out my original intention of exploring the eastern bend of the Euphrates, I made careful inquiries about possible routes over the intervening mountains, and the likelihood of my being able

THE CASTLE, KIAKHTA

to discover any traces of a former road by the side of the river. The replies which I received compelled me to relinquish the idea, and though I afterwards regretted my decision, the information subsequently given to me at Malatia and Gerger fully corroborated what I had been told at Kiakhta, and inclined me to believe

that the journey, if undertaken at all, must be commenced on the eastern, not on the western bank.
There is—so the natives allege—no practicable track
for pack-horses across the mountains ; it would be
necessary to lead them on foot up and down the steep
sides, making long and frequent detours, and the few
villages which exist in this district are so widely scattered, that it would be often impossible to obtain a
night's lodging or food, either for animals or men.
Similar accounts are so frequently given to deter travellers from going into regions where brigandage is
rife, and where an attack upon them would involve
the authorities in serious trouble, that I should have
discounted these difficulties, and attempted the journey in spite of them, had it not been for a positive
assurance that, even in the event of my reaching the
Euphrates, I should find myself debarred from farther
progress. The cliffs, I was told, descend so abruptly
into the water that they admit of no passage between ; and since Von Moltke made his expedition by
raft, starting from Kummer Khan near Malatia, great
masses of rock have been dislodged from the crests
and hurled into the bed of the river. It is scarcely
probable that this story, repeated to me at both the
above-mentioned places, can be a mere invention, and
if it is true, the General's achievements will not easily
be repeated. In any case, the attempt would have to
be made during the melting of the snows, for, as I
discovered later, the stream at Kummer Khan is too
shallow during the summer to allow of raft navigation,
even if rafts were procurable without long notice
beforehand.

But admitting the possibility of descending the
rapids in this way, and avoiding the sunken rocks,
which, in the event of a collision, would at once pierce

the inflated skins by which the raft is floated, I doubt very much whether any fresh light would be thrown on the vexed problem of the Roman road. I talked to more than one educated native who had travelled through the villages on the eastern bank between Gerger and Malatia, and they all agreed that there were no traces of anything of the kind, and that a French scientist had made a careful but fruitless investigation a few years ago. That any strategic road can ever have traversed a mountainous district which is now believed to be impassable for horses seems to me, I confess, well-nigh incredible; and while the bridge over the Bolam Su is inexplicable except on the assumption that it formed part of a great highway, it can scarcely be supposed that any consideration of military convenience would have induced a people so practical as the Romans to make the short cut through Adiaman to Kiakhta only to turn aside again to Gerger and follow the tortuous curve of the Euphrates to the north. It appears to me far more probable that the continuation of the road, if any remnant of it still survives, will ultimately be discovered on the line of the head-waters of the Bolam Su. No two travellers follow the same track over the hills, for there are so many, and they cross and recross so often, that the zaptieh, unless pressed for time, will choose that with which he is personally most familiar or which is most convenient at the particular time of year. Mr. Hogarth's party crossed in the spring, when the snow still lay deep on the ground, and it must be remembered that, as pasturage is extremely scanty on the bare ridges of the Taurus even in summer, the selection of halting-places is necessarily regulated by the movements of the tribal Kurds, in whose camps alone can any provisions be obtained. This occasionally leads one over the higher tops, which the military road in all probability avoided. There is no trace of it on the eastern bank of the Bolam Su close to the bridge, but it is possible that, after turning slightly aside to Kiakhta, it rejoined the stream farther up, to the left of the ordinary tracks across the watershed, and came down upon the Malatia plain west of the town, where the modern roads from Marash and Albistan converge.

The route which I followed occupied a little under eighteen hours, and would, I imagine, at an earlier season of the year, be completely blocked by snow. The scenery is desolate to a degree unparalleled except on the Kop Dagh, between the Black Sea and Erzerum, having all the savagery without the grandeur of the north-eastern range, and affording no relief to the eye except a patch or two of millet or maize by the side of the resonant burns that have furrowed a course through the shaly basin of the deep ravines. Riding N.N.W. for an hour and a half, and leaving the small village of Shad on your left, you cross a ridge of 4300 feet, and continuing due northward for three hours, descend to the stream at Sinjak Deresi. Here the surface is broken by large outcrops of red and green marble streaked with white veins, and you begin the laborious ascent of a steep incline on which the track narrows to a foot's breadth. From 5300 feet it drops again with equal suddenness, and turning westward, climbs along the banks of another burn till it reaches the top of the watershed (5900 feet), a slightly sloping tableland of verdant grass dotted with the black goats'-hair tents of the Kurds. Presenting ourselves at the chief's tent, in which two women were busily weaving a carpet, we obtained a young kid for our dinner, the flesh of which was scarcely distinguishable from inferior mutton. During the night the thermometer fell to 55° Fahr., the mercury rising 30° at a leap between 6 and 6.30 (sunrise) next morning.

The trend of the second day's journey was throughout in a north-westerly direction. A slight rise brought us to the highest point, just 6000 feet, followed by a descent of 1600 feet, and fording a small but rapid stream, we followed an easier track, past several clusters of Kurdish gravestones, bearing the sculptured devices of scimitars and gridirons, to the northern edge of the mountain range. Here the shelving rocks are splashed with some kind of mineral purple, and in the centre of the broad valley, a little to the westward, the eye, weary of the arid landscape, rests gladly upon the grateful contrast of gardens and orchards surrounding the city of Malatia. On reaching the Kharput road, we discovered the president of the Belidie awaiting us with a small cavalry escort, and after a three-mile ride in their company found ourselves comfortably ensconced on divans round a bubbling spring in the courtyard of his house and regaled with glasses of cool syrup and sherbet.

The town (3300 feet) lies on a flat, surrounded on all sides by mountain chains and embowered in poplars and fruit trees of various kinds. Pears, apples, melons, and grapes flourish luxuriantly, and out of a total of about 6000 houses more than a quarter are inhabited by Armenians. The only interesting sight, however, is the gathering on market-days of the Taurus Kurds, with their flashing black eyes and neat twisted moustaches, some of them carrying hawks on their wrists, and arrayed in baggy blue or white trousers bound at the waist with gay coloured sashes of silk.

The Kharput road, one of the best in the interior, runs straight across the plain and over a slight elevation to Kadi Keui, where there is a ferry over the

Euphrates.   The boats are of the same Noah's ark
type as those used on the lower reaches near Birejik—
great flat-bottomed hulks, with prows nearly level with
the water and sterns arched up overhead at a height of
some twelve feet or more above the stream, propelled
by poles of the size of a small poplar stem.   Near the
banks is a circular mound, obviously artificial, which
might repay exploration in view of its proximity to the

EUPHRATES FERRY-BOAT

Assyrian monument close to Kummer Khan, six miles
farther up.   This was first seen and described by Von
Moltke, an inscription in Vannic cuneiform of about
fifty lines cut on a panel six feet high by four broad on
the face of a rocky bluff five hundred yards from the
river.   It is exactly like the panel which I afterwards
saw on the castle cliff at Palu, and the so-called "door"
of Meker Kapusi on the outskirts of Van.   It has, I

believe, been recently copied by Herr Belck, the German professor, but in a few more years will have become so weather-worn as to be no longer decipherable.

The inn at Kummer Khan is situated on the edge of the stream a little beyond the point where it enters a fine rugged cleft through the Taurus, and the surrounding country has been converted into a huge garden for the cultivation of water-melons. The *chaussée* now turns up a beautiful glen watered by brawling torrents, and for thirty miles traverses a wide reach of undulating corn-land dotted with well-built and prosperous-looking villages, to the headquarters of the vilayet at Mezreh.[1] This is a very small and modern settlement, the growth of the last thirty years ; and the neighbouring town of Kharput, feeling desperately aggrieved at the slight implied by its rejection as the seat of government and the residence of the Vali, has been long agitating to be allowed at least a Kaimakam of its own.

Kharput is an extraordinary place, not the least striking in point of size, for the population numbers scarcely more than 20,000, but in situation almost rivalling that of Mardin on the road between Mosul and Diarbekr. Perched on the very summit of an isolated hill 4700 feet above the sea, it commands in every direction an unbroken view of the vast low-lying plains, a smiling sea of green circled by an apparently limitless mountain range. A little below the eastern face nestle the tiny villages of Husseinieh and Senamut, tenanted chiefly by Armenians, and from the brow of a line of precipitous cliffs crowning the summit and known as Kayer Bashi—the Head of Rocks—rises a small serried cluster of houses. A portion of the town

---

[1] Two battalions of Nizams (regulars) are supposed to be stationed at Mezreh, but their actual strength is only 700 men.

which runs straggling over the slopes and crevices was reduced to ashes at the time of the massacres. It was not one of the worst outbreaks, for no more than eighty-five persons were killed, although a certain number of Armenians are said to have been destroyed in the surrounding villages by Kurds, and a girls' school and six other buildings belonging to the American Mission were burnt down. "These outrages," said a local Mussulman to me, "have put back the civilisation of the country for fifty years, but they would never have occurred at all but for the suspicion that some of the Powers were conniving at disloyalty, while others were only scheming to obtain a pretext for interference. What we require is money to enable us to build railways, and if your country were friendly to us or really cared anything about reforms she would come to our assistance. It is only our poverty that stands in the way of reform."

There was, however, no evidence that revolutionary intrigue existed in Kharput itself, for although two young members of the Hintchakist Committee made their appearance shortly before the outbreak, steps were at once taken to inform Raouf Pasha[1] of the fact, in order that he might prevent mischief arising from their presence in the town.

The destruction would perhaps have been greater than was actually the case had it not been that for some reason or other the attack which the ringleaders had fixed for Sunday was postponed till the following Monday, and during the interval many Armenians were apprised of it and hastened to place themselves under the protection of Mussulman friends. The American College, which provides accommodation for five hundred scholars, occupies a spur of the western promontory,

[1] Now Vali of Erzerum.

and here the missionaries themselves and a number of Christians took refuge while the Kurds were pillaging the town.   Mr. Barnum's [1] house still bears unmistakable evidence of the deliberate intention of the rioters to wreck the European quarter—the window frames of his study being riddled with shot, and fragments of shell remaining buried in the walls.   The officer in command of the troops had previously declared that he would be cut to pieces sooner than allow a massacre to take place, but there is no doubt that his men co-operated with the Kurds from outside, and that if the authorities had acted with energy the disturbance would never have occurred.

Since that time the Government have unfortunately displayed a deplorable hostility to the work of the Mission, and the orphanages at Kharput, Choonkoosh, and Palu, the latter under the temporary charge of Herr Jacob, a German, in the Diarbekr vilayet have been temporarily closed.[2]   The only excuse which can possibly be made for them is that they may have been misinformed of the facts, and that, as I have good reason to believe, they were told that the opening of these orphanages was merely a pretext for the distribution of funds in aid of the revolutionary propaganda. It is sincerely to be hoped that they will in future disabuse their minds of this idea.   It has no foundation in fact, and they ought to realise that action of this kind constitutes an inevitable presumption of an anti-Christian crusade on their part, which they have throughout been most anxious to repudiate.   The persistent refusal of the Turkish Government to meet the demands of the American Government for an indemnity

---

[1] The superintendent of the Mission.

[2] The Germans are also desirous of opening a school at Mezreh, but have not yet succeeded in obtaining the requisite permission.

for the losses sustained by the Mission has been generally attributed to a disinclination to make concessions which might be interpreted as a direct or indirect admission of responsibility for what occurred. The payment of this sum would of course involve no confession of the kind, any more than the payment by Great Britain of the claims of France in respect of losses suffered by the Jesuit missionaries in Uganda constituted an acknowledgment of our connivance in the destruction of their property. Those who believe that the massacres were instigated by the authorities at Constantinople will certainly not be persuaded to the contrary by refusals to compensate innocent people for the injuries they have sustained, while those who hold that accusations against the Porte ought never to have been made in the absence of conclusive proof, can only regret their apparent inability to distinguish between connivance with crime and responsibility for the preservation of public order.

By removing, in most cases, the civil governors and military officers, whose bigotry or apathy encouraged the perpetration of excesses, the executive have not hesitated to admit the guilt or incompetence of those whom they had themselves appointed to those posts. Having already swallowed the camel, they now display the most extraordinary perversity in straining at the gnat. It is obvious that open refusal on the part of any Government to accept pecuniary liability for outrages committed by its own subjects must constitute a tacit encouragement to lawlessness, and is therefore fatal to its claim to be considered as a civilised Power. Germany, which has assumed the special rôle of the patron of Turkey, is consequently making a great mistake, if her professions of friendship are genuine, in not pressing, like America, for the fulfilment of legitimate claims on the part of her subjects in the interior. She may, indeed, by humouring the prejudices and suscepti- bilities of her protégé, win a temporary political advantage for herself, but it is a short-sighted policy, and the very reverse of that which she has pursued in. China, and by which she initiated and precipitated the partition of that Empire. Missionaries, as such, have indeed no claim whatever on the support of their home Government, and the interests of Christianity have long suffered, and will always suffer, by being made the plea for national aggression. But as subjects of a foreign State, they have a right to demand the same protection and the enjoyment of the same treaty rights which have been secured by their fellow-citizens in the country in which they carry on their work. To over- look the violation of these rights in their case is as fatal in its consequences as to make such violation an excuse for territorial encroachment; for the one leads as surely, if less directly, than the other to the break-up of the Empire whose independence it is Germany's object to maintain, by paralysing the forces of progress and alienating the sympathy of other nations.

If Turkey exhibits a disinclination to sanction the extension of missionary influence and the opening of new educational institutions, it is possibly inexpedient to press her in this direction. Whatever the faults and follies of individual missionaries may be, I am firmly convinced that the wisest and most experienced among them are sincerely anxious to do nothing to weaken by their teaching the authority of the central Government. On the other hand, it is idle to deny that education, in the modern sense, must tend to encourage political speculation, and that Turkey is not the only autocratic

Government which regards the influence of such speculation as subversive of discipline and loyalty. Wherever a bad governor proceeds to extremities against Armenians, in nine cases out of ten he can probably produce some idiotic letter containing political allusions—harmless, it may be, in themselves, but capable of seditious construction—to justify his action in the eyes of his superiors. Missionaries and agents of relief societies who are new to the country are not always as careful as they should be of the character and antecedents of those whom they employ, and thereby lay themselves open to additional suspicions, which no asseverations on their part are likely to dispel.

But it is manifest that Turkey cannot go back upon a step which she has already taken, and that, having permitted the opening of schools, she is bound to proteet them from the intolerance and fanaticism of the populace. She will best serve her own interests by frankly recognising the fact, and by directing her officials to deal openly with the Europeans who are working within the sphere of their jurisdiction. So long as they keep them at arm's length, they encourage the Armenians to regard the missionaries as political sympathisers, and to look upon them as a standing witness of the interest of Europe in their cause. Let it once be known that the authorities are in constant and friendly communication with the directors of these educational establishments, and this tendency will soon disappear. The authorities will obtain a greater insight into the character of these institutions, and the missionaries will be encouraged to keep a stricter watch on the conduct of their pupils, and to prevent indiscretions on their part which would forfeit the goodwill of the Government.

At present about 500 children of the victims of the massacre have been boarded out and are being supported by the relief funds at the disposal of the Mission, while employment has been afforded to many of the destitute in cutting stone terraces on the hillside facing the plain, and in making a road along the slope to the summer quarters of the Americans, about half a mile west of the town. Surpassingly beautiful is the panorama seen, as we saw it, from this spot, the purple folds of the Taurus to the south and of the Anti-Taurus to the north, shot through heavy banks of thunder-cloud with golden transitory gleams from the setting sun. We were most hospitably entertained by Mr. and Mrs. Barnum, who, owing to their residence of more than thirty years in Asiatic Turkey, have an intimate knowledge of the country and people to which few foreigners can pretend, and are singularly free from that bitterness of feeling which repeated and almost continuous provocation and disappointment might naturally have been expected to produce.

The native bazaars, in which English is largely spoken, as many of the shopkeepers have been educated at the Mission, are of small extent, and the principal imports appear to be German chemicals and Manchester cottons. Passing by the mosque of Sarahatoun, now in course of reconstruction, you reach the castle, very old and ruinous, standing at the edge of a limestone cliff between the Mussulman quarter, which covers the sides of the ravine, and the Armenian, dominated by the handsome white façade of the American college.

Its chief interest to Englishmen lies in its connection with the history of the Crusaders, Baldwin de Bourg, Count of Edessa; and Jocelyn de Courtnay, who were for some time imprisoned within its walls, and eventually released by a band of Armenians from Besne. It is said to have been erected by Tigranes, but the Armenians attribute to this king every building whose origin is unknown ; and the only feature which may perhaps be taken as corroborative evidence of the truth of this tradition is a gigantic bas-relief on the western flank, between two thin round turrets, of a bearded man wearing a long flowing robe and a tall conical hat.

His appearance and attitude alike recall the figures of the Zoroastrian Magi portrayed on the sculptures and intaglios of Persia. Two centuries and a half before the battle of Arbela, Tigranes I., the founder of the Haikian dynasty of Armenia, had adopted the religion of Cyrus, and aided him in extending the borders of his empire as far westward as the Halys. During the interval which elapsed between the death of Alexander and the reconstruction of a united Armenian kingdom by the second Tigranes, the son-in-law of Mithridates, it was still from the country of the vanquished Darius, not from that of the victorious Macedonian, that the petty kinglets, his successors, borrowed their art and their religion. Antiochus of Commagene, the royal architect of those barbaric colossi hewn from the naked peaks of the Nimrud Dagh, bowed himself like the greatest of the Achæmenians before the altars of the Uncreated Source of Light and Day. For over two hundred years a Persian dynasty had occupied the throne of Eumenes in Cappadocia, and when Carcathiocerta (Kharput) became the capital of Lesser Armenia, Zadriades, its ruler, may also have been among the votaries of that purer monotheism which reigned side by side with the debased and sensual worship of the great Earth Goddess of Comana.

The name of the town has been changed repeatedly, and its modern form, Kharput or Kharpert, which first appears as "Karpote" in the History of Cedrenus, is locally explained as signifying the "mule god" or the "stone castle."

CHAPTER VIII

AFTER a ride of six hours we reached the eastern end
of the plain and put up at the Armenian village of
Asharli Soghaji ("the lower village"), which lies near
the foot of the Taurus, surrounded with cotton planta-
tions, and overlooks the narrow streak of the Euphrates
to the north. The current, drained by the long drought,
wound its way through a vast stretch of dry stony bed,
the mountains rising pink and violet against a grey
sky-line, and pushing out scarred ashen-coloured ridges
to the water's edge. Following the left bank for about
a mile, we crossed in the usual high-sterned ferry-boat
and traversed a fertile plateau sprinkled with villages
and gardens of poplar and mulberry. The houses are
built in picturesque ledges along the slopes, their roofs
dotted with beehives that yield copious and excellent
honey. Another hour, and we came in sight of Palu
(3200 feet), a fair-sized town, hugging on three sides
the base of a remarkable crag that falls steeply from
a height of nearly a thousand feet to the brink of the
stream. On the opposite bank the hills come even
closer down, huge rifted masses dashed with the most
wonderful and vivid mineral tints of mauve and purple,
and shrouding their feet in the dense poplar groves
that line the bend of the Euphrates. Several *keleks*
(rafts) were drifting on its surface, for the water teems
with fish, and all along the western sky the storm

clouds hung curtain-like in blue and lurid folds. On rising ground to the east stand the new Government offices, and from this point the best general view of the town is obtained. The river, sweeping from the western gorges round a projecting crag, passes a number of steep isolated cliffs of sandstone, and flows beneath the arches of a crazy bridge about 180 yards in length. Thence it can be seen from the castle summit twisting and turning for nearly twenty miles to westward, till it is lost among the narrowing ridges of the Kharput plain. The cuneiform inscription already alluded to is cut on a panel of the rock which falls precipitously on the north-west side, and the face of the hill is perforated by a quantity of large caverns, approached by steps, which are supposed to have contained the remains of the old princes of Palu.

The Kaimakam, who assigned to us a house which, as I afterwards learnt, had been built for the accommodation of the Armenian orphans, made no secret of his hostility to Herr Jacob's work. The erection of an orphanage and the distribution of relief was looked upon as a covert design for setting up schools without permission from Constantinople, and it is said—I do not know with what truth—that inhabitants of a neighbouring village had been chosen to distribute money who were known by the Government to have been prominently identified with revolutionary intrigue. But the Kaimakam, being only a subordinate, may have been acting under the directions of the Vali of Diarbekr, who seems to be one of the most unsatisfactory of all the present governors in the interior, and has recently come into conflict with the missionaries of Mardin. If the German Government is not willing to take up the matter, it is difficult to see what real good can be effected by a private individual, while harm may result to the Armenians themselves from persistent defiance of the wishes of the authorities.

Descending the hill at the back of the town, the road turns E.N.E. by the village of Demirji, and running over undulating country till it reaches the bed of a small stream, follows the right bank, through a shrubbery of hawthorn and medlar trees, to the Moslem village of Tekiyah (5600 feet). During the ride I picked up a huge caterpillar, apparently of the privet or hawk-moth species, from six to seven inches in length, with a line of large round spots, blood-orange ringed with black, running down each side, on a cream-coloured ground, black feet and long upright black tail. Our night's lodging, provided by an old blind man, cursed with a termagant and garrulous wife, was rich in specimens of natural history of a different kind. The walls literally swarmed with vermin, and waking from a brief interlude of slumber, I discovered a brindled cat curled up under my bed, growling in ecstatic enjoyment over a monstrous rat which it had just caught and decapitated.

The ground behind the village rises to a height of 6300 feet, a wild and bleak spot infested by robbers. Having surmounted the ridge, we wound along the hillside, barely escaping a heavy thunder-storm, which burst with magnificent effect in the hazy valley below. A descent of 3000 feet to a strip of well-watered meadow-land, followed by an ascent through oak forests and over shaly carmine-coloured slopes, brought us to the edge of the Chabakchur plain, where the village of Chevlik occupies the farther bank of a river of the same name. Here the governor of Palu had assured us that we should find fresh horses, but of course there was no such thing. We therefore addressed ourselves to the Kaimakam, partly with a view to securing a house in which to pass the night, as more rain was blowing up, and partly to inducing him to compel our recalcitrant muleteers to go with us as far as Mush, since otherwise we should be left stranded indefinitely without any means of procuring substitutes for either animals or men.

Having examined our passports and hinted his distrust of their genuineness, the little brute, a Lazi from the neighbourhood of Trebizond, proceeded to offer for our accommodation a hovel which was almost as filthy as that in which we had slept at Tekiyah. While we were debating between ourselves whether we should accept this proposal or run the risk of being flooded out of our tent, our servant hurried in with a scared face, saying that the governor, who had just stepped out upon the roof of the house below, insisted on confiscating our books and examining all the luggage we had brought with us. I sent back word that I was surprised he had not himself informed us of his intention, and that I refused to recognise any such authority on his part. Our passports were perfectly correct, and our belongings had already been examined and passed by the proper authorities. The next minute they returned together, the governor purple with indignation, and our servant accusing him of having used the most outrageous terms of abuse, threatening to have him flogged and to put us in prison. Meanwhile the subject of this denunciation was already stalking out of the room with the suspected literature under his arm. I followed him at once, and found him in the act of directing the muleteers to open our trunks in the presence of a large and excited crowd. This of course afforded me an opportunity of appealing to Cæsar, of which I at once took advantage. Raising my voice so that every one might hear, I told our friend that in the course of three years' travel in Turkish territory I had never been exposed to such an insult before, and that, having received an assurance from the Sultan before I left the capital that everything would be made easy for my journey, I should seize the first opportunity when I reached a telegraph station of acquainting the authorities with the impertinence of their employé, unless I at once received a full apology for what had happened.

It was a bold card to play, because there was no telegraph station within a considerable radius, and if the governor chose to detain us, we should have had to wait until the Ambassador received notice of our non-arrival at Bitlis. But the game of bluff succeeded admirably. There was a moment's pause, during which the commissioner of police took his superior aside and apparently addressed to him a few words of earnest remonstrance. Choking down his wrath with difficulty, the Kaimakam then turned to me and said that he felt it to be his duty at least to take away the books and examine them, in order that he might satisfy himself that they were not of a seditious character. I replied that I had already said all that was necessary. If he chose to persist he must take the responsibility and abide the consequences. But, I added, it would perhaps save him a good deal of inconvenience if I told him at once that the books in question (which of course he could not read) were English novels and maps of Asia Minor. He collapsed at once. "Pek ala" (very well), he replied ; and seeing that the victory was won, I offered him a cup of tea, and we made up the quarrel over a large brass samovar, compromising the question of lodgings by agreeing to sleep in the house, provided that it was properly swept out and cleaned before we went to bed.

We started early next morning, and the governor, still looking very sulky, came to see us off. He had insisted that the muleteers should go on with us, and had provided three sowars or gendarmes on foot to act as escort. One of these had a rifle, which he found too heavy to carry and consigned to the care of the muleteers, another had a sword, and the third a hatchet ! With this imposing caravan we crossed the plain to Manderan, and passing the Chabakchur river, reached, in four hours, the ford over the Murad Su at Dik, where the stream divides into three channels. Making a short cut across the spurs of the Darkash Dagh on the left bank through copses of oak, we crossed a small burn, and ascending a sharp incline, rode through the village of Shemsor to Girnus.

Both these villages, and indeed all the hilly tracts in this region, are inhabited by the Zaza Kurds, belonging to the Shiah sect, and the houses, as a rule, have only two rooms each, opening into one another, the front one exposed to the open air and raised on a platform about six feet from the ground. The people are strikingly handsome, the men wearing long bushy beards and low white caps swathed in bands of coloured silk, while the women, who go unveiled, have clear olive complexions and straight-cut, almost Grecian profiles. They have no traditions whatever of their own origin, but in an interesting report written in 1881, Major Trotter says that almost all the Kurds, except those of Hakkiari, came originally from the neighbourhood of Diarbekr. The number of the Zaza-speaking Kurds he estimates at about 100,000, and asserts that their dialect, being closely akin to the

Persian, would not be understood by the more numerous Kermanjis, who adhere to the Sunnite form of
Mahommedanism. Whether this is so I cannot say;
but the Turks had no difficulty in making themselves
understood by the Zazas, and the Kurmanjis themselves use so many Persian words (*e.g.* the numerals)
that it is difficult to believe that the difference between
the two dialects can be as great as he represents.

From the crest above Girnus (6400 feet), where
the rocky soil is covered with coarse bedstraw and
pretty brick-red poppies, a long descent brings the
traveller down upon the broad table-land (4600 feet)
upon which Guenj, a small rambling village, and the
headquarters of the sandjak, lies. The Mutessarif received us with great courtesy, gave us luncheon, and
sent us on our way with three more sowars, if possible
more ragged and disreputable-looking than the last.
Presently the rain began to descend in torrents, and
finding a village at the foot of the gorge, where the
Euphrates runs swiftly beneath a precipitous crag, we
took refuge in a ruinous and deserted house, and inquired whether decent quarters could be found for
the night. We were informed that we might sleep
in the mosque if we pleased; but as it looked cold,
damp, and uninviting, and there was a temporary lull
in the storm, we decided to continue our journey. The
men were very sulky, and one of their mules dead
lame, having just executed a somersault down the
slippery side of the ravine. But we were told that
there was a good halting-place not an hour off, and
this encouraging assurance was repeated at intervals
by every one whom we passed on the road. At the
end of four hours, after following the river through
woods of oak, walnut, and hawthorn, it became apparent that the village existed only in the imagination

of our informants. A few semi-subterranean mud hovels there were, and we had almost decided to pitch our tent beside them, although the men and animals would have to go without food for the night, when one of the sowars recollected that not half an hour away we should really find a village, as well as a house belonging to a very rich man. At last nightfall put an end to the futile quest, and we drew up at the door of a solitary mud cabin, occupied by a ruffianly looking gentleman, who cheerfully explained that he was living alone, because his two brothers had been imprisoned for a murder which he himself had committed. This was hardly reassuring. The baggage animals were a long way behind, and when they arrived it took two hours to put up the tent, for neither threats nor persuasion would induce the sowars, who sat warming themselves at a large fire of dried branches, to lend a helping hand. No provisions of any kind could be obtained, and it was obvious that a strict look-out would have to be maintained all night if we wished to prevent our baggage from being stolen with the connivance of our own escort.

Sleep would, however, have been out of the question in any case, for before midnight we were in the thick of the most terrific thunderstorm I ever remember. For seven hours it raged without a moment's intermission, the whole landscape illuminated with the blue glare of the lightning, which forked and flashed, as it seemed, from every quarter of the heavens at once, now a blinding streak that darted across the door of the tent, now a broad blaze of rose-coloured light that dyed the heavy cloud banks from north to south: The roar and clash of the thunder was deafening, while the rain, descending like a waterspout, wrenched the pegs from the ground and made

PALU : BRIDGE OVER THE EUPHRATES.

a standing pool below our feet. And through it all the muleteers lay in the open beside their horses, lest the friends of the gentleman next door might make a raid while the zaptiehs slept!

Next morning it was necessary to find breakfast somewhere, and striking inland from the river, we rode up a little side valley, at the head of which we came upon an encampment of Bekeranli Kurds. The Sheikh, a magnificent old man with a long white beard that reached to his waist, was sitting at the door of a bamboo tent of enormous size, roofed with black goats'-hair canvas, and divided into two partitions by a frame of cane covered with brilliant-coloured threads of wool. Behind this screen the women sat cooking, and swinging a large skin of milk over the fire, preparatory to converting it into the sour *yaourt*, which is the staple food of the Kurds. I have never, by the way, been able to understand how this delicacy was originally made, because it now seems to be an essential condition of the process that after the milk has been warmed a bit of old *yaourt* shall be inserted. Sitting in a circle round their father were a group of stalwart young men, clad in short jackets of shaggy black goats'-hair and white pantaloons, and wearing their hair behind, like the Bakhtiaris of Persia, in long lank and stiff locks with a slight curl at the tips. Two ragged little boys squatted in the background, playing with a couple of tame partridges, and from the pole over their heads hung a sword and three round battered wicker shields, crossed by thin bands of iron that connected the boss with the outer rim.[1]

The Sheikh at once invited us to enter, and set before us coffee and a dish of frizzled eggs. He

[1] These shields are also used by the Nestorian Christians of Hakkiari, but are generally covered with gay tassels and used in the native dances.

explained that his tribe was still occupying their summer quarters on the Antogh Dagh, but that they were about to move southward to the plain of Diarbekr for the winter, and as an evidence of their perpetual feuds with their neighbours he showed us with great pride the deep scars left by old sword-cuts on his bronzed arms. It is during these annual "flittings" that depredations are committed upon the settled villages,[1] and the sanguinary feuds fought out between different tribes, of which we had terrible evidence later on. In the scheme of reforms drawn up by the English, French, and Russian Embassies in 1896,[2] and subsequently accepted by the Porte in a modified form, a special effort was made to deal with this evil. The places to which the tribes might migrate were to be fixed beforehand, hostages were to be given for their good behaviour, and a commissary of police with an armed force was to accompany them. At the same time they were to be induced, if possible, to abandon their nomadic life, on condition that certain Government lands were assigned to them for their occupation. This had already been done in the case of the Circassians, and a modification of the same plan was adopted by Selim I. when, after the wars of 1514 against Shah Ismail of Persia, the Kurds, then for the first time subjected to Ottoman suzerainty, were persuaded to emigrate from the province of Diarbekr

[1] According to Consul Hallward's account, the disturbance in the Sassun district in 1894 originated in a raid by these same Bekeranli Kurds upon the Armenians, who were thereby provoked to reprisals. Sir P. Currie estimated the number of Kurds in the sandjak of Guendj, which includes that of Talori and Sassun, at 15,000, and of Armenians at 3000. He mentions the fact that the Kurds pay no taxes to the Government and are practically independent, while Consul Graves believed that the authorities at Bitlis encouraged the Kurds in their depredations, in order to provide themselves with an excuse for destroying their autonomy.

[2] Turkey, No. 1, 1896.

to the pasture-lands near Erzerum, and were assured of immunity from taxation, provided that they would act as a militia for the protection of the frontier.[1] The police regulations have been since carried out in a very few cases, but the Kurds have never been disarmed, and the available zaptieh force on the spot is too small to undertake the work thoroughly. The difficulty is not unlike that which meets us on the Indian frontier. Over many of the eastern districts the Turks have never effectively established their rule, and they have alternated between the practice of despatching occasional punitive expeditions, like that under Reshid Mehemed Pasha, who in 1834 marched with 20,000 men from Sivas *viâ* Kharput and Diarbekr to restore the interrupted communication between Bagdad and the capital, and the practice of overlooking minor offences rather than expose themselves to the trouble and expense of asserting their authority.

In some parts the Armenian and other villages are still in a position of quasi-vassalage to the Kurds. They pay a kind of blackmail to one tribe in order to secure protection, and they may find that, after all, their patrons are too weak to defend them from the attacks of more powerful neighbours. This blackmail up to a recent period consisted of two kinds— the *hafir*, levied by the aghas as overlords, and the *hala*, a tax upon bridegrooms amounting to half the sum paid to the bride's parents. These are now illegal and their existence is denied by the Kurds, but the fact remains that in some form or other a toll is levied on the hill villages throughout the country of the Dersim south of Erzingian and the districts lying between Mush and Diarbekr.[2]

[1] Major Trotter's Report on Kurdistan, 1881, No. 6.

[2] During my voyage through this district I made inquiries as to the names of the various Kurdish tribes residing temporarily or permanently

The nomads pay no taxes except the sheep-tax, which is collected at Jezire and other places, where they have to cross the Tigris in the spring-time on their return from the Mosul plains. But for this necessity, they would certainly escape taxation altogether, except in those instances in which pressure can be brought to bear upon individuals when they carry in their wool to the local markets. As it is, they display the most wonderful astuteness in evading the sheep-tax by concealing their flocks in the mountain caves, so that all efforts to schedule their possessions are triumphantly baffled. The attempt to induce them to enlist as regular soldiers under proper discipline having proved abortive, the Government in the vicinity of the Mush plain. Some of these are plainly derived from the places of their migration and are mentioned by Major Trotter and other writers. The list is as follows :—

	Winter Quarters.	Summer Quarters.
Bekeranli . . .	Diarbekr.	Antogh Dagh.
Shirdudananli.		
Kaikani.		
Gessani.		
Panjinarli . . .	(Trotter)—Bisheri.	Sassun and Mush.
Rashkotani . .	(Trotter)—Winter in Bisheri near the Tigris and go to summer quarters at Sassun and Mush.	
Sarmali.		
Mussinli.		
Djellali	Trotter puts them near Bayezid.	
Sassunli.		
Bellaki.		
Malayusuf.		
Parsenkli.		
Topli.		
Mutkeli.		
Khrianli.		
Ulpli.		
Padkani.		
Hevedani.		
Pecharni.		

has now intensified their power for harm by recognising many of them as volunteers and unpaid
irregulars, and giving them a direct appeal to the
court-martial at Erzingian when arrested for any
delinquency. This has enabled Zekki Pasha, the
Mushir of the fourth army corps, to win their confidence and allegiance by sheltering them from the
consequences of their attacks upon the rayats, and
the authorities probably support him under the impression that by this means alone can they prevent
the Kurds from defying them openly, and committing
even worse outrages than they do at present. One
of the most enlightened Pashas with whom I con-
versed on the subject told me that he was convinced
that any remedy that could be applied must be a
gradual one. The tribes were too numerous, too
heterogeneous, and too antagonistic to one another
to render it possible to select one or two chiefs and
make them responsible for misdeeds, while the
nomadic and lawless instinct was so strong that it
could not be overcome by any inducements which
the Government might offer. Pending the introduction of roads and railways, which would gradually
restrict the area and opportunities of disorder and
plunder, an attempt was being made to educate the
rising generation by attracting the sons of the chiefs
to a school for Kurds instituted by the Sultan at
the capital, and it was hoped that the Hamidieh
Kurds, who were brought to Constantinople to form
the guard at Yildiz a few years ago, would on their
return carry back to their own country the habits of
civilised life which they had learnt on the Bosporus.
It is said that when they first arrived at Stambul
they used to act like savages, swaggering insolently
about the streets and pushing the conductors off

the trams if they ventured to ask them for their fares. After a time, however, they sobered down and fraternised amicably with the officers and men of the Turkish troops. Since then they have been replaced at the palace by Albanians and Arabs, and have returned, no doubt with heartfelt relief, to a position of greater freedom and less responsibility. The Government can hardly be expected to solve the problem off-hand when, as the Pasha remarked to me, "It took the Russians nearly a hundred years to make anything of the Circassians, and they are not up to very much even now."

Much has been done in the west during the last fifty years to destroy the power of the Kurds, and the invariable practice of taking advantage of their mutual discords gradually to reduce the tribes to submission will, in the course of time, bring about a more settled state of affairs throughout the interior. But financial reform can alone provide a more rapid remedy, by allowing sufficient funds for the maintenance, as in the days of the Abbaside Khalifs, of a responsible officer with an adequate force at his command to control the nomads, and for the payment of a subsidy to the chiefs in return for an undertaking on their part to keep the roads open and protect traffic.

Bidding farewell to our hosts, we returned a little on our tracks, and commenced the ascent of the last ridge that separated us from the Mush plain, at first through stunted oak, and later over bare ground, from which tiny curls of vapour still fluttered like tufts of wool, until we reached an altitude of 6600 feet, the highest point we had yet attained. A superb prospect lay beneath, the Euphrates flowing W.N.W. to E.S.E. between scrub-covered hills of about the same elevation as that on which we stood, while to the north-east the road dipped sharply over 2000 feet into the broad valley, where the southern branch of the river —the Kara Su[1]—makes its way from the watershed of the western shores of Lake Van, backed in the far distance by a low monotonous mountain chain. Following the foot of the spurs, we passed through several Kurdish and Armenian villages, each of them a mere congeries of earth burrows, of which the reddish-brown mud-domed roofs would be scarcely distinguishable from the adjacent soil were it not for the big earthenware jars which, after their bottoms have been knocked out, are thrust through the surface of the ground to serve as chimneys.

After lunching at the village of Kizil Agatch, we crossed a muddy poplar-fringed stream, and reached Gelsor at sunset. The Armenians here are the finest-looking and most attractive specimens of the race I have ever seen. Although their poverty was manifest, they were excessively anxious to show us hospitality ; but, with every desire to avoid hurting their feelings, we found it difficult to conceal our disgust at the prospect of spending a night in the place. Many of the houses had been sacked during the troubles, for the Mush plain has unfortunately been a happy hunting-ground of the detestable and cowardly agents of the Revolutionary Committees. Such was the natural squalor and dilapidation of the whole village that the signs of

---

[1] The Kara Su. Two branches of the Euphrates are called by this name, although in practice the natives always use the term " Phrat" for every tributary of the great river. The main branches are the northern (Kara Su), which flows from Erzerum, and the eastern, the Murad Chai, which flows from the neighbourhood of Bayazid, the two joining between Egin and Kharput before they enter the Taurus near Malatia. There is, however, a third branch also called the Kara Su, which takes its rise in the S.E., from the volcanic basins near the Nimrud Dagh, and flows by the northern edge of the Mush plain.

human destruction were scarcely noticeable. We inspected two underground stables stretching far into the bowels of the earth, which were offered as the best quarters available, but as they were provided with neither windows nor any means of ventilation, the heavy reek drove us out panting for fresh air before we had advanced more than twenty yards beyond the entrance. A previous experience, which had landed me in an unwary moment with one leg down a chimney, had taught me the disadvantages of sleeping on a dark night on the housetop, and here the rounded form of the roofs made it impossible to do so even had we wished. So finally we selected a hovel raised just ten feet from the ground, and spread our beds on an open platform six inches above the courtyard, which for accumulated filth could scarcely have been surpassed even by the Augean stables.

The town of Mush, the capital of the sandjak and the headquarters of a battalion of Nizams, lies an hour and a half to the east, picturesquely perched on a small projecting spur of the hills and ringed round with a few vineyards and fields of tobacco. Above it stand the ruins of an old Armenian castle, but the only interesting building is a caravanserai of the Arab or Seljuk period, the handsome arched gateway of which spans one of the streets of the bazaar, and is surmounted by the figure of a bull between two rudely sculptured heraldic lions. The winter climate is intensely severe, and must occasion great suffering to the badly clothed and ill-fed population.[1] Their condition is the more deplorable when contrasted with the natural

---

[1] The expenses of the Turkish Commission in 1895 were, it is said, largely defrayed out of the taxes of the Mush and Guendj districts, and the relief funds were no doubt in great measure appropriated partly by the collectors and partly by the agents of the Revolutionary Committees.

advantages by which they are surrounded, for the plain is wonderfully fertile, and as we rode eastward I was astonished by the vast numbers of cattle and buffaloes engaged in ploughing or drawing little creaking wooden carts heaped high with loads of straw.

Passing Haz Keui, where there are sulphur springs, we put up for the night near a zaptieh guardhouse at Arkevank. The state of the district is so insecure that we were warned to pitch our tent close to their door, for every village is at deadly feud with its neighbours, and raids are of constant occurrence. Soon after midnight we were turned out of our beds by the sharp report of a pistol, and in a few seconds the post galloped up. They had run the gauntlet of a small marauding party of Kurds, and stopped to give a few hurried directions and change horses before proceeding on their road to Bitlis.

Beyond the Kurdish hamlet of Kotni, which lies in a lateral valley to the south-east of the Mush plain, there is a curious circular pool of the most transparently clear spring water, the cradle of the Kara Su, and close by it the fine but dilapidated tomb of Karabedani Agha, dating from the end of the thirteenth century. Behind it stretches a broad plateau, of the same elevation as Erzerum, which forms a connecting link between the southern ranges of Lake Van and those that run northward from the Nimrud Dagh towards Ararat. This high ground is called the *Rahva*, and from it in every direction flow little trickles of water to the Tigris, the Lake, and the Euphrates. The volcanic peak of Nimrud, the crater of which is occupied by several lakes surrounded with stunted oak and overhanging rocks—a favourite hibernating place of the Syrian bear—was hardly visible, owing to the clouds that surrounded it, but we caught the sun's glint on the snows of the sister cone of Sippan Dagh as we turned down the gorge of the Bitlis Su. The small stream leaps and plunges down the cleft, shut in by narrow rocky walls and crossed and recrossed by solid well-constructed bridges of stone. Near one of these, about a mile and a half from the town, stands a fine old caravanserai with a richly carved doorway, probably the same mentioned by Tavernier in the eighteenth century as being the one most frequented by the merchants, owing to the liability of another in the town to be flooded by the sudden rise of the stream. Here we found the Vali's son, who had been sent to escort us into the capital, and descending the narrow streets lined with fine stone houses which overlook the gully on either side, we dismounted at the municipal buildings, and were welcomed by the president of the Belidie and other members of the Council.

CHAPTER IX

BITLIS

BITLIS, or, as the Armenians call it, Paghesh, the birthplace of the famous Kurdish historian, Edrisi, is said by the natives to have been built by a son of Skander Beg. Beautiful as its situation is, it possesses no remarkable building except the old castle, of which Tavernier gave an interesting description more than two centuries ago. At that time Bitlis was ruled by the most powerful of all the petty chiefs of the country, and recognised the authority of neither Sultan nor Shah. Holding the key of the main trade route between Tabriz and Aleppo, he could dictate his own terms to both these potentates, and his friendship was the more indispensable to the ruler of Constantinople because, in the event of a Persian attack upon Van, he could either bring against the invader the 25,000 cavalry and the large force of infantry at his command, or refuse a passage to the Osmanli troops through his territory. I have before alluded to the immense strategic importance of Bitlis at the present day, owing to the command which its occupiers would possess of both the southern and western passes, and it is curious to find the old French writer emphasising the extreme facility of an attack upon Van from the Persian side, and the practical impregnability of those mountain passes, which, to use his own hyperbolic phrase, "ten men could hold against a thousand."

A capable engineer is now engaged in the construction of a military road from Diarbekr to Bitlis, a difficult task owing to the amount of blasting which is necessary in the narrow gorges of the Tigris. This is proof that the authorities are more alive than is commonly supposed to the urgent need for preparation, in view of the possibility of a Russian advance from the direction of Van. On the other hand, their apathy, when contrasted with the activity displayed by the Russians in Trans-Caucasia, is amazing. Besides the battalions at Erzerum, a place so ill-fortified that one can make the whole circuit of the town within easy range of artillery and yet remain screened from the hill forts all the time, there are only one battalion at Bitlis, four at Van, another incomplete one stationed on the frontier, and a small battery of field-guns. Add to this that artillery practice is almost unheard of and that the men are quite untrained, and you have some idea of the hopeless inadequacy of the Turkish defences in this quarter. Meanwhile, Russia has two full army corps (one at Tiflis and the other at Alexandropol), and quite recently has more than doubled all her frontier garrisons. The alarm aroused by these preparations is probably responsible for the sudden decision of the Turks to enrol for the first time conscripts who in ordinary years have been drawn for service but excused upon family grounds, and for the recent order for new quick-firing guns from Germany. If competent foreign officers can be obtained in time, who will introduce into the provincial army the same methods of discipline and training which they have already imparted to the soldiery at the capital, the prospect of successful resistance to an invader may yet become less of a chimera than it appears to be at the present moment.

The castle, which stands on a rocky plateau almost in the centre of the town, was at the time of Tavernier's

BITLIS.

visit the official residence of the Bey and its approach was guarded by three drawbridges. Two large courts gave access to a smaller one facing the governor's apartments, and no one except his esquire and himself was allowed to enter on horseback. It is now a mere shell of moss-covered walls, flanked by numerous round or octagonal towers, and below it the river falls in hundreds of tiny cascades between long avenues of white-stemmed poplars and under the pointed arches of numerous stone bridges. One of these, just below the municipal buildings, forms a covered bazaar street like the Ponte Vecchio at Florence, and near it on the left bank are a plain square edifice which is dignified by the name of the Armenian monastery and two mosques, the Ulu and the Yeshil Jami. High up on the mountain side to the south-east stands the American mission-house, presided over by Mr. and Mrs. Cole, and commanding a magnificent view of the long stretch of tier-built houses on either side of the ravine, the grim ranges of the Kurdistan hills blocking the southern horizon, and the great twin peaks of Nabat and Meleto rising in the Modeki Kaza to the westward.

The bazaars are narrow steep lanes covered over with matting and branches, and always thronged with a vast concourse of Kurds from every part of the vilayet. Silluks and Nahali from the immediate neighbourhood, the dreaded Artoushas from the south, the Hassananli and Haideranli from the north of Lake Van, all dressed in wide baggy trousers fastened by tight gaudily coloured sashes at the waist, laced waist-coats and black rough woollen capes with high shoulders, jostle in the crowd with Jacobite Syrians and Armenians of the town. Of Nestorians I saw very few, for they live almost entirely south of the Bohtan river, and rarely risk the dangers of the caravan route in order to bring their produce to the Bitlis market.

Although the present Vali and the commandant of the troops have exercised their authority to preserve order since the disturbances, it cannot be said that confidence has been entirely restored, or that any great advance has been made towards assuring tranquillity in the district. About 800 Armenians are believed to have perished in the massacres, but any exact computation of numbers was impossible, as some of the bodies were no doubt thrown into the stream, while the Government were accused of having falsely described many of the victims as Turks. Since that date an additional blow was dealt to their influence by the open defiance of the Kurds of Modeki, who forcibly and successfully resisted the installation of a new governor, even when accompanied by troops,[1] and the acquiescence of the authorities in this flagrant act of insubordination is only too likely to encourage others to assert their independence in a similar manner.

Under these circumstances, the temporary withdrawal of the British representative from the consulate, which may ultimately be altogether abolished, seems a little premature, and might conceivably lead to most unfortunate results. It must be remembered that during the sittings, at Mush, of the Commission appointed to investigate the history of the Sassun disturbances in the spring and summer of 1895, the vice-consuls who attended the inquiry reported the intimidation of Armenians who wished to give evidence, and that in consequence Mr. Hampson was appointed as vice-consul at Mush to prevent reprisals against the Christians after the departure of the Commission. It is not denied that the outbreaks in

[1] See " Notes from a Diary in Asiatic Turkey."

1893–94 were partly attributable to the murder of
Kurds by Damadian and Murad, the Armenian revolutionists, although Consul Graves believed that
the attack of the Kurds upon Talori supplied the
motive for their retaliation.   Vice-Consul Shipley,
who attended as the British representative at the
inquiry, entirely confirmed the accusation made by
the Porte against those men, and stated that the
suspicion with which American missionaries were
regarded was due to their repudiation of all knowledge of the existence of seditious agitation.   There
is no reason to believe that this suspicion has been
since dispelled, and it is therefore of the utmost importance that some European should be present on
the spot, in whose impartiality more confidence is
reposed by the authorities.

There is no longer any vice-consul at Mush,
although the necessity for supervision has by no
means disappeared.   Several revolutionists had been
arrested in the vicinity shortly before our visit, and
the feeling of the Moslem population was evidenced by
the attack of the Kurds of Nimrud upon the German
professor, Herr Belek, in the previous year, owing,
it is said, to their having mistaken his dress for that
of an Armenian from the Russian border.   The chief
culprit in this incident was, I believe, a certain Kasim
Bey, a Hamidieh captain belonging to the tribe of
Hussein Pasha, a chief of the Haideranli Kurds.   The
professor, wearing a Russian cap and boots, seems to
have strayed away from his escort, and to have been
surprised by two men on the hillside, to whom he
at once surrendered his pistol.   They then shot him
through the neck, and on his falling down and feign-
ing death, fired a parting shot at him at about a foot's
distance, narrowly missing him, and blackening his

face with powder. Their suspicions of his nationality were probably founded on the common knowledge that Armenian revolutionists were prowling about the country at the time. Some fifty families had recently crossed from Russian territory and returned to their old homes at Bulanuk, near the northern shore of the lake, whence they were promptly sent back by the authorities. A secret agitation was then commenced by eight individuals in the plain of Mush, and the Government officers entering the house in which they were assembled, are said to have killed them all.

Another incident which must have disquieted the executive, but with which they dealt promptly and effectively, was an armed incursion by a band, headed by a Russianised Kurd named Makou, over the Russian frontier at Serai. Information had also been received of the probable attempt by a renegade Chaldean priest in the Urmi district, of whom I shall have more to say later on, to smuggle presents and literature of a seditious character into the Tiyari region with a view to converting the followers of Mar Shimun to the Russian ecclesiastical propaganda. Consequently there was a general feeling of restlessness abroad, which rendered the Mussulmans exceptionally suspicious of the intrusion of foreigners into the district.

When Herr Belck's case was reported, the Government do not appear to have exhibited any reluctance to bring the principal offender to justice, but they wished to do so in their own fashion by means of a preliminary trial in the shape of a court-martial, which, resulting in his military degradation, would have rendered him liable to arrest by the zaptiehs—a procedure from which, under existing circumstances, he was protected by his rank as an officer of the Hamidieh.

To this course the professor refused to assent, declaring that he would insist on having a regular trial at which he himself should have the right of cross-examining. The result was that Hussein Pasha, on being interrogated as to his complicity in the affair, merely replied, "Do you think that I am come here in order to incriminate myself?" and thereafter steadily refused to answer a single other question. The trial dragged on for a considerable time, reducing the Turkish officials to a condition of pitiable perplexity and paralysis, until at last, sentence being pronounced on Kasim Bey, it was discovered that he was no longer in the country, having already taken the precaution to retire into Persia! Rumour, however, declares that he has since returned and is now hiding in the mountains, making repeated but fruitless overtures to the unfortunate professor to compromise the matter for a pecuniary consideration.

These occurrences cannot but tend to encourage the Kurds in their lawlessness. So long as the Revolutionary Committees maintain their activity, the innocent Armenian population will always be liable to suffer for the patriotism or fanaticism of the surrounding population ; and while a good governor may find himself powerless to protect them, a bad one will know that he can earn a cheap popularity by re-imprisoning the men who were released after the inquiry, or by inflicting penalties on those who were suspected of intrigue or of having given evidence against the Kurds. Rightly or wrongly, the natives believe the Russians to be interested in maintaining sedition among the Armenians, and the latter are consequently credited with Muscovite sympathies, which are certainly not entertained by the majority of those with whom I have come in contact. The governing class at Constantinople may rest assured that the feeling among the Armenian peasants of the interior, if it be one of discontent, is at least not a pro-Russian one. Some of the wealthier may still cherish the dream of an independent Armenia, though its impracticability has long been recognised by the majority, and can never seriously threaten the stability of the present system. But nationalism is a very different thing from a desire for foreign control, and I am confident that neither ideal has obtained a hold upon the imagination of the mass of the Christian population. Deliver them from the intolerable and perpetual menace of Kurdish raids, safeguard them from the extortion of governors and tax-collectors, and they will be, not merely passive spectators, but as strenuous opponents of foreign aggression as the most loyal of the Mussulman population.

But however well intentioned the Government at the capital, can they control the actions of their delegates in the remote provinces of Bitlis and Diarbekr? If they cannot or will not, they will be again confronted by a crisis which will shake the empire to its foundation, and compel the intervention, be the consequences what they may, of European Powers which remained inactive in 1896. Meanwhile it is our interest and duty no less than theirs to prevent the occurrence of such a catastrophe. We have no special responsibility towards the Armenians, but we have a responsibility towards the whole Mussulman and Christian population of Turkey. In common with Europe, we have pledged ourselves at Berlin to watch over the introduction of reforms, and that pledge was repeated and emphasised in the Convention of Cyprus. Reform to us means, or ought to mean, everything which will improve the moral and physical condition of the people, without distinction of race or creed. We cannot enforce it, but we are bound to urge it, to support it, to aid it by every means in our power. We sent our military consuls—after 1878—into the country in order to redeem this very obligation, and by withdrawing them in 1882 for political reasons, we deprived ourselves of a means of influencing the local administration which might altogether have averted the disasters of 1895.

Our consuls and vice-consuls in the interior provinces of Asiatic Turkey are there in a different capacity from those on the seaboard or in other foreign countries. The amount of English trade in those parts is not, has never been, and probably never will be sufficient in itself to necessitate their presence, and were it not for the political interests at stake we should certainly not devote money to maintaining a consular staff in Kurdistan which we refuse to spend in the south-east and south-west of Persia. The fact is that the consuls in Asiatic Turkey are, or should be, active promoters of internal reform. While the Ambassador at Constantinople exercises his influence with the executive, they ought to exercise theirs with the local administrators. It is their duty to keep the Ambassador constantly informed of misgovernment by the officials in the provinces, so that he may be in a position to warn the Porte of acts on the part of their delegates of which they may be themselves in entire ignorance. Their presence and constant supervision operate as a check and a deterrent in cases of attempted abuse of power, tyranny, and injustice, and their position enables them to discourage or prevent seditious agitation, which might lead to disturbance and massacre. I know of several cases in which consuls have gained the confidence of the Vali by opportune information

K

of the intention of agents of the Revolutionary Committees to cross the border into Turkish territory, or of intrigues on their part to disturb the peace of the vilayet. They are always at hand to give advice if it is required, and although it may be disregarded by a bad governor, it does in many instances produce effects of which we at home hear nothing. No class of public servants are placed in a more trying situation or receive less credit for what they do. They have the disheartening experience of witnessing the accumulated results of corrupt administration, and making constant recommendations, of which, owing to considerations of diplomatic expediency, they are aware that little or no notice can be taken. Yet they perform a most valuable and indispensable work in maintaining the prestige of their country, and arresting, even if they cannot prevent, the decline of Turkey. To withdraw them or to lessen their number is to withdraw or lessen the influence which Great Britain has hitherto wielded through them, and which once forfeited will not easily be retrieved.

No doubt every case must be judged on its own merits, and to maintain two consuls in a district where one can do the work of both would be a useless and culpable extravagance. But this hardly applies to the Bitlis vilayet. Its great extent and the difficulty and delay entailed in traversing the more mountainous districts render it practically impossible for any one not resident either at Mush or at Bitlis itself to keep himself acquainted with all that is going on. The only consul who could possibly be called upon to undertake the task is the one stationed at Van on the eastern shore of the lake, and he has plenty to do already in his own sphere, which includes a large portion of the wild Nestorian country of Hakkiari to the south, as well as the plains adjacent to the Persian frontier, which have been the scene of repeated Kurdish forays or inroads by armed Armenian revolutionaries from the province of Azerbaijan. On the western side of Bitlis, both the large vilayets of Kharput and Diarbekr are entrusted to the supervision of a single British consul, who divides his time equally between the two capitals. So that at present we have only two men on whom we can rely for our information or for the exercise of our influence in a tract of country measuring some 300 miles in length, and comprising the most fanatical and turbulent population to be found in the whole of the Sultan's Asiatic dominions. This is scarcely a condition of things which can be regarded as altogether satisfactory, and were disturbances by any misfortune to break out again in these regions,[1] it would be difficult for us to feel that we had done all in our power to prevent them, or that we had been justified in crippling, for the sake of a paltry economy, our power of timely and effective intervention.

The present Vali of Bitlis, Mejjid Bey, seems to be a well-intentioned man, for he has recently taken some steps to alleviate the appalling misery and destitution resulting from the tyranny and extortion of the tax-farmers, which in the current year had produced such a scarcity of bread that it had been found necessary to forbid all exportation of corn from the vilayet. Similar steps have also been taken by the Vali of Van. He has publicly announced that in future the Government will themselves undertake the collection

[1] These views, to which I gave expression in the debate on the Foreign Office estimates in July 1900, were speedily confirmed by the conflict reported in the press two months afterwards between the Turkish troops and the Armenians of Spaghank in the Bitlis vilayet—the only one from which we have withdrawn our consular representative.

of the tithes, instead of letting them out, as heretofore, to the Haideranli chieftain, Hussein Pasha, who had used his power to rob the villagers of everything upon which he could lay his hands. The inhabitants were, of course, overjoyed at this decision, and Hussein, although proportionately incensed, found himself powerless to resist the decision. More recently, several instances have occurred in which Hamidieh privates have been arrested by the zaptiehs and fined for non-payment of taxes, which had just become due on the expiration of their stipulated seven years' period of exemption.

During our conversation with the Vali of Bitlis, a messenger called to collect the contribution from the local treasury in aid of the relief funds for sufferers from the recent earthquake in the district of Aidin, which had resulted in the total wreck of more than 9000 houses. The governor handed over a bag of money with unnecessary ostentation, turning at the same time to us and asking whether there was any parallel in England for such public-spirited generosity, to which I replied that the well-known Mansion House Fund in London was constantly opened to meet emergencies of this kind arising not only at home, but in every part of the Empire.

The ordinary route eastward follows the shores of the lake from Tadvan, the port from which the small native boats ply between Bitlis and Van, but being anxious to see some of the less well-known districts to the south, we made a slight circuit through the mountains before rejoining the main road at Vostan.

The autumn rains had set in much earlier than usual, and we waited in vain for several days for the weather to clear. The roads were a sea of mud, and when, after threading the vegetable gardens carefully banked up from the stream, we commenced the steep ascent of the hill to the south-west, the mules could hardly keep their footing on the slippery soil. From the crest (6900 feet) the distant town, entirely concealed by poplar groves, looked a mere oasis of green in that desolate landscape, and beyond it, their indigo tints darkening almost to black against the white cliffs of the foreground, dashed with the vivid emerald of tufted grasses, rose the peaks of Modeki, blurred in a mist of rain. The summit, known as the "Gultik Meidan" or "Plateau," is exactly like the crater of an extinct volcano, a basin rimmed on every side by low pointed bluffs, and on the farther side, deep down in a luxuriant valley, circled by a long range which terminates in a line of whitish-grey serrated peaks to the south-west, nestle seven Kurdish villages and the little Armenian hamlet of Gultik. The houses are solid structures of stone with flat mud roofs resting on poplar beams or poles that project across the streets, and in one of them our zaptieh, a native of the Circassian settlements near Ardjisch, north of Lake Van, succeeded in procuring for us tolerably clean and comfortable quarters.

Next day we set out again under a heavy leaden sky, followed for some distance by a procession of men and women carrying their babies on their backs, *en route* for Lake Urmi. Turning eastward, the road passes to the right of the Kurdish village of Ivris, a single row of houses perched under naked overhanging rocks, and having surmounted a ridge (5800 feet), winds along a lovely glen between gentle undulating slopes dotted with oak woods, till it enters the valley of the Ghinzel Dere Su.[1] The level patches are

---

[1] "The Valley of the Beautiful River." The villages of this valley are Shimek (Kurd), Wanek (Armenian), Vervan, Pass, and Mishgunesh (Kurd), and many others.

thickly sown with flourishing tobacco crops, which, however, grow smaller and more closely packed than those of the Baltic provinces. A more scientific method of cultivation would probably produce a larger and better quality of yield, but the prevalence of contraband dealing is fast ruining the *regie*, and tending to reintroduce the old system of free competition. At the Armenian village of Gelhod there is a tiny church of the Nestorian type, with low entrance and bare interior, scarcely distinguishable from an ordinary house. The chief was a picturesque old gentleman, wearing a carved wooden powder-flask round his waist and armed with a long muzzle-loading gun inlaid with bone and wood.

From the village of Keshtonik (Kurd), a little beyond, there is another ascent over stony ground to 6350 feet, from whence the first glimpse is obtained of the snow peaks to the south-east; and then a long ride through a fertile valley dotted with fine clumps of oak, mulberry, beech, and walnut. At the eastern end, upon the slopes of two low hills, lies the village of Kara Su, the seat of a Kaimakam, on the border of the Van vilayet. It was necessary to find some shelter, for a heavy thunderstorm was already brooding over the hills, forked tongues of lightning seaming the inky clouds, which seemed to clash and break away into streaming ribbons, and then to gather again and wheel in a circle till they rounded the valley and burst in a deluge of rain over our heads. The only sleeping-place we could find was an empty, windowless room in an unfinished house on the outskirts, and the roar and rattle of thunder continued incessantly all through the night. When day broke there was a brief lull, but another and more threatening storm was rapidly creeping up, and before long we had actually to leave the room and take refuge in the passage. A sudden splash of rain, changing to a perfect cataract of hailstones, so large that in a few seconds the ground was covered to the depth of more than four inches, drove clattering and hissing through the open casements, while the water pouring from the roofs of the houses ran in a rivulet down the main street of the village. A small clear burn at the foot of the hill, transformed in an instant to a rushing chocolate-coloured flood, burst its banks, tore down the poplars along its margin, and carried destruction over the sur-rounding fields. It was a grand display, but luckily the last. The storm ceased as suddenly as it had begun, and we set out again under a blue and sunny sky.

There is a direct route to Kochanes through Spairt (Armenian) and Shattakh, which we had intended to take, in order to make the acquaintance of a Kurd, Mortulla Beg of Mukus, who played a conspicuous part during the disturbances in sheltering and protect-ing the Christians. Hearing, however, that he had left the district, and that the road to Shattakh, which, under ordinary circumstances, occupies about seven-teen hours, would be practically impassable for bag-gage animals after the recent bad weather, we decided to turn northward through Karchikhan. Making our way over the white slopes, we crossed the foaming waters of the Khoros Su by a foot-bridge and climbed the left bank, winding along the mountain-side at a great height through forests of stunted oak and patches of vineyard. Descending again, and re-crossing by another bridge at a point where the Khoros Su meets the Khiessan Su in a rocky defile, we followed the track, a mere ledge on the muddy slope, till it dipped once more to the edge of the stream, and en-tered a fine thickly-wooded glen.

Here we were brought to a sudden and unexpected halt. Owing either to the bursting of a mountain rill, or more probably to the descent of a small waterspout, the whole ground, from above the centre of the hill to its base, had been torn up to a depth of more than twelve feet. Huge boulders were heaped in tumbled masses below the banks, while right across our path stretched a quagmire of deep mud ooze, in the centre

"BOGGED"

of which lay a tall willow tree torn up by its roots. Not realising the trap, one of our zaptiehs attempted to force his horse through, but had hardly advanced more than a few paces before the animal became bogged, and lay feebly on his side, making scarcely an effort to free himself, or even to raise his nostrils above the surface. Luckily for us, there were two houses on the opposite bank, and the inhabitants coming to our assistance, after much trouble, shouting, hauling with ropes, and flogging, the horse finally emerged, a pitiable object, caked from head to foot in a thick brown plaster of slime.

We managed to circumvent the debris higher up, but were forced to flounder through several other similar but less formidable bogs before we reached stonier ground planted with walnut, terebinth shrubs, and small pear-like trees bearing round berries of the flavour of dates. This belt of wood runs half way up the hill, and swarms with hoopoes, jays, and partridges, but the cliffs crowning the summit are bare and jagged and apparently of dolomite formation. At the end of seven hours we reached the Kurdish village of Tekke (4500 feet), standing close to the water's edge in a valley, the farther end of which is blocked by a lofty crest crowned with the remains of the ancient Armenian fortress and village of Somban. The villagers, an ugly and truculent-looking crew, gave us a room which they used as a granary, and supplied us grudgingly with a little milk and some of the walnuts with which every roof top was littered. The repulsiveness of their physiognomy was only equalled by the grotesqueness and brilliancy of their costume. Some went about naked to the waist in trousers of mandarin-yellow, while others wore dark blue breeches striped with broad scarlet bands, black woollen tufted capes with puffed shoulders, and jackets of primrose-yellow cording seamed with green.

Turning off to the left before reaching the Sombau mountain, the road enters the valley of the Karchikan Su. The steep wooded inclines on either side, dotted with small crofts, gradually narrow together, leaving but a scanty space of level and cultivated ground near the banks of the stream. The bridges are constructed

entirely of tree trunks, and large holes yawning between the flat stones, which are laid irregularly along
the twig-covered footway, present many pitfalls for the
horses' feet. We passed several groups of Kurdish
women and children gathering the sour red berries of
the *drenind*, the former very handsome, with big dark
eyes set far apart and short aquiline noses, and wearing curious high tiara-like hats, from which white
linen veils fell down over their shoulders. A little
beyond the hamlets of Adjian and Sahaled, picturesquely bowered in groves of cherry, pear, and ilex, the
road enters bare down country, still following the left
bank of the stream, although the villages are all built
on the right. At the end of five hours we rode into
Kinderas (5800 feet), the head-quarters of the Kaza,
where I was greeted effusively by two zaptiehs whom
I had met on a former occasion at Mehemet Bey's
house, between Van and Baskhala, and having procured for us a good luncheon of *dolmas* of grated
meat, they obtained permission to accompany us to
our night's halting-place at the end of the plain, in
the large Armenian village of Geulu.

LAKE VAN.

CHAPTER X

Soon after leaving Geulu we reached the top of a low crest (6600 feet) strewn with grey slabs of slate and covered with straggling oak scrub and sweet-scented juniper.

Before and beneath us lay the whole mountain cradle of the great inland sea, a landscape of unrivalled beauty and solemn grandeur. Far into the hazy east, where the town of Van lies, on the edge of the marshy shore, steep craggy headlands, pushing out one behind another into the shimmering expanse, formed little bays of translucent blue, through which the eye could distinguish every pebble on the shingly bottom. Northward, towering to a height of over 12,000 feet, its unclouded crest a glistering pyramid of snow that cast grey purplish gleams and dashes of light across the waters rippling to its base, rose the majestic volcano of the Sippan Dagh, and beyond it stretched a low faint line of hills, backed in their turn by more snow peaks, Nature's grand barrier between the plains of Russia and Kurdistan, range on range flashing into sight as the level rays glanced upon their summits, and blocking from view the higher crests of Greater and Lesser Ararat.

The road follows for some distance the irregular bends of the promontories, and then striking away from the lake, ascends a steep shoulder (7300 feet) formed of mica schist, where the lie of the ground presents such difficulties to laying the telegraph wires, that in places there is an interval of more than 300 yards between pole and pole. Again descending sharply, it leaves the village of Kanjek to the left, and following the course of a small stream for two hours, debouches once more upon the lake. Here the shore is low, a fringe of pink mud with patches of grey shingle, and scattered over a surface of shifting shades of turquoise-blue and peacock-greens and purples, rise the rocky heads of a number of tiny islets, of which the largest and rockiest is the sharp splintered cliff of Akhtamar, backed to eastward by the dark snow-speckled crags of the Varak Dagh, and crowned by the buildings of the famous monastery church of the Armenian Catholicate.

Dismounting at the monastery itself, a low straggling farmhouse in the village of Pashavank, close to the water's edge, we were hospitably greeted by the monks, and regaled with dishes of cheese, honey, and clotted cream like pie-crust that had much the same flavour as tallow. The rooms contained hardly any furniture, and the walls were quite bare, except for a single full-length photograph of the old Catholicos, the rival of the potentate at Echmiadzin, a most striking figure in his full vestments, with long white beard and dark meditative eyes. On hearing of our wish to visit the island, the monks invited us to sleep at the monastery, and got ready their small sailing-boat, which is the only one available for the crossing. Several of them accompanied us, and the oars, made of poplar, with blades in separate pieces, were taken by two of the brethren and two small boys. A sail was hoisted, but the breeze being fitful, it was more than an hour before we reached our destination, and dropped anchor in a lovely little bay facing the village of Vostan on the opposite shore, and tenanted by flocks of pretty reddish-brown ducks with white heads.

The church, a perfect specimen of the Ani type, occupies a rocky pinnacle at the eastern end of the island, rising above a long low line of buildings in which the staff of the monastery are housed. About forty of the monks live here, and get their provisions from the mainland, where the remaining sixty mem-

CHURCH OF AKHTAMAR

bers of the fraternity are stationed. The shape of the church is cruciform, covered with a cupola and conical dome, and a belfry of more modern date has been added in front of the northern entrance which leads into the monastery square. The surrounding buildings have a rude wooden gallery running the length of two sides, and the roof is almost on a level with the base of the western front of the church. Along each of

its four faces, between exquisitely carved mouldings
and friezes, run bold sculptures in relief of various
size and character, totally devoid of any symmetry of
design.   Framed in long scrolls of heraldic figures—
bears, dwarfs, peacocks, and hares—are six representations of scriptural scenes and heroes modelled on

AKHTAMAR CHURCH, WEST FRONT

a gigantic scale.   On the northern side a miniature
David battles with Goliath, and Jonah issues from
the belly of a strange whale adorned with long asses'
ears.   On the western side, beneath the projecting
heads of prehistoric bulls and horses, stands the figure
of our Lord between tall six-winged seraphim, while
on the eastern He appears again surrounded by the

four Evangelists, each of them attended by their own
symbolic effigies in the shape of animals of unknown
species.   For the most part, these sculptures are excel-
lently preserved, but some damage has been inflicted
on the northern face, and the wall is riddled with
holes from the rifle bullets of the Mukus Kurds, who
landed on the island four years ago, and finding that
the monks had closed the church and fled to the hills
for safety, wreaked their spite as best they could upon
the exterior.   Inside, the building is high and narrow.
Four lofty and graceful arches support the roof, with
smaller and slighter ones between, and light is admitted
by a circle of small slit windows round the cupola.
On the northern side is a balcony—formerly the king's
pew [1]—adorned with the projecting heads of horses.
A silvery metal ball hangs before the altar, and beside
it is placed a tawdry and hideous doll representing
a seraph.

In the courtyard, where some thirty small boys
were drawn up for inspection, dressed in grey jackets
and brown felt hats, are a number of exquisite tomb-
stones covered with tracery and lacework of Celtic
character, and in a small room, which the monks have
set apart as a messroom, are two large and interesting stones covered with cuneiform inscriptions.   The
biggest of these, a massive block of marble, is said to
have been found on the spot, and to contain a record
by the Vannic King Menuas, while the smaller, apparently part of a broken altar with a line of writing
along the sides, was, we were told, brought from the
village of Norkiogh, on the road between Van and
Bashkala, where another similar stone is built into
the walls of a church.

[1] The church was erected by Gagig, first king of the Arzrunian
dynasty, in 928 A.D.

The sun sank in a gorgeous pageantry of changing colour as we rowed back to Pashavank. Glittering bars of light struck down from the edges of the sombre precipices of the southern range, and forked into long lanes of gold across the motionless calm of the sea. Little fleecy clouds of rose and pink, sailing across the pale liquid blue of the sky, mirrored themselves in the glassy surface, and the same delicate, almost transparent, tints flushed the confronting snows of Sippan and Ardost, till the moon's rim peered over the eastern horizon and touched the whole with a tremulous sheen of silver.

Next morning we rode on to Vostan to secure fresh zaptiehs for the journey to Kochanes. Vostan is a pretty low-lying village near the shores of the lake, surrounded by gardens and orchards, which render it a favourite summer resort of the Vali and the official class at Van. Following the main route to the capital of the vilayet for about an hour, the road then turns southward through a long, naked ravine to the Kurdish village of Geurundash, perched high up on the hillside (7700 feet), where, finding no decent house, we pitched our tent, in spite of the severe frost which had already set in. A second and narrower gorge brought us to the banks of the Bohtan Su, the main tributary of the Tigris, which it eventually joins, after a somewhat devious course, a little to the south of Sert. Here it is nothing more than a mountain burn, broken into innumerable cascades as it plunges down the rapidly shelving bed of the ravine towards the whitened line of spires that overlook the Armenian village of Shattakh (5300 feet). While we were still more than a mile away, we suddenly caught the combined notes of drums and flageolets, and before long came upon the Kaimakam and a crowd of natives busily engaged in making a new road, and apparently deriving much solace and encouragement in their work from the dulcet strains of the band. The governor hastened to inform us that the English Consul from Van (Captain Maunsell) had arrived the previous day in the hope of seeing us, and passing the avenue of houses near the stream, and over a small bridge fronting the old Armenian fortress of Zel upon the crest of a neighbouring hill, we put up in a room already secured for us by Spordoni, his Italian dragoman.

Shattakh was, not long ago, the centre of a flourishing shawl industry, but this has now become extinct, and I saw no Angora goats in the district. The Armenian population have not suffered much except from Kurdish raids, and it is believed that this year instructions had been issued to the tribesmen by Zekki Pasha, the Mushir at Erzingian, their special protector and patron, impressing upon them the uecessity of keeping quiet. Mustapha Pasha, the chieftain of the Meran Kurds, is said to have written to the Kaimakam promising to abstain from committing depredations within the sphere of his jurisdiction during the current twelvemonths; but, as will appear later, the rival chieftain of the dreaded Artoushas, Hadji Agha, has not proved equally tractable, and it is possible that his instructions have been of a different character.

Before leaving the village with Captain Maunsell, who had very kindly given us the pleasure of his company for a short distance, we called at the Kaimakam's house to bid him farewell, but that indefatigable official had already risen betimes and resumed his occupation of superintending the construction of the road. From the river banks the pass lies over a crest from 9300 to 9400 feet in height, commanding a superb view of the Bohtan valley and the villages of Shattakh and Arnus, while to the north-east the horizon is barred by the snow-covered peaks of the Chukh Dagh, between Van and Bashkala. After lunching at a small spring on the high plateau, we descended by the village of Gowan, following a small affluent of the Bohtan (called by the natives Tikris or Tigris), which flows under bare rounded hills, presenting a most curious appearance from the slanting line of the strata, and the large boulders which are ranged as if by hand in parallel rows along the slopes. A remarkable and solitary cliff of limestone, which, in spite of the apparent inaccessibility of its sides, is crowned with the ruins of two native houses, marks the point at which the track, if such it can be called, strikes eastward over rolling hummocks, and, after another steep ascent, enters the Armenian village of Pirbadilaun (7400 feet), presided over by a Kurdish Mukhtar or headman, and containing the most ruffianly looking set of banditti one could wish to avoid. It had been a very long day's march—over ten hours— and the late arrival of our baggage animals occasioned us some anxiety, although luckily there was a glorious full moon, which glittered on the surrounding snows and lit up the whole country. The bitter cold tempted us to spread our beds in a large underground stable, containing a deep oven in the centre of the floor, enormous oak-boles supporting the wooden rafters, from which hung an inflated and filthy sheepskin, and two large earthen corn bins, on which all the resident poultry were roosting. We bitterly regretted our weakness, and spent most of the night trying to read by the light of a guttering candle, the flame of which was repeatedly extinguished by the constant drip of fleas from the roof.

Leaving the village and its little church, over the roof of which a wooden board[1] is suspended and beaten to summon the congregation to prayer, we rode up a gentle grassy slope to the miserable collection of mud cabins at the Chaldean village of Mervanen (8000 feet), the centre of a mudirlik in the Norduzd Kaza. Here it was necessary to call upon the Mudir to ask him for fresh mules and men to take us on to Kochanes, as the natives we had with us refused to go any farther. There were, however, no animals in the place, and after he had vainly admonished the muleteers that they must accompany us until we could procure others, we were obliged to resort to the high-handed proceeding of leaving them behind and driving their mules before us ourselves. Any one who has tried knows that it is almost as difficult an art as that of driving pigs, and had not the muleteers speedily repented and followed us, we should have soon been reduced to desperation.

The zaptiehs were quite useless, being new to this part of the country and ignorant of the roads. Consequently we missed the direct one which runs *viâ* Kochanes, and were obliged to diverge considerably after leaving the Armenian village of Ustayan, in order to strike the Van road near Sekunis. Thence the path crosses a green rolling plateau to the Kurdish village of Zakh (8900 feet). The natives called themselves " Khanian " Kurds and were very civil, offering us a large room in the chief's house, though we preferred to sleep in the porch rather than in the company of

---

[1] This form of *semantron* is common in Chaldean churches and is termed *nagusha*. The authors of the " Catholicos of the East and his People " quote from the book of the " Heavenly Intelligences "—" As Noah beat wood on wood to warn people to enter the ark, so we beat the semantron. It is a type of the trumpets on the day of judgment."

the cattle which were stalled in the inner apartment.
The "khanum," a lovely little lady and not in the
least shy, was very anxious to be photographed with
her children, but her husband would not hear of such
a thing. The men are almost always more suspicious
of a camera than the women, for although the latter
sometimes believe that by a kind of X-ray process
their apparel will be ignored in the portrait, the
former are convinced that the object of the artist is to
portray the soul, which will consequently pass from
the possession of its owner, to the prejudice of his
existence in a future life. During the night most of
the inhabitants kept vigilant watch to prevent the
repetition of an attack by neighbouring Kurds such
as had lately resulted in the capture of five hundred
of their sheep.

At the summit of the pass (9800 feet) we reached
snow-level and caught the first glimpse of the glorious
Jelu peaks, a chain of jagged needles rising like the
wreathed spires of Milan Cathedral against a dark and
ragged mass of cloud. The hill shelves rapidly to a
green lawn-like promontory on which the little colony
of Berwar stands, surrounded on every side, like
Kochanes, by deep chasms, and facing a superb vista
of hills to the east. We presently discovered that the
muleteers had again lost their way, and, taking a small
Chaldean boy to act as guide, we retraced our steps up
to the head of a stream which dashes along the southern
slopes of the platform, and began the most toilsome
ascent of all. Winding along narrow corkscrew-like
curves, we regained the snow and looked straight
across to the Jelu, now reddening into a fiery blaze
caught from the western sky, while the rising moon
hung, a great round shield, in the dim distance over
the mountains of Gavar at the head of the Kochanes

valley. Myriads of tiny birds, like snow-white sparrows,
flitted over the slopes, apparently quite at their ease in
spite of the depressing drizzle of hail which had begun
to fall ; and presently I met two old acquaintances of
mine, Chaldeans from Kochanes, who almost fell on
my neck in their pleasure at seeing me again. They
told me, to my great disappointment, that Mr. Browne,
the English mission-priest, had just left the village in
the company of Mr. Heazell, a fellow-missionary from
Urmi, who was about to take up his residence in the
Tiari valley at Lizan. They offered to turn back with
us, but recognising the peaks above the pass to Jula-
merik, I declined their offer and trusted to make out
the path without the assistance of our guide, whom
we had left behind with the baggage. But the great
height at which we stood rendered it difficult to realise
the features of the landscape as one sees them from
Kochanes itself. One of the cliffs, which forms a precipice lower down, seemed a mere hummock sloping
gradually into two forking valleys, and the Jelu peaks
rose so lofty and clear that one could not distinguish
any intermediate crest high enough to altogether conceal them from view at Kochanes. After several fruitless attempts in the gathering darkness, we luckily
found a Chaldean still busy on his threshing-floor, and
under his escort passed safely through the slush and
bogs of the hollows and gained the door of Mar
Shimun's house. I had just told our friend to announce us, when Petros the steward, hearing my voice,
rushed out, followed closely by little Benjamin, the
Patriarch - designate, and his sister Surma, both delighted at seeing us again, and begging us to come in
at once to their uncle.

The Catholicos of the East, whom I now saw for
the first time, as on the occasion of my last visit he

was away collecting his revenues, rose as we entered, shook us warmly by the hand, and motioned us to be seated, while a crowd of familiar faces gathered round the door—Petros, Quasha Ishu the priest, and many others, among whom I missed only the old jester, Shliemun. "Good-bye," we had said as we left him two years before, and his parting joke, "Rook go pai" ("Spit in my face")—a feeble pun on the sound of the English word—was to be his final farewell. Our arrival was quite unexpected, for a letter which I had written more than two months before had never reached its destination. This, however, made no difference to the warmth of our reception, and we were lodged in my old quarters in Ishy's large Persian-decorated room, whither Surma accompanied us, asking endless questions and telling the news in almost perfect English, of which when I was last here she hardly spoke a syllable. Petros and Benjamin, still a very slight but handsome little figure, had both been down with typhoid fever, caught after a visit to Jelu, but had weathered the attack through the devoted nursing of Mr. Browne, although Petros had lost most of his shaggy black beard, and had bartered his magnificent silver *khanja* for a new horse.

Our conversation was suddenly interrupted by a great hubbub in the stone-vaulted passage outside, and a little crowd burst into the room telling us that our caravan had arrived, but that one of the zaptiehs had been fired at by a band of Artousha Kurds—the balls whizzing past within an inch of his head—and 1500 sheep had been driven off from the village. The most intense hubbub and excitement prevailed. Only one or two of the Kochanes men possessed guns, and Surma begged me to order the zaptiehs to go, or at least to lend their rifles, saying that a few of her uncle's people properly armed would be a match for any number of the Kurds. I told her that I was afraid the zaptiehs would refuse to go themselves or to lose sight of their weapons, and this proved to be the case. Indeed, they declared that not even at the orders of the Sultan himself would they part from their firearms, and while we were still arguing, news arrived that the whole alarm was a false one, and that no sheep had been carried off after all!

This was a great relief, for while the possibility of a raid of the kind had long been foreseen, Kochanes had never yet been attacked. It had, however, been reported that Hadji Agha, the Artousha chief, many of whose followers are Hamidieh, had this year received a message from Erzingian, to the effect that he might do anything he pleased, a permission upon which he would be likely to place the most liberal interpretation. The general situation was also complicated by internal intrigue. Nimrud, the brother of Mar Shimun, having attempted to raise a rebellion against the Catholicos a year or two before, had for some time been in disgrace, but was now pardoned and had returned to Kochanes, where he was still busily intriguing with the French Jesuits at Van and the Russian priests across the frontier. Nominally himself a convert to the Romish Church, but in practice declaring his readiness to embrace any creed or nationality, if by so doing he could further his ambitious aims, he was now living in a most disreputable manner, often intoxicated, and only protected from a sentence of banishment or excommunication by the timidity or generosity of his kinsman. The result has been not only to paralyse the authority of Mar Shimun among his own people, but also to induce the Turkish authorities to believe, quite unjustly, that a general movement is on foot among the Chaldeans to place themselves under foreign protection by embracing the tenets of the French or Russian missionaries.

Whether the former have really acted in the manner reported to me from various sources I do not know, but I give the story for what it is worth, since it not only explains recent events, but is a curious illustration of the methods employed in the name of religion in order to obtain political or ecclesiastical ascendency over a people, who, be it remembered, if nominally heretics, are yet sincere believers in the fundamental doctrines of Christianity.

After the massacres which took place at Van and the neighbouring villages, the Armenians were reduced to a state of pitiable destitution, augmented by subsequent forays on the part of their inveterate foes the Kurds. The Chaldeans, though, not being regarded as revolutionaries, they had escaped actual attack upon their lives and properties, were nevertheless miserably poor, and no doubt uneasy about their safety in the future. This of course afforded a magnificent opportunity for proselytism of a not over-scrupulous kind. Large funds had been sent out by charitable friends to be distributed in relief of distress, and it is said that in return for such assistance the Armenian villagers were induced in many instances to hand over their *hamediehs* or title-deeds of lands, which have to be produced in order to substantiate a claim for exemption from military service. Some of the Chaldeans also had been induced by the prospect of relief to abjure their peculiar tenets,[1] and in the summer of 1898 one of the Dominicans made a complaint to the Vali that Hadji Agha, the Artousha, acting, as he declared, in league with Mar Shimun, had not only

[1] *Vide* Appendix.

stolen sheep from the Levin valley in Tiyari, but had forced the inhabitants to subscribe to two statements : one that they had no ground of complaint, as he had merely reimbursed himself for advances made to them in the preceding autumn, and the other that they would never become Catholics, under pain of forfeiting their lives and property.

The Vali at once ordered an inquiry, and entrusted its conduct to a member of the Medjliss, who, so the story runs, was soon induced by the bribe of a horse to close the proceedings and declare the charge to have been unfounded. The Catholic priest was staying at the time at the village of Khananis, where he was joined by Nimrud and other chiefs, who had already professed themselves converts. A night attack by five or six Moslems resulted in a scrimmage, during which a few of the Christians were wounded, and a bullet passed through the Frenchman's tent without doing any further damage. Meanwhile the inhabitants of a Chaldean village in Tiyari had retaliated upon Hadji Agha by carrying off nearly 800 of his sheep, after which they had decamped, leaving the unfortunate rayats of the Levin valley to bear the brunt of his vengeance in the pillage of their houses and the desecration of their churches. The officer in command of the local Turkish soldiery refused to interfere ; but another trial took place at Baskhala, which resulted in the imprisonment of Nimrud, to whose intrigues and plots in a great measure the disturbance was probably due, while Hadji Agha went scot free. The Roman Catholics, therefore, while they failed to get any satisfaction, succeeded in compromising Mar Shimun and the Chaldeans generally in the eyes of the Turkish Government, and the Kurds, although no doubt the original malefactors, were able to point to a breach of order by the Christians not much less grave than that committed by themselves.

The Russian Church seems for the present to have confined its attentions mainly to the Chaldeans in the Persian districts surrounding Lake Urmi,[1] although attempts are made from time to time to employ the influence of recent proselytes to win over their co-religionists in Turkey to the new propaganda. Hitherto all such efforts have signally failed, and the apparent intention of the Orthodox priests to revolutionise the Chaldean liturgy, despite the fact that it contains hardly anything offensive to their own doctrinal tenets, is not likely to contribute to greater success in the future. In addition to this attack upon the ancient and venerable form of service, to which the Chaldeans are sincerely attached, the converts are now compelled not only to adopt the use of ikons—a practice entirely foreign to their ideas—but also to ascribe to the Blessed Virgin the epithet "Theotokos," the " Mother of God." This is a phrase the use of which they have always repudiated, not from any desire to deny the human or Divine nature of our Lord, but because the word Θεος (God), in their own language, signifies either the first Person of the Trinity or the whole three Persons together. Consequently, they insist that the application of the epithet "Theotokos" to Mary would be equiva-

[1] Since the above was written the Russians have practically withdrawn their mission from Urmi, leaving as their representative a single Chaldean Orthodox bishop. Their intrusion has been disastrous to the Chaldeans both politically and ecclesiastically. It has hampered the unsectarian educational work of the English mission, it has sown dissensions which may never be healed in a hitherto united Church, and it has undermined the self-respect of many by inducing them to barter their spiritual convictions for delusive temporal advantages. The Russian Church may yet be destined to play a great part in the conversion of Eastern Asia, but it must be by other methods and in a loftier spirit than that which has characterised her recent crusade in Azerbaijan.

lent to a denial on their part of the Fatherhood of Him who was "neither made, nor created, nor begotten."

It is probably in part due to these causes, and partly to their disappointment at discovering that a change of theology has not carried with it the benefits of foreign protection which they had at first expected, that many of those Chaldeans who so eagerly welcomed the Russian bishops on their arrival have since cooled in their ardour or reverted to their allegiance to the Catholicos. The Russian Government is probably anxious not unnecessarily or prematurely to outrage the susceptibilities of the Persians, from whom they are busily engaged in extracting concessions which will eventually give them a substantial control over the country, by lending official support to their ecclesiastical pioneers. It is sufficient for them that the presence and influence of the missions gives them a right of interference in the affairs of Southern Azerbaijan whenever a favourable opportunity for doing so arrives, and the recent withdrawal of the Archbishop of Canterbury's mission from the larger part of its sphere of work at Urmi to the western frontier districts of Mergavar and Tergavar [1] is not calculated to increase the waning prestige of Great Britain.

The English mission, unlike every other, has consistently pursued the policy of educating and strengthcuing the native Church without making any attempt to win converts to the Anglican communion. They cannot be blamed, therefore, for declining to embark on a competition with the Orthodox Church, even in a field upon which they were the first to enter. But,

---

[1] The three districts between the frontier and Lake Urmi are Mergavar, Tergavar, and Bradost. The last is the most northerly of the three, and must not be confounded with the Turkish district of the same name to the south of Neri.

viewed from a political standpoint, the decision of the Primate, whom the average Chaldean hardly distinguishes from the Prime Minister himself, is liable to be construed as a surrender to Russia, and an admission of our unwillingness or inability to resist the encroachments of our formidable rival in Persia. If Turkey would only reflect that the activity of English missionaries among the Chaldeans on her side of the frontier—being, as it is, unselfish and non-political— is the surest antidote to the extension of Muscovite influence in these regions, she might be induced to withdraw her short-sighted opposition to an increase in their number. They make no attempt to convert Mahometans from their faith, and their work is entirely confined to those who are Christians already. The English Government, in relation to missionary work, adopts the attitude of Gamaliel, and cares for none of these things. It has no desire, and no incentive to press for "firmans" for schools or missions in Hakkiari, and yet for this very reason it might be a good stroke of policy for Turkey to grant them of her own accord. If any blame attaches to the missionaries in this connection, it is that they are not perhaps always very wise in the methods they adopt for extending their work. Instances have occurred in which they have sought to open schools in new districts without having previously applied for a "firman," and nothing is more deeply resented by the Government. Every foreigner has a treaty right to travel through the country, but he has no right to set up religious or educational establishments without permission from the Porte. To do so secretly, in defiance or evasion of express regulations to the contrary, is scarcely right in principle, and it is certainly impolitic, for it confirms the natural suspicions of the authorities that mission-

aries are propagandists of revolutionary and subversive
theories, a suspicion which does no good to the pro-
tégés in whose interests they act.

Having already traversed the greater part of the
Ashiret districts of Tiyari and Tkhoma, I was especially anxious to supplement my knowledge of the
country lying between the Zab and the Persian frontier
by crossing the high range of the Jelu mountains.   A
direct road runs from Kochanes up the valley of the
Deezen or Diz, joining the easier route from Julamerk,
the headquarters of the Kaza, which lies about four
miles to the south of Mar Shimun's village.   It was
necessary, however, to obtain a change of zaptiehs
familiar with the district, and as those who had accompanied us from Mervanen refused to run the risk of
being attacked on the pass behind Kochanes, I persuaded Quashi Ishu, the priest, a regular type of the
old Assyrians, with a hawk nose and a jet black
pointed beard, to go over to Julamerk next morning
and ask the Kaimakam to send us fresh mules and an
escort.   At the same time I despatched a note by a
messenger to Mr. Browne, at Tkhoma Gawaia, begging
him, if he could spare a few days, to return by way of
Baz and to meet us on the Jelu road.

Next morning Shaoul, a Chaldean servant of Mar
Shimun's, persuaded us to go out partridge-shooting
on the slopes of the northern ravine.   There were
quantities of crows, pigeons, and magpies, fighting
with the big white pariah dogs and hens for the
refuse on the dungheaps, but not a single partridge.
However, we shot some of the pigeons, and on our
return were mildly reprimanded by the Catholicos for
this unwitting act of sacrilege, Surma explaining that
the Chaldeans never molested these birds, as they
were in the habit of roosting on the little church of

Mar Shalita, and were venerated as types of the Third Person of the Trinity. We expressed due contrition, and the victims were served up for our dinner and proved excellent eating.

In the afternoon, Mar Shimun, who spends the earlier part of the day in his devotions, paid us a visit, and I took the opportunity to urge him to go to Van before the winter set in, so that he might obtain an interview with the Vali, who had, I knew, expressed his readiness to see him, and explain that he had no sympathy or part either with Nimrud's projects or with the Russophil movement among his people on the Persian side. He told me that he had already made up his mind to go, but that he was waiting until an escort should be sent from Van. During our conversation the room was crowded with Chaldeans, smoking their long clay pipes, each and all of them introduced to us by Surma as "my second cousin," while the Catholicos himself reclined on a divan at our side, a listless, indolent-looking figure, with a drawn and rather flaccid countenance, iron-grey hair and beard, and large light-grey eyes, haunted by a perpetual expression of worry and bewilderment. He was dressed quite simply in a garb of uniform dark blue, a black cloth round his turban, and large loose slippers on his feet. Presently a messenger came in from Jelu bringing a report which at once created the greatest consternation. The Mutessarif of Bashkala, having received orders to compel the Kurds of Oramar to restore sheep which they had recently stolen from the Christian villages of Deezen, between Jelu and Kochanes, had apparently quartered himself at Diza, and sent troops into Jelu, which were now harrying the Chaldeans, on the pretext that they owed tribute to the Government, notwithstanding the fact that the annual contribution of 150 goats had—so the Catholicos assured me—already been paid. He now sent a message to Mar Shimun himself, demanding the instant payment of a sum of £800, which he alleged had been promised to the Government on behalf of the Chaldeans of Tiyari, and threatening that if compliance was refused he would at once send soldiers to occupy Kochanes, and another detachment to levy the money by force in the valley of the Zab. The promise referred to had been made by Nimrud, no doubt in order at once to ingratiate himself with the authorities, and to place his brother in a difficulty. If he intervened on behalf of his own subjects, whose debts, paid through him to the Government every three years, and collected by the Maliks whom he appoints triennially, had already been liquidated, Nimrud would at once denounce him for inciting his people to repudiate their obligations. If, on the contrary, he acquiesced in their oppression, he would be confessing his own impotence, and tacitly acknowledging the usurped authority of his cousin, while the latter was at the same time industriously circulating reports that this *roi fainéant* took good care to line his own pockets by appropriating a substantial share of the moneys that passed through his hands.

In the case of the plunder of the Levin valley by the Artousha, to which I have just referred, the Catholicos found himself in the same dilemma. The Mutessarif having punished the Kurds and imprisoned Nimrud, with whom he had been formerly on the best of terms, and in whose house he had stayed at Kochanes, requested Mar Shimun, on his part, to order the Christians to restore the sheep which they had stolen from the Artousha. Fearing lest he should appear to endorse the calumnies of Nimrud by taking the part of the Government against his own people, he refused this very reasonable request, and thereby played into the hands of his ingenious adversary by corroborating his accusations of disloyalty.

Shortly before our arrival an incident had occurred which showed the growing insolence and daring of this inveterate schemer. Mr. Browne, accompanied by Mr. Heazell, had started from Kochanes on his way to the Leezan valley, when they were stopped and robbed by the emissaries of Malik —— of Upper Tzari and Malik —— of Tkhoma, both followers and adherents of Nimrud, and no doubt acting on his instigation. Up to that time the English missionary, relying on the good faith and affection of the people among whom he has passed the best years of his solitary life, and to whose interests he has devoted himself with un-wearying patience and fidelity, had travelled every-where in perfect security without the protection of any escort from the Government. The actual annoy-ance in the present instance amounted to nothing more than a temporary inconvenience, but it illustrates the disastrous change which has taken place in Hak-kiari owing to the intrigues and divisions among the Christians themselves. The stolen things were eventu-ally restored, but the two Maliks persistently denied, and have not been punished for, their own complicity in the affair. One of them being openly accused by a native of Kochanes, attempted to prove his innocence by ordering his own son to recover the lost property from the thieves, and threatening to cut his throat if he returned empty-handed. Unfortunately for him, the ingenuous and undaunted youth promptly requested his parent not to talk nonsense, saying, "You know very well that you did it yourself."

We were still discussing the situation when a fresh

complication was introduced by the return of Quasha Ishu from Julamerk. The news from Jelu had obviously reached the Kaimakam, and had excited his suspicion of ourselves. He returned an absolute refusal to our request for an escort, saying that our desire to enter Jelu must be due to the instigation of Mar Shimun, which of course was quite untrue, and that if we wished to go there we must first obtain a firman from the Sultan himself. Meanwhile Mr. Browne, if he obtained my note, would probably be soon on his way to the centre of the disturbance, and unless I proceeded to Julamerk it would be impossible to communicate by telegraph either with the local government at Van or with Constantinople.

M

CHAPTER XI

THE ALPS OF HAKKIARI

THE rain descended in torrents all the following day, the lightning flickering in scimitar-flashes over the Jelu hills and the snow deepening on the high pass between Kochanes and Julamerk. I revisited all my old haunts, the tiny church, built, according to the Catholicos, 260 years ago, and 140 after the arrival of his people in the district; Mr. Browne's house, now completed; and the house of Asiah, Surma's mother, perched on the very edge of the precipice fronting the steep barrier between the valley of the Zab and the Deezen—a frequent resort of bears and covered with the thin smoke-wreaths of the shepherds' fires.

The mules from Julamerk arrived late in the evening, and we sat down to compose the telegrams which we should send on our arrival, if the Kaimakam still proved refractory. The difficulty was to obtain a Turkish or Chaldean translation, for our Albanian servant could write neither. Mar Shimun's secretary, a fox-like Kurd, refused to do so, on the ground that his handwriting would be recognised and that he would get into trouble if he assisted in framing a message which would be tantamount to a complaint against the Kaimakam. The Chaldeans were equally reluctant to implicate themselves, and Mar Shimun interrupted the discussion every now and then by sending some well-meant but irrelevant advice from the inner room, where an old priest sat copying a manuscript with gall-ink and a pointed wooden stile on paper made from the grasses of Mosul. Eventually it was decided, on Surma's suggestion, to write the telegram in French, on the chance that the telegraph clerk would not plead ignorance of that language.

Mar Shimun paid us another call before we left, and I again implored him to act with decision and attempt to come to a clear understanding with the Vali of Van, who probably misconceived the situation, and would be able to set matters right if the true facts of the case were placed before him. The Catholicos, muttering interjaculatory prayers between his sentences, promised to do so as soon as he obtained a safe-conduct, but I left him with considerable doubt of the probable permanence of his decision.

It was a lovely morning, and we set out attended by a servant of Mar Shimun to act as guide and two puny Kurdish muleteers. There proved to be but little snow on the pass, and we met only a group of ragged Kurds warming themselves by a fire of tragacanth grasses. The view from the summit was magnificent— the green tableland of Kochanes surrounded by precipices, the snow peaks of Gavar far away to the north, the Deezen crags to the east, and in the southwest the giant cliffs of Chella and Berecella looking towards the Levin valley and radiant in sunshine. Soon after mid-day we rode into Julamerk and went straight to the telegraph office, where, to my great relief, I found that the clerk was the same whom I had met there two years before. He greeted me with great cordiality, and I told him that I proposed to lunch in the office while I sent my servant to remonstrate with the governor for his act of discourtesy. He at once assented to this proposal, and ordered a dish of poached eggs, evidently anxious not to associate

himself more than he could help with the policy of his
superior.   Having given my servant careful instructions as to the terms in which he was to couch his
message, I hoped that the Kaimakam would shrink
from pressing matters to extremities, and that he
would prove as tractable as the Lazi at Chabakchur.
But I was doomed to disappointment.   Scarcely a
quarter of an hour had elapsed before the Montenegrin
returned with the following terse and graphic description of the interview :—

"J'ai trouvé le Kaimakam faisant le promenade. Je
l'ai approché avec le grand air. Je lui ai dit tout ce
que vous m'avez commandé—comment vous êtes venus
avec la permission de S.M. le Sultan, et tout cela.
J'ai demandé pour vous des zaptiehs pour aller à Jelu.
Mais il restait comme ça—les mains derrière son dos.
Il m'a regardé sévèrement et il m'a dit—'Non, certaine-
ment je ne leur donnerai pas des zaptiehs pour cette
route la ; seulement s'ils veulent aller par Diza, c'est
à dire par Gavver ; autrement faut qu'ils restent
ici.' "

"Very well," I said to the clerk ; "then you must
send off these telegrams at once to the Consul at Van
and the Ambassador, saying that the Kaimakam refuses
to give us an escort to Jelu."

"Peke" (All right), he replied, "only I will add,
'Without the permission of the Vali.' "

To this we made no objection, and stayed till the
telegrams had been sent and a voucher for them
handed to us.   I did not wish to place myself under
any obligation to the governor or to expose myself to
another rebuff, so I persuaded the clerk to give us a
room next to the office, where we sat down with some
amusement to await developments.   With scarcely a
moment's interruption throughout the whole evening,

we heard the instrument on the other side of the frail partition ticking off frantic messages, and were on the point of sending in to say that either there must be a time limit to this sort of thing, or else some quieter quarters must be found for us, when two zaptiehs arrived with our dinner, and a yuzbashi (colonel) sent by the Kaimakam to inform us that a wire had just been received from the Mutessarif at Diza ordering him, to his great consternation, to go there instantly and render an account of his conduct. The explanation was obvious. The telegram to the Consul had been taken off the wires at Bashkala and a copy at once forwarded to the Mutessarif at Diza, who, realising the danger of an official inquiry, had promptly turned the vials of his wrath upon the unlucky Kaimakam for having ventured to detain us. Five minutes had not elapsed before the telegraph clerk bustled in with the news that a telegram had also arrived for us from the Mutessarif inviting us to pay him a visit at Diza.

"Tell him," I said, "that we are much obliged for his courtesy, and that, if we find later that we have time to spare, we will avail ourselves of the offer, but that we cannot alter our route. We decided to go through the Jelu long ago, and to that determination we intend to adhere."

No sooner had this message been despatched than a zaptieh brought word that the Kaimakam was waiting below in a state of abject despair, and entreated that we would graciously consent to see him. We did so, and he crawled in, almost literally on all fours, his face the colour of white paste, an underhand, treacherous-looking fellow, whom it would have been a real pleasure to kick. We let him have his say, and he explained that his misunderstanding of our request sent from

Kochanes was due entirely to the badness of the weather. The idiotcy of the excuse proved that he had almost lost his wits in the extremity of his apprehension, and that argument would be wasted upon him; so I told him that I thought it best that he should clearly understand our views; that we had no desire to be blocked by the snows in Hakkiari, and that we could not afford to waste time by having perpetually to change our zaptiehs and depend on the whims of subordinate officials to give them or not as they pleased. He must, therefore, not only consent to let us travel by the road we chose, but also give us men who could accompany us beyond Jelu either to Diza or Neri, according as we might subsequently decide. He looked daggers, but submitted nevertheless, and crawled out of the room again, making an undignified rush as he reached the door. A second telegram from the Mutessarif arrived before we retired to bed, giving us the unnecessary information that the shortest road to Diza was not through Jelu but by the Gavver plain. Of this we took no notice. We had won the game, and outside sat the three zaptiehs, the stakes for which we had played.

Just as we were starting next morning, a telegram arrived from the Consul conveying the now superfluous permit from the Vali, but adding the startling news—so our Montenegrin servant interpreted it—that England was at war, and that under those circumstances the Jelu road might be dangerous owing to the probable excitement among the Kurds, if the information should leak out. Luckily, suspecting that our man had his own reasons for wishing to avoid any risk if possible, I made the clerk read it out to me, and discovered that the message was merely to the effect that war might be declared at any time, but

expressing no opinion whatever on the desirability of
a change in our plans.

So at last we set off, and riding straight down to
the Zab began the ascent of the valley northward,

VALLEY OF THE UPPER ZAB

between naked walls of dark crumbling slate, the road
turning and twisting over the splinters and shavings,
sometimes a ledge running under overhanging cor-
nices, sometimes an artificial rock staircase protected

by a low natural parapet from the sheer drop beneath. Far above us the magnificent snow-canopied crests towered into the sky, reminding one of the peaks of Monte Civetta, their bases rimmed with forests of dwarf oak, while over the shelving edges of the stream the vines trailed their long tendrils and mellowing leaves, a blaze of green and gold. Every now and then the water cleaves a narrow passage between fronting precipices, and as one winds along the face by a track scarcely wide enough to allow of two mules passing abreast, one meets a long string of men and animals coming from the opposite direction, and a hopeless block and an angry debate ensues as to which party is to give way to the other, and back into a wider space. For two hours and a half not a village appears in sight; only one small and deserted church; till you reach a deep ford over the Zab at the point where the Suringa Su comes in from the south-east, forming the Deezen valley, at right angles to that of the main stream.

On the right bank of the Suringa stands the small Kurdish village of Ras, surrounded by fine walnut trees and flourishing plots of Indian corn, while on a spur behind it rises the ruined castle of Moodebba Bey, the contemporary and ally of the old "mira" of Jula-merk, Nurulla Bey, in his quarrels with the famous Bedr Khan of Bohtan. Of the former many stories are told by the natives, of which the following is an example. In those days the castle of Julamerk, of which scarcely a stone now remains, stood on a steep cliff above the village, and from its summit, as from the Tarpeian rock, it was the practice to hurl criminals to their doom. On one occasion, however, by some extraordinary chance the culprit reached the bottom unharmed, and the Mir, turning to a mullah who stood beside him, expressed his determination to let the man go free as a recognition of the interposition of Providence on his behalf. The mullah ridiculed the suggestion, saying that the miracle could be easily explained on the hypothesis that the wind blowing under the skirts of the victim's dress had broken the rapidity of his descent.

"Very good," replied the Mir, "let us see whether the wind will buoy you up in the same way!" and disregarding the protests and appeals of the unhappy ecclesiastic, he triumphantly demonstrated to the bystanders the falsity of the materialistic hypothesis.

Passing by the Chaldean hamlet of Madis we saw ahead of us, blocking the valley to the south-west, two strange cliffs, shaped like sugar-loaves, and curiously resembling the "Tre Sorori" of the Austrian Tyrol. The nearest, a sheer precipice on one side, is called the Suringa Kaleh (castle), some say because there was once an old Kurdish fort there, of which, however, there are no longer any traces, except the merest indication of what may have been a staircase or passage leading down to the water. It was, like the precipice near Lizan, in Tiyari, the scene of a great slaughter of the Christians by the Kurds in 1842. Sulti, Mar Shimun's sister, then a mere child, was found under the bodies of the slain, and rescued by a Kurd, who brought her to Kochanes, asking as his reward nothing more than the girdle which she wore.

The whole bottom of the valley along the banks of the stream was aglow with the red-gold autumn tints of poplar and maple, and the peasants' houses nestling among them are so numerous and so straggling, that it is difficult to tell exactly where one village ends and another begins. We passed one more Kurd village (Kerassagh), and then crossing to the left bank

put up for the night in a house in the Chaldean settlement of Kirisse.   Here the chief, Malik Ulmiss or
Hormuzd, paid us a visit, and informed us that the
village could supply but one chicken for our dinner,
the sole survivor of a raid by the Oramar Kurds, who
had carried off everything they could lay their hands on.

THE SURINGA KALEH

Before reaching the head of the valley[1] the road
crosses the stream three times by plank bridges formed
of single poplar trunks, and running under the cliff

[1] The journey from Julamerk to the head of the Deezen valley occupies
about eight hours.   The principal villages of the Deezen are as follows
(the names are variously given by the natives) :—
    Rus (Kurd).
    Rabban Durdishu (uncle of Jesus), to the left.   There is an old church

of Suringa, passes a number of caves hollowed out of the hill face and overgrown with mosses. A jagged pinnacle of rock blocks all exit to the east, though a goat track, impassable for laden animals, runs round

GORGE OF THE DEEZEN SU

its southern flank, and is, I believe, the most direct to Jelu. The Deezen valley branches off sharply to the

here, built before the time of Melka Baluk (*i.e.* before the days of Mahomet), who had his summer quarters near Oramar.

Madis, right.

Kiriass, or Chamba de Chiri Chiri (chamba, level fields cut under rocks. *Cf.* Chamba de Susina ("the level of the hawthorns") in Upper Tiari. The same word is used in India), left.

Chiri Chiri, up the hill to the left.

north, the stream plunging in a series of lovely cascades over huge boulders shaded by magnificent walnuts. A little above it is the small village of Kursin, lately sacked by the Oramar Kurds in revenge for a raid by the Christians upon their own flocks. Twenty of the inhabitants were said to have been killed, besides two wounded, and many of the houses had been gutted by fire. A Chaldean passed us on the road, flying with his little girl from the troops, who were quartered at Jelu, and he urged us to turn back to save our own throats from being cut. As we climbed higher the scenery increased in grandeur. In front the water flashed in a succession of swirling pools rimmed by gigantic white rocks, and through a vista of tawny gold foliage glittered the rugged snowy needles of the Jelu. Just under their southern slopes, at the head of the stream, lies the village of Sumna, surrounded by fields of tobacco, and behind it the path rises ladder-like to a height of 8300 feet, where a broad plateau opens out, carefully cultivated, and commanding a marvellous panorama of the surrounding country. On our right a wall of grim precipices crowned with splintered points and dashed with purple gulfs of shadow, behind us a long line of glistening peaks, the Maidan above Julamerk and the Norduzd hills overlooking Kochanes, scarcely twenty miles off as the crow flies, and straight ahead the white snow fields and crags of the highest mountains of southern Kurdistan.

After a short rest to breathe our animals we continned the climb over a hard frozen crust, the springs trickling between a tangle of icicles that hung from the long coarse grasses by their margin. The wind blew icily as we passed under the southern face of a rocky inaccessible pinnacle, the Shinna Jelu, that rises

PEAK OF JELU.

to a height of between 500 and 1000 feet above the level of the snow plateau where the aneroid marked 10,200 feet. Struggling through deep drifts we reached the edge of the summit and looked down over a shining surge of mountains, that rolled without a break to the farthest verge of the horizon. Immediately to the right ran a continuous barrier of sombre icebound crags with fantastic wreathed and riven

ON THE PASS

tops, and beyond them to the east rose the great white cone of Mount Garar,[1] that overlooks the valley of Baz between Jelu and Tkhoma.[2] Farther northward stretched the cliffs of the Oramar district, practically unknown to Europeans, and behind them, ridge on ridge, some bare, some green, some dented like the

[1] Nestorian "gar" or "roof"—cf. the "Pamirs"—the Roof of the World.

[2] The valley of Baz lies about three hours distant, and Tkhoma one day's journey, from Jelu.

teeth of a comb and streaked with horizontal pencil-
lings of shadow, others sheeted in a gilded canopy of
snow, the hills of Gavver and Shemsdin melted into
the dim blue haze of twilight along the Persian frontier.

The descent is appalling, a ladder of rocky steps
worn by the tread of passing caravans wherever any

MOUNT GABAR FROM JELU

natural crevice allows a foothold, but the rungs so far
apart that the mules have to drop from one to the
other with their forelegs close together, dragging their
hinder ones after them.   Just under the crest are two
enormous natural grottoes, ideal haunts for brigands,
where we found a motley crowd of Chaldeans, all
refugees from Jelu, and armed with rifles.   The stair-

case falls about 150 feet, after which the track pursues a less precipitous course, zigzagging along the out-cropping ridges of crumbling strata that line the sides of massive shoulders' pushing out into the fertile val-leys below. Looking back you would say that no one—certainly not a horse or mule—could accomplish the ascent, for there is no vestige of a made path, only the projecting knife edges of the slippery slopes ; and one of our mules, which had accidentally trodden on a crumbling fragment, would inevitably have rolled down several ·thousand feet, but that by good luck it was brought to a sudden standstill against a solitary boulder after it had executed a few rapid somersaults.

Owing to the trend of the strata it was impossible to make much progress downward, and we were still at an elevation of 9000 feet, and within an hour of sunset, before we obtained a view of the Zerani valley,[1]

---

[1] The Ashiret district of Jelu is divided into two portions, the Greater Jelu and the Lesser Jelu, on the borders of the Oramar territory. Oramar, Jelu, and Doskan, or Dustik, are combined in one *mudirlik*. The following are the principal villages of Jelu :—

1. Zerani (with the churches of Mar Audishu and Mar Aziza).
2. Marta (with the combined churches of Mar Zaia and Mar Marta in one. The seat of a malik and bishop).
3. Nahra (one church).
4. Alsen (one church).
5. Medi.
6. Talana } (one church).
7. Bebukra }
8. Zir (two churches).
9. Neriki (one church).
10. Marmuria.
11. Uri (only six houses).
12. Omut (twenty houses and the church of Mar Aura).
13. Serpal.
14. Bubawa }
15. Matriya } (part of Ishtazin between Oramar and Diza).
16. Samsiki }
17. Mospiren }
18. Saten (half Christian and half Kurd, near Oramar).

and began the descent in earnest. At this point we met two more Chaldean fugitives, and I hurriedly cross-questioned them as to what had occurred in the villages below. Like many of their neighbours they had already been three days in hiding among the mountains, for the soldiers, under a bimbashi (or colonel), had occupied every house in Mar Zaia (Marta) and Zir during the last nine days. According to their account, the troops had not killed any one except three men in the Deezen valley, but had wrecked several buildings and collected from seven of the villages about £90 or £100. They believed that the force had now marched off to Oramar, but this information I found subsequently to be in-correct. Many other Chaldeans straggled past us as we neared the bottom, among them a large number of women wearing little nose-ornaments of coloured glass. They did not appear to be much alarmed, and I began to suspect, what afterwards proved to be the case, that, however annoying the presence of the mili-tary might have been, no serious acts of violence had been committed.

Zerani is built on the picturesque grassy lawns and ledges of one side of a ravine that falls steeply into the forked valley leading in the direction of Baz. We were immediately greeted on our arrival by a large crowd, and the malik, Mirza by name, set low stools for us outside his house while the large inner room was being prepared for our reception. Conversation was made easier by the presence of the malik's son, Simon, a fine dark-haired man of about twenty-five, who had travelled largely in Europe and America, and could speak about six languages with equal ease and fluency. The Jelu men are well known for their fond-ness for foreign travel, during which they seem to be singularly successful in collecting contributions from charitable people, which it is to be feared they are apt to squander as soon as they return to their own homes.

The soldiers, we heard, were still at Mar Zaia, and this was the third or fourth time that year that they had come to collect the tribute. On the present occasion it was believed that Mar Shimun had himself asked that they should be sent, to compel the Kurds of Oramar to restore the sheep which they had raided from Deezen, but that Sootoo Bey, the Oramar chief, had persuaded the bimbashi by a bribe of £100 to turn his forces back into Jelu. The Christians were in despair. Many of them asserted that if this system of extortion was allowed to continue unchecked they would be forced to leave the country, and one actually asked me to take him with me to England. I questioned them as to whether they had ever offered resistance to the government, but they replied they kept their ammunition for the Kurds. The Jelu Ashirets number about 1500 men, and are well armed with rifles of various patterns, purchased in Persia. Some of them possess Mausers or Martinis, besides pistols, which they hide whenever the soldiers come, and use partly in hunting the wild ibex and partly in combating the nomad tribes, for whose courage they have the most profound contempt. There is no doubt, however, that the Kurds sometimes prove more than a match for them, and their intestine quarrels render them an easy prey to any powerful combination. The evidence, for instance, goes to show that on the occasion which gave rise to the present disturbance—the attack of the Oramars upon the Deezen people—the Jelu chiefs, if they had not actually permitted, at all events had done nothing to oppose the passage of the Kurds through their own territory.

Of the five Ashiret tribes, numbering about 20,000, who pay tribute instead of ordinary taxes like the Rayats, viz. Jelu, Tiari, Tkhoma, Diz,[1] and Baz, the three first are by far the most powerful, well-armed, and independent, and from time immemorial have exercised a determining influence over the politics of the community. The history of the election of Mar Auram, the immediate predecessor of Mar Shimun, to the Catholicate is a curious illustration of the method employed by the rival factions. At the time when the office fell vacant he was but a boy, the son of a poverty-stricken widow; and a violent dispute arose as to who should be chosen to fill the chair at Kochanes. The men of Tiyari planned a *coup d'état*. They marched up to the village, took off the lad's rags, lent him clothes of their own, and having secured his consecration in the church of Mar Shalita, met the opposition party on their arrival with the news that the question was already decided.

Upon one point the Jelu men of to-day are absolutely firm and unanimous. Whatever hold Nimrud may have obtained over the headmen of Tiari, he has, I believe, only one adherent in Jelu, and all those with whom I talked were vehement in their denunciation of his treasonable conduct towards his brother and spiritual chief, and strongly opposed to the proselytism of the Russian and Roman Churches.

As we sat in the large room of Malik Mirza, eating our dinner of " bulgar " pilaf and potatoes, while the snowy cone of Garar, framed in the wide open square of window, glimmered ghost-like above the darkening valley, I thought I had never seen such a striking group as that which gathered round us. A red-

[1] Diz or Deezen, not to be confused with Diza (Gavver), which is Rayat.

bearded priest with light blue eyes and wavy hair played with Simon's little children, feasting them on large lumps of beet-sugar; and almost all the men, stalwart fellows, wearing huge khanjas with silver studded handles of ebony in their girdles, were of the same unusually fair type. It is impossible to believe that they can be of the same origin as the inhabitants of Tiari and Tkhoma, with whose characteristic type—black plaited masses of hair, reaching to the shoulders, eagle noses, and jet-dark eyes—they have scarcely anything in common. Their headdress too is of a different kind, for instead of the high white and black conical felt hats of the southern valleys, they wear caps like those of the Kurds swathed in rags of various colours, generally red. So far as I am aware there is no legend affording a clue to their identity, their history, or the date of their immigration.[1] The people of Baz, on the other hand, are said to have originally come from Nisibis, and, if the Assyrian origin of their neighbours be admitted, the shorter stature and darker features of the natives of Tkhoma, as compared with those of Tiari, may possibly correspond to a similar difference

[1] On the question of the date of the "Nestorian" immigration, the authors of the "Catholicos of the East" remark: "We believe Dr. Badger is in error in stating that there are no architectural or monumental records which argue a longer residence of Nestorians in Kurdistan than Tamerlane's time. There are several churches, some said to be built by kings, which claim to date from before Mohammed, as Mar Gwergis (George) of Khanamis and two churches in the district of Diz or 'Diza.' These were probably built before the immigration of refugees from the south." The original settlements were few in number, and tradition still preserves the names of those from which the various valleys were gradually peopled. Thus Salabegan and Tkhoma are inhabited by the descendants of the villagers of Bealitha; Lizan is an offshoot from Marta de Kaar; Mergi, Kurhi, and Mineanish, in the Ashitha valley, are colonies of the "Sons of Ligippa" (the Cave); while Upper Tiyari was filled by the "Sons of Belealatha and Rumta" (lit. "High Place" of Joseph of Rumta = Arimathea).

of type which is supposed to have existed between the dwellers in Babylon and Nineveh.

The following morning broke dark and cloudy, the mists filling the valley and circling about the three pointed crags, the Douruk, the Sappa Douruk, and the Shinna Jelu, that tower up behind the village. A few steps below the malik's house stands the great church of Mar Aziza, a square building of rough-

HOUSE-TOP, ZERANI

hewn blocks, in the centre of a courtyard. Over the lintel of the doorway, which is larger than the entrance of most Chaldean churches, several much damaged ibex horns are fixed, and on a table in the porch lie a couple of crosses, one of metal and one of stone, with a curious Persian glazed tile bearing two portraits and an inscription unintelligible to the natives. Across the west end of the interior is stretched a cord strung with a number of sheep bells, which are tinkled by pious people on entering the church, and also rung at intervals during divine service. To the right of the sanctuary, which contains the sacred books, and is curtained off from the nave, the baptistery is entered through two folding doors made of black oak, apparently of great age, and elaborately carved with quaint representations of birds, animals, and crosses. In

CHALDEAN WOMEN

front of it stands a lectern, supporting an old Bible dating from the middle of the eleventh century, and containing a reference to the reign of the Emperor Alexander Yonan.

On our return from the church we found the village in a great stir of excitement. Women bent double under huge loads of firewood stopped to gossip with the groups gathered round the door of the malik's house, and the room in which we had passed the night was thronged by a number of the headmen, assembled in vociferous conclave. Two Chaldeans had just arrived from Saten, bringing fresh demands for money from the officer of the government troops, and the news had been received with the utmost indignation. A protracted and heated debate ensued, in the course of which the malik delivered a passionate oration, which for expression and gesture would have graced the efforts of Demosthenes himself. It was an extraordinary scene. The orator held his long *kaluna* in his left hand, and his audience smoked and refilled theirs with unabated energy, every one shouting and screaming at once, and paying no regard to what his neighbour was saying or to the spasmodic interruptions and interjections of the two envoys. Several aged crones tottered into the room during the discussion, their withered and bony features contorted with excitement, as they whined and shook the men by the shoulders to arrest their attention, until the patience of the statesmen gave way altogether, and belabouring their helpmeets with hazel sticks they bade them go about their household affairs. Finally the Zerani men brought in two heavy iron fetters, and therewith shackled the feet of the Saten messengers, saying that they should go back to those who sent them, as an eloquent demonstration that there was nothing more valuable to be extracted from Jelu ! And when we left the village the two scapegoats were still squatting in their fetters outside, smoking, laughing, and eating mouldy cheese and bread, apparently not in the least perturbed at the dark prospect in store for them.

CHAPTER XII

MARTA, or Mar Zaia (7000 feet), the principal village in Jelu, lies at a distance of about two and a half hours on the rugged hill slope east of Zerani. As we came over the last crest we heard a bugle sounded, and saw a company of troops in the act of being drawn up to the salute. The whole place seemed to be alive with soldiers. A crowd of them was collected in the church enclosure, and the red gleam of their fezzes showed on the flat roof of every house. Indeed so effective and thorough had been the occupation, that there was no room vacant, and we had to go on about a quarter of a mile to the house of the little boy bishop, Zaia Mar Sergis,[1] which is built on the farther side of a gully facing the village. The bimbashi (colonel) sent to offer us a guard, which we declined as unnecessary, and presently started back with our little host, a child of fourteen (surely the most diminutive recruit ever enlisted in the ranks of the Episcopate), to see the famous church of Mar Zaia.

It stands high, the old square stone walls bulging

---

[1] Besides Mar Sergis of Jelu and Baz there are two bishops, Mar Sliwa (Cross) and Mar Saurishu (Hope of Jesus), in Gawar, and a metropolitan, Mar Abunanishu (Mercy of Jesus), in Shemsdin, whose jurisdiction extends over the Persian districts of Mergavar and Tergavar. At present I believe there are no bishops in either Tkhoma or Lower Tiari. Mar Auram (Abraham) of Berwari, near Kochanes, was at one time patriarch-designate, but has fallen into disgrace owing to his complicity with the intrigues of Nimrud.

outward, and the porch, the paving of which has been worn into shiny and slippery hollows by the feet of countless worshippers, is so low, that you cannot enter without stooping. Though apparently a single building, it consists in reality of two churches, separated by a thick partition wall. The first, nearest to the

ZAIA MAR SERGIS

entrance, stands on a lower level than the other, and is never used except on very special occasions. At its eastern end is the sacristy, where the communion bread is prepared, and the sanctuary, containing two ancient liturgies of enormous proportions. It is almost entirely dark, for it derives little benefit from the two small deep window slits which light the upper and larger building. This is said to be the biggest of all the Chaldean churches, and is probably also the oldest. According to local tradition, it was erected 1620 years ago by Sen Mar Zaia, a pilgrim from Palestine or Syria, who, having passed through Bagdad and Mosul, "seeking rest and finding none," eventually determined to spend the remainder of his life in the secluded highlands of Jelu, and now sleeps in his coffin, beneath a canopy of embroideries, before the dim sanctuary. Upon it rests a manuscript of the Bible, written in the oldest Aramaic character, and three old metal-wrought crosses, while suspended from the roof overhead sway a quantity of ostrich eggs curiously decorated with pin-prick designs. These are said to have been originally imported from China in the palmy days of the Chaldean Church, when its missionary activity was so great and so successful that it counted twenty-five metropolitan sees within its jurisdiction, and established flourishing Christian communities throughout Central Asia and Far Cathay. Across the west end is stretched a string of bells as at Zerani and Kochanes, and the walls are all tapestried with hangings, many of them moth-eaten and threadbare with age. The only piece of furniture is the lectern, at which the bishop, priests, and deacons stand together while the Gospel is read. There are no seats, and the congregation stands or kneels during the entire course of the service.

By far the most curious relic is a handkerchief covered with an inscription in the Arabic character, and believed by the people to be a firman for the protection of the church by the Prophet Mahomet himself. Unfortunately I was not able to obtain a sight of it, for it had been already seized and carried off by the colonel, who had probably entered the building in search of concealed treasure. During the nine days that the troops had occupied the village the people had not dared to hold a service, for fear that they might thereby provoke the soldiers to enter and profane the church, but recollecting that it was customary to use incense morning and evening, they now lighted a small quantity in the censer and proceeded to fumigate everything high and low.

On our way back, it was curious to observe how every one rushed up to kiss reverently the little bishop's hand, while the Turks looked on with an air of un-disguised amazement, not unmixed with contempt. He carried his dignity lightly and without any airs, saying a few pleasant words to each, and inviting one or two to spend the evening with us at his house. He changed his clothes before dinner, and came down in a superb frockcoat of sky blue, recited a grace which lasted ten minutes or more, and ate a spare meal of eggs and honey. The conversation turned naturally on the critical condition of affairs and the probable intentions of the government. Hearing that we were likely to pass through Shemsdin the guests expressed themselves in very strong terms about the conduct of the matran (metropolitan) there, saying that " he had left his sheep to the wolves," or in other words, that he had left the Urmi district, which forms part of his see, without having made any determined effort to win back the Chaldeans of Persia from their recently professed allegiance to the doctrines of the Russian Church. They seemed to recognise that this move-ment on the part of their co-religionists had drawn the suspicion of the Turks upon themselves, and did not conceal their belief that the conversions had been dictated by pecuniary motives rather than by any sincere change of religious conviction. With regard to their own plight they told me that the old arrangement under which the tribute of the various Ashirets used to be collected and paid to the government by Mar Shimun had been lately abandoned, and that the Turks now collected it themselves, as best they could, directly from the headmen of each tribe.

We passed the night in a large inner room, ventilated only by two tiny apertures in the wall, and were nearly suffocated in consequence.

The day of our departure began with a row.

If any difficulty is to be raised by your muleteers, you may be quite sure that they will carefully refrain from mentioning it until the hour fixed for the start has arrived, and, if possible, until you are yourself already in the saddle. So it happened on the present occasion. Everything had been arranged the evening before ; the zaptiehs and muleteers had been informed of the route we proposed to take through the country of the Oramar Kurds, and neither had offered any objection. But at the last moment their hearts failed them. One of the zaptiehs, himself a Kurd, and brother of Mar Shimun's secretary, declared that the road to Oramar was so dangerous that nothing would persuade him to go that way. The other, a Christian and an excellent fellow, said that he would go anywhere we pleased, but that before doing so he must get explicit leave from the authorities. The muleteers, both Kurds from Julamerk, flatly refused to put their foot across the Oramar border, for the excellent reason that one at least of their mules had been stolen by them from the Oramar Kurds themselves, and would certainly be recognised and appropriated by its owner. There was no way out of the dilemma but to send to the colonel in command of the troops and ask his assistance. He replied that he was quite willing to allow us to go to Oramar and to compel the zaptiehs to accompany us, but he begged us not to attempt the passage of the country lying between Oramar and Neri, as it was so infested by marauding bands of the Herki Kurds that it would be impossible to guarantee the safety either of our lives or property.[1] We agreed, therefore, to strike back to Diza up the Ishtazin valley after visiting Oramar, and the mule question was settled by putting all the baggage on four of the animals and leaving the stolen one behind.

The track continues eastward over the Jelu spurs at an average height of 7000 feet. We had not gone far when a messenger came up with us, bearing a letter from Mr. Browne, who had arrived the previous evening at the lower village of Nahra, but had not come to Mar Zaia for fear that his mules might be requisitioned by the soldiers for transport. I scribbled a line asking him to meet us if possible at Ishtazin, and we then proceeded on our journey, descending the hill at the end of three hours to the Chaldean hamlet of Zir. It is a pretty little place, clustered under the shadow of huge grey boulders at the foot of a deep cleft which runs down from the crags of Jelu, and above it stands an old church on a platform of green sward. The entire population appeared to be discussing affairs on the corn-heaped threshing floors, while some twenty-five soldiers squatted on the housetops, having, I was informed, received the tribute on the first day of their arrival, but nevertheless stayed on for another eight, ordering the best of everything, and enjoying themselves prodigiously. Only it must be admitted to their credit that they had abstained

[1] The direct .road to Diza from Mar Zaia lies through Zir and Ishtazin.

from doing any wanton damage to property, and the general appearance of every village we passed through bespoke infinitely greater prosperity than is to be found in most Mussulman or Kurdish settlements.

Threading the narrow ladder-like streets we turned down along the banks of a stream (the Zir Su), riding due south through lovely glen scenery. Old walnuts and planes, stretching the twisted roots of their huge

PEAKS OF ORAMAR

and often hollow boles across the water, formed a succession of glittering falls, while to right and left rose steep wooded slopes crowned by naked crags, and along the southern sky the view was bounded by the bare rocky walls and serrated summits of the precipices of Oramar. A little below Zir, on the hill to the left, stands the church of Mar Auram, and beyond it that of Mar Johann. At the end of about ten miles the stream cuts a dark passage between sheer cliffs, scarcely twenty yards in width, and wading along the shallow channel we forced our way with difficulty through the thick tangle at the foot of a gigantic plane, literally hung from top to bottom with a trailing curtain of vines. On reaching the end of this extraordinary defile we found ourselves confronted by three stupendous greyish-white precipices, stretching eastward to meet the darker red-streaked peaks of the Oramar Dagh, upon whose fissured surface the snow lay in small and scattered patches. Below, the Ishtazin Su flows in a rapid torrent from north-east to south-west, ultimately joining the Zab in the neighbourhood of Rezan ; and looking down its tortuous course one could hardly imagine how the water found an opening through the forest of crowded sharp-edged and pinnacled crags that rose straight up from the gloomy hollows to the level of the snows.[1]

The track follows the right bank for a short distance, in places only affording sufficient footing for a man, so that the animals have to swim round the projecting boulders, till the ford and wicker bridge is reached near the hamlet of Pirezan. From this point it turns to the right, and running up the hillside, passes a considerable belt of vineyards and plots of cultivated ground before entering the village of Oramar (5500 feet). Here a crowd of Kurds, tall lanky men with rather languid blue eyes, soon collected, and an interminable discussion ensued (a drizzle of rain and sleet was falling all the time) as to where we should pass the night. Some suggested the mosque, formerly a Chaldean church, while others scouted the

[1] Probably none of these are of great height, for the level of the stream at Oramar is only 3800 feet, and except in the spring and winter they would be free from snow.

idea of such profanation, and sent for the headman to decide the question. His first proposal was that we should share a stable already tenanted by a large family and a number of sheep and poultry, but on our declining the offer he eventually consented to find us quarters in his own house, magnificently situated on the very verge of a cliff facing the twin peaks of the Oramar Dagh (the Jalta or Jaita (slippery) and the Kalabiri oroch) and the snow range above the Ishtazin valley to the east. Here we passed the night comfortably enough in a room, the roof of which was fantastically decorated with the prints of human hands following the lines of the rafters.

The Oramar Kurds are not Hamidiehs like the Artousha,[1] and being a pastoral people usually migrate to the Mosul plain during the winter. Their chief, Sootoo Beg, divides his time between Oramar and the village of Nerwa, distant a two days' journey on the road to Zibar, in the Dustanga or Dustik Ashiret. This is the route usually followed by the tribe to the lowlands of the Tigris, but they sometimes choose the more westerly one through the Rekan country and Amadigah. On the south-west they have for their neighbours the Apneanish or Apenshai and the Dustik Kurds, and to the east, beyond Ishtazin, the fierce Herki, who descend into the plains through the district of Shemsdin, and often lay waste the settled villages on their way. The country between Oramar and Zibar has, so far as I know, never been explored by Europeans, and the frequency of faction fights between the rival tribes would probably render it a perilous journey even if the protection of some of the chiefs could be secured. The Oramar were the

---

[1] The Artousha live mainly in the district of Baz and on the western side of the Zab.

only ones with whom I came into contact, and they certainly showed no signs of fanaticism, and surprisingly little curiosity, considering that, according to their own account, we were the first "Firenghis" who had ever visited the place. They appeared to be extremely poor, and prided themselves especially on their worked silver khanja-sheaths with twisted chains, which I believe are bought at Sert, and which they value so highly that they will not part with them for less than four or five pounds apiece.

Descending below the steep front of the Jalta precipices we pursued a north-westerly course between lofty snow-capped crags till we regained the banks of the Ishtazin river, littered with brilliant red and green slabs of jasper and porphyry. After a two hours' ride the road crossed to the right bank by a swinging bridge, and the narrowing walls of rock soon shut out the sparkling mist-circled peaks behind. The natural gloom of the defile was intensified by lowering thunderclouds overhead, and the rain, pouring off the worn and rounded boulders of the *stangi* made the track so slippery, that it was not long before one of our baggage mules had rolled over the edge and was rescued with difficulty from perishing in the stream below.

We had just accomplished the task, and were refreshing ourselves with a meagre repast of bread and raisins, when I saw a familiar figure approaching in the shape of Gauriel, Mr. Browne's Tiyari servant, followed closely by the missionary himself. My conscience reproached me for having induced him to come, as he had only one mule for himself and his baggage, the remaining animals having been withheld by the katir-jis lest they should be seized and requisitioned for transport. Our letter from Kochaues had reached him late, for he was not at Lezan as we had supposed, but was staying with Mr. Heazell at the house of my old acquaintance, Malik Berkle, at Salabegan, near Tkhoma Gawaia.   On receiving my message he had come on

GORGE OF THE ISHTAZIN SU

as fast as he could by way of the Baz valley, and having missed us by a day at Jelu, had taken the short cut from Zir to Ishtazin.   With him we went on to our destination at the little Christian village of Shemsiki (4700 feet), situated at the mouth of the gorge at a

o

slight elevation above the stream, facing a long snow range in front and backed to the south-west by a huge tapering cone of bare cliff. While a room was being swept out for us in the malik's house, and we were seated over a samovar on the roof outside, the mudir of Ishtazin [1] arrived to pay his respects. A Kurd by nationality, his appearance was not prepossessing, and the Chaldeans, who form the large majority of the population of the Ishtazin valley, have been subjected by him to many acts of petty oppression. Quite recently he arrested several who had come from Urmi with properly signed tezkarés, and rated them roundly as *giaours*, while he is suspected of constantly taking as toll from the Kurds of Oramar a portion of the flocks which they have raided from their Christian neighbours.

About three miles above the village the stream forks into two channels, the one branch flowing down from its source in the country of the Dustik Kurds, while the other, which we followed for a short distance, descends from the north. After riding along the left bank for about an hour we crossed, and immediately began the steep ascent of the great peak of Kaleano (or Kaleashin), which rises to an altitude of 8800 feet. Snow lay deep on the crest, and on the farther side, looking towards the Gavver plain, reached nearly to the base of the hills, though elsewhere the ground was bare, save for a bristly growth of large thistles and tufts of the prickly gum tragacanth, which is much appreciated by the mules and horses, especially during the spring when the thorns are soft. We used

[1] The mudirlik of Ishtazin comprises also the districts of Jelu and Oramar. There are three castles in Ishtazin, all of them said to date from the pre-Mahommetan period, and each of the valleys possesses two churches. The names of the villages are as follows :—Bubawa, Shemsiki, Marteriyi, Mospiren, Bibakshi, Serpa.

it to make a fire at the top of the pass, and brewed some coffee to keep out the bitter cold. Numbers of Dervishes and miserable-looking Kurds, dressed in rags and tatters that would hardly keep together, and accompanied by their women and children, passed us going westward, and stopped to beg a few copper *gurush* or a fill of tobacco. The view on both sides was splendid. To the south-west the dazzling crests of Oramar, and beyond them the faint blue line of the distant hills of Apneanish and Dustik, while to the north-east the eye travelled over the white surface of a small frozen lake to the long low range that stretches from Albek, Baskala, and Kochanes to the snowy mountains between Diza and the Persian Salmas, terminating in the lofty peaks of Shemsdinan. At our feet lay the broad expanse of the Gavver (Gawar) plain, once a lake bed, flat as the palm of your hand and extraordinarily fertile, running almost due north and south, at a practically uniform level of 6500 feet. Numbers of villages, Chaldean and Kurdish, are scattered along the edges of its green surface, which during the spring is often entirely submerged by the water from the melting snow. At the entrance to the sloping gorge, by which we descended, we were greeted in fluent English, learnt at Urmi, by the malik of the Christian village of Mamikan ; and wading laboriously through large shallow sheets of water, vocal with the cry of shieldrake, snipe, and big bustard, we came to the banks of the Nila river, which flows in a northerly direction to the Zab. The attempt to ford it was disastrous, for the mules, losing their footing in the deep mud, floundered about, wetting us to the waist, before they settled down to swim, while Gauriel rode pillion behind. Twilight had closed in before we reached Gargoran, the seat of Mar Sliwa, one of the two Chaldean bishops of Gawar, and the sky was suffused with the last flush of a gorgeous and wintry sunset, the white ranges glimmering like sheeted spectres against a great circle of bluish-green sky from which broad streamers of rosy light shot out east, north, and south, turning their highest tops to a fiery red above the gathering darkness of the plain.

A number of Mar Shimun's servants, who had come to the village to collect their master's corn, met and conducted us to the bishop's house, a mere mud hovel like the rest, where we were not sorry to dry ourselves after our icy bath in the river. The village of Gargorau is now the property of the Catholicos, who obtained the title-deeds on the understanding that he would take over the standing debts of the proprietors. Under favourable circumstances the fertility of the soil is such that the produce ought in itself to suffice for the maintenance of his family. But although things are much better than they were, the inhabitants still complain that they are left to protect themselves against raiding and robbery by the Kurds. Only a few weeks before three Kurds had tried to break into a house, when the proprietor hearing a noise rushed out, collared one of the culprits, and called the neighbours to his assistance. They proceeded to haul the prisoner back to the scene of his operations, and found that in the meantime his associates, making the best of their opportunity, had effected an entrance, and, having barricaded the door, were threatening to kill the first man who attempted to burst it. But they were answered by a piteous appeal from their companion, who implored them not to shoot, as his captors had thoughtfully placed him in the direct line of fire. By this means all three were secured, and duly handed over to the authorities at Diza for punishment.

The village is only just recovering from its pillage by the Kurds three years ago, after which the inhabitants deserted it altogether.   Since their return the local government appears to have blackmailed them by threatening to refuse the regular allowance of three days' supply of water for irrigation per fortnight unless they consented to pay an extra sum for the privilege.   In other cases the government has acted with inconsistent leniency and toleration.   At Kerpil, a village three miles from Gargoran, on the road to Kochanes, it has placed a force of ten soldiers to protect the Armenians from outrage by the Kurds; and in Marbishu,[1] eight hours east of Diza, they have not only reinstated in their homes the Chaldeans who had fled, but are reported to have actually granted them, for the time being, complete immunity from taxation.   The principal topic of discussion at Gargoran was the news that Quasha ——, the Chaldean priest sent by Nimrud to treat with the Russians in Urmi, had been arrested by the orders of the mutessarif as he was crossing the frontier, but, much to their disgust, had been almost immediately released.

An escort was sent out next day to bring us into Diza, where we dismounted at the konak, and found the kadi (judge) waiting to receive us, as the mutessarif was temporarily indisposed.   With him were seated an officer of the customs, smoking from a cigarette-holder made of areca-nut wood, and two Kurdish chiefs from Basherga and Kardian in the Gawar plain, Tamar Beg[2] and Nejjid Beg, descendants of the old mira, Moodebba.   Tall men with heavy and stupid but good-natured countenances, they have a great idea of their

---

[1] Not to be confused with Mar Ishu, the matran's house

[2] *Beg* is a title given to those who are either kaimakai or, like Moussa Beg of Khumaroo, descendants of the Abl

own importance, although stripped of the reality of power which their ancestors enjoyed. The Turks look upon them with contemptuous amusement. "Proud, stuck-up old things," as a high official described them to me, "they are of no use to any one, and we are gradually getting rid of them all." But the natives still regard them with respect. During our interview a servant brought to Tamar Beg a piece of wood, a kind of charm, upon which he first drew a pentagon with portentous solemnity, then blew upon it, cut it in two with an enormous pair of scissors, pronounced over the pieces the name of the Prophet, and handed them back to the messenger, informing us that they were intended for the benefit of a sick child, who *Inshallah* (please God) would speedily recover.

Being very anxious to talk matters over with the mutessarif and see if anything could be done to prevent a conflict between the soldiers and the Chaldeans of Tiyari, who would be not unlikely to resist their entry into the Zab valley, I sent word that I proposed to call upon him in the evening. Accordingly we walked over to his house, which was close to the konak, and were cordially, if a little hysterically, welcomed by Mohammed Pasha in a room richly furnished with carpeted divans and a small table covered with liqueur glasses, bottles of raki, and excellent old brandy. The preliminary courtesies over, I begged that the servants might be dismissed, as we should then be able to converse more freely. He readily assented, and during the interview, although he became very excited, and perpetually crossed and recrossed his legs, cased in long Russian riding-boots, spoke perfectly frankly, and never lost his temper. He impressed me on the whole very favourably as a strong man who knew his own mind, and had a definite

policy which he intended to carry out, not, as I had
feared he might be, a petty and rapacious official who
was merely acting in his own interests, and would
resent any discussion or criticism of his actions.

I began by telling him that I had heard of his
having arrested and subsequently released Quasha ——,
and that I thought he probably did not realise the
trouble which might arise if men who were regarded

DIZA

as emissaries of Nimrud, and engaged in plots against
the authority of the Catholicos, were not discouraged
to the best of their ability by the Turkish authorities.
To this he replied that he had no proof against Nimrud,
who might, or might not be, a mere weathercock, and
willing to turn to any one whom he thought likely to
serve his own interests. But he could not undertake
to investigate the domestic quarrel   Shimun's
family, and he had good reason   that if

Nimrud was intriguing against his cousin and misrepresenting him to the authorities, the latter was at the same time acting disloyally towards the government. One letter signed with his seal and addressed to the Russian bishops had been lately intercepted, and even allowing that this might have been a forgery, since Nimrud is known to possess several copies of Mar Shimun's signet, a second had left no room for doubt. This was in the handwriting of the Catholicos, and contained an express order to the Chaldeans of Tiyari not to pay their tribute at the bidding of Nimrud.

"Well," I said, " but I do not see that, if this be the case, Mar Shimun is to blame. It is he and not Nimrud who is responsible to the government for the tribute, and if you encourage the latter to interfere in such matters you are helping to undermine the legitimate authority of the Catholicos, which has been recognised and admitted by the Sultan."

"That is not quite the case," he returned. " Not only did I punish and imprison the Artousha for their raid on the property of the Christians in the Levin valley, but I also placed Nimrud in confinement, and Mar Shimun, if he had had any courage, might have excommunicated him at once when he abjured his creed and joined the Roman Catholics. But what has he done? He has taken from his own people 85,000 piastres (about £800) worth of mules, corn, raisins, &c., during the last five years, and the whole of this money goes into his own pockets. He devotes none of it to the public good. All the churches that I have seen are old buildings ; many of them falling into disrepair ; no new schools are built ; no expenditure is devoted to objects such as every Turkish governor is expected to promote ; and, on the other hand, how is our tribute paid? Formerly we received £700 per annum from the Chaldean Ashirets. During the whole of the last six years we have received only £500. And yet every one knows that the men of Jelu, for instance, are by no means poor. They are constantly bringing back large sums of money from America, and in spite of this they grumble if we ask them to pay us what they owe."

I answered that of course I was not competent to judge of the extent to which the Christians had been to blame, nor did it become me to question any policy which the government might think it necessary or desirable to adopt towards them. If the tribute of Jelu and Tiyari was in arrear, there could be no doubt of their right to enforce its payment, though the manner in which the Catholicos dealt with his own property did not appear to me to be relevant to the subject. Provided that the government received their stipulated share of the money, the uses to which the remainder might be put was clearly a matter which only concerned the Christians themselves.

On the other hand, admitting the duty of the government to protect its own interests, the method which they had adopted for doing so might, I thought, be impugned on the grounds both of policy and justice. The individual peasants were not and could not be made directly responsible, and the attempt to collect the tribute by a military occupation of the villages involved the infliction of great injustice and suffering upon a number of persons who might have loyally fulfilled their obligations, while it afforded no guarantee for punctual payment in the future. This could only be secured by insisting upon the responsibility of the village maliks or of Mar Shimun himself, and by bringing direct pressure to bear upon them in the event of their refusal to comply with legitimate demands.

"Instead of this," I pointed out, "you send your troops to a small hamlet like Zir. They remain there for ten days, eating up all that the people have, and then, I believe, you propose to order them to proceed to Tiyari, where the inhabitants, being of an independent spirit and unaccustomed to such treatment, are by no means unlikely to offer resistance, and bloodshed will ensue. Every European newspaper will announce a massacre of the Christians of Tiyari, and what shall I or any other friend of Turkey be able to plead in your defence? You know," I added, " how great was the indignation abroad when the Armenians were massacred. The defence put forward on that occasion was that the Armenians were punished not as Christians, but as revolutionaries appealing for foreign sympathy. No such plea could be advanced in the case of similar treatment of the Chaldeans. So far from being revolutionaries or intriguers, they are bitterly hostile to those of their own nationality in Persia who have adopted an alien faith, and Mar Shimun himself, in virtue of his position as head of the Chaldean Church, is notoriously and necessarily averse to external influence. If you now take steps which, however harmless or justifiable in themselves, may lead to another period of conflict and massacre, you will at once and for ever alienate the sympathies of all those in Europe who still desire the maintenance and prosperity of the Turkish Empire."

"I entirely appreciate," he replied, "the weight of your arguments, though as for newspapers, they must say what they please. That is not my affair. I have simply to do my duty. It is not for myself that I want the money. I come of an ancient family in

Damascus, and in my office here as governor I will not tolerate a state of things which has already gone on too long. As for bloodshed, of course if the people attack the soldiers, they will have to take the consequences. But do not be alarmed. I have no desire to provoke a conflict, and I think that matters will be arranged peaceably, and that when you next come back to these parts you will find a better state of things prevailing. I wish we could make you a present of vilayets like this and Adana.[1] They are a perpetual source of worry to us, but, now that we have succeeded in introducing order into the greater part of the provinces, it is impossible that we should allow insubordination in Hakkiari, and these incessant raids between Kurds and Christians to continue unchecked. I will tell you my idea "—here he produced a sketch-map of the Hakkiari district, drawn up, he said, by the American missionaries at Urmi—" I shall place a kaimakam at these two villages—Marta and Bedoo (at the junction of the Levin valley with the Zab)—and after that I hope that all will go smoothly, and that neither you nor any of our friends will for the future have anything to complain of."

I thanked him for the courtesy and frankness with which he had discussed the question, and felt that it was of little use to pursue the topic. Indeed I could not but recognise that the policy he had outlined, however inimical to the prospects of continued independence for the Chaldean Ashirets, was, sooner or later, almost inevitable. No government can put up for ever with the *imperium in imperio* which has hitherto prevailed in Hakkiari, and which has certainly not conduced to the peace and security of the district. If the Turks now determine to curtail the quasi-autonomy

[1] The province containing the Armenian revolutionist city of ?

of the Christian tribes, they are, after all, only doing
in their case what they have long ago accomplished in
the case of the Mussulman Kurds, by abolishing the
independent jurisdiction of the old miras and dere
beys. The possibility of resistance by the men of
Tiyari was the chief danger to be apprehended, but,
although more excitable and stubborn than those of
Jelu, they are also much less well armed, for their
guns consist chiefly of old flintlocks and muzzle-
loaders, whereas the eastern Ashiret has provided itself
with modern rifles of various patterns imported from
Persia. On the other hand, the soldiers, although they
had quartered themselves for an unnecessarily long time
upon the villages, had carefully abstained from committing wanton outrage either on life or property, and
there was, therefore, no indication of any desire to
precipitate a conflict which would provide an excuse
for more stringent measures. The allegation that the
troops had been originally sent at Mar Shimun's request to compel restitution from the Oramar Kurds,
and that the officer in command had been bribed by
Sootoo Bey to turn his attentions to Jelu, was one
which I could not substantiate, and which did not
appear to tally with the evidence of a carefully thought-
out policy on the part of the mutessarif.

If Mar Shimun were a stronger man he might
preserve the independence of his people by sternly
asserting an authority, the absence or inefficiency of
which supplies an almost unanswerable justification
for the introduction of Turkish jurisdiction and control. It cannot be said that the Chaldean population
has been unfairly or excessively taxed in comparison
with the Kurds, for, like the Armenians of the towns,
they possess most of the wealth ; and, although no
doubt this is due to their superior industry and talent,

the principle of easing or exempting the poorer at the expense of the propertied classes is one for which precedents are not lacking even at home. The fact that the wealthier minority in Turkey happens to be also Christian, lends colour to accusations of religious persecution which are not altogether justified. If the proceeds of their industry were applied to the improvement of the country, instead of being wasted on an extravagant and corrupt system of administration, and if they were protected from pillage by the Kurds, the Christians would have but little ground for complaint. Unfortunately, as I have already remarked, they are not infrequently themselves disturbers of the peace, and it can hardly be expected of the government that they should show themselves less lenient to their Mussulman than to their Christian subjects.

During the greater part of the century they have been engaged in reducing to subjection the Kurds in other parts of the interior, and, at the present moment, the sole relics of tribal independence are to be found in the wild districts of Hakkiari and the Dersim. It was the policy initiated by Mahmoud, the Reformer, and, like many well meant but precipitate reforms in Turkey, it has created an evil, worse in some respects than that which it sought to remedy, by substituting for the strong paternal authority of the clan-leaders the corruption and incompetence of a centralised bureaucracy. But it is a policy which, however questionable, cannot now be reversed, and which does not admit of half measures. At least it cannot be justly urged that the attack is directed against the Christians alone, and, if the method applied in their case is peculiar, it must be admitted that whereas pressure can be easily and effectively applied to the Christian by a demand on his pocket, the effort to extort money from a Kurd is in most cases about as profitable as the attempt to squeeze the proverbial dry orange.   It must be remembered also that while the government is not afraid of either the Kurds or the Christians singly, they view with considerable apprehension the possibility of an understanding between the two races for purposes of common defence.   Improbable as the idea may appear of such a lying-down together of the lion and the lamb, I know that overtures have more than once been made by the Kurdish chiefs to the village headmen, though the Christians have always most wisely decided to reject them.

And the inducement for co-operation is obvious. The Kurds believe, and rightly, that when the Chaldeans have been deprived of all power of giving trouble, their own turn will come next; and they will be reduced to the same condition as the rayat Kurds of the Taurus.   Meantime the independence of the Christians serves as a kind of barrier for their own nomadic license, while it enables them to live without effort on the fruit of their neighbour's industry.   This calculation, which is already alarming the Kurds, is, no doubt, the determining factor in the policy of the government.   To flatter their cupidity and fanaticism, to encourage their factions and rivalries, and to deprive them of possible, though uncongenial, allies is a necessary preliminary to attacking those who are still capable of making a determined and even a successful resistance.   Hence the readiness with which excuses on their part are accepted, because, however trivial they may be, it is not as yet safe or politic to reject them.

A curious instance of this is said to have occurred not long ago.   Sherif Agha, chief of the Shikkah Kurds, being under a temporary cloud owing to his misdeeds, bethought him of an ingenious trick by which he might regain his credit with the government. He sent a letter to the Armenian revolutionists in the neighbourhood of Salmas, inviting them to make a raid from Persia into Turkish territory, and when they incautiously acted on the hint, he promptly met and defeated them with an overpowering force. Unluckily for him, one of the Armenians who had been captured divulged the particulars of the plot. Sherif Agha was immediately arrested, and while every one was discussing his approaching trial and the chances of condemnation, a firman arrived from Constantinople according him a free pardon, prompted, it was believed, by the Mushir Zekki Pasha, the patron saint and protector of every blackguard in the country who wears the Hamidieh uniform.

And here I might bring the chapter to a close, were it not that the critical situation in the affairs of Hakkiari, which I have described, has been considerably modified by events which occurred shortly after my return to England.

Early in December 1899 a report reached our friend, the mutessarif of Bashkala, that Malik Ismail with six hundred Tiyari Christians had descended upon the Levin valley, raiding and levying blackmail on the Mussulman villages. The real facts were these. Tajir, the Kurdish agha of Levin, had not long before killed several of the Tiyari tribesmen and driven off one hundred and twenty of their sheep. Malik Ismail then offered to compromise the feud, if he would consent to pay blood-money and restore all but twenty of the stolen animals. After some discussion, which took place in a boundary village of Tiyari, these terms were eventually accepted, and at the close of the interview Tajir was presented by Malik Ismael with a costly khanja, in token of renewed friendship. At the same time it was arranged that the latter should send up a few of his followers to Levin next day to receive the compensation upon which the chieftains had mutually agreed. When they presented themselves, however, Tajir, excusing himself on the ground that he had not the money ready, despatched a messenger to Julamerk to his friend Hadji Mohammed Agha, who immediately imparted to the kaimakam there the garbled version of the story which I have given above. That energetic official setting out for the scene of action with mounted zaptiehs from Bashkala was met half-way, in the Selai country, by a sowar bearing a written statement from the police-mamur that the raiding party consisted of nothing more formidable than some dozen Tiyari corn-buyers and mule-sellers scattered about the village on their several errands. To this explicit information he paid no regard, intent on a master-stroke of policy which would enable him by seizing the Tiyari men to hold them as hostages for the punctual payment of the tribal tribute. But his calculations were forestalled. A portion of the ruffianly rabble of Kurds that accompanied him pushed on in advance, found their unsuspecting victims dispersed among the various houses, and massacred two in cold blood, wounding four others out of sheer wantonness, one of whom died not long after, while the rest were stripped to the skin and thrown into prison at Julamerk.

Meanwhile a brother chieftain, Malik Suleiman, having sent word to Tajir that *his* sheep were also being "lifted" by the Tiyari tribesmen, the Kurdish horde hurried off from Levin, and, overtaking the culprits, killed and wounded several—among them the nephew of Malik Suleiman himself! This gentleman, unable to endure the constant pilfering and persecution to which he was subjected by his uncle, had for two years lived in refuge among the Christians; and the recent agreement between Malik Ismail and Tajir had presented itself to his revengeful mind as a favourable opportunity of recouping himself for the losses he had sustained, and retaliating, with the aid of his Tiyari friends, by a foray on his kinsman's flocks. To assist any one in recovering his goods, however illegally, is regarded by Chaldeans and Kurds alike as a very different thing from raiding, and although Malik Ismail made a tardy effort to prevent a breach of the peace, his envoys arrived only just in time to share the fate of those against whose action they had come to protest. After some delay the Christians were put upon their trial at Julamerk, and by dint of hard lying on the part of Hadji Mohammed and the Kaimakam, were duly convicted and sentenced to terms of from ten to thirteen years' imprisonment. But, much to the surprise and disgust of every local official, the Sultan, apprised no doubt of the miserable travesty of justice which had been enacted, annulled the verdict, and ordered the whole batch of prisoners to be set at liberty !

The Kurds, however, were none the less delighted with the success of their treachery. Emboldened by the attitude of the local administration they determined, as soon as the spring began and the roads were open, to concoct another ingenious story—to which some indiscretion on the part of the Ashirets in the interval would be sure to lend colour and plausibility —and obtain from the authorities an order for a general levée of the surrounding hillmen, who, under the ægis of a handful of regulars, would soon make a clean sweep of every Chaldean settlement.

Shortly before Lent, while these plots were hatch-

P

ing, Mar Shimun had arrived in Julamerk. In face
of the dire emergency he had, for once, shaken off his
habitual indecision, and was in direct communication
with Constantinople. Pistol-shots were fired outside
his window. Every artifice short of open violence was
employed to shake his resolution and terrify him into
taking refuge at Kochanes. The officers of the local
corps of nizam and redifs alone stood by him. They
posted sentry outside the miserable house in which he
had secured temporary lodgings at Pagi, a suburb of
Julamerk, sleeping at night without mattress or anything but a thin strip of carpet between his body and
the hard floor ; and they furnished him with a guard
while he celebrated his Eucharist at Easter and Whit-
suntide on a rock outside the village. His indomit-
able courage and perseverance were at last rewarded.
The release of his own subjects by the Sultan's interposition was followed by the dismissal from their posts
of the Kaimakam of Julamerk, and the Mutessarif
of Bashkala,[1] and the conferment of special marks of
royal favour upon Mar Shimun himself.

The result has been to enormously increase his
waning prestige and influence among his own people as
well as the Kurds, by disabusing their minds of the
idea that an appeal to the higher poweis can result in
nothing but approval and confirmation of the decrees of
petty local officialdom. Almost for the first time in his
life the Christian Catholicos has boldly and frankly
placed his case in the hands of the Padishah, and he
has not found his confidence misplaced. The establishment of more cordial and intimate relations between
the Palace and the semi-autonomous Patriarchal Court
has strengthened the authority of both, while it has
baffled alike the sinister calculations of the Kurds, the

[1] Now of Diza (Gawar).

meddlesome intrigues of foreign ecclesiastics, and the treachery of their Chaldean dupes and proselytes.

Of these Nimrud has been the first to feel the altered situation. In pursuit of his usual tactics he had lately concluded an advantageous bargain with certain French and Armenian speculators, by which in return for a payment of £4000 they obtained a concession giving them the right to the produce of all the walnut trees in the various Ashiret districts. A company was formed, and the promoters, after arranging with the authorities the necessary preliminaries in the way of backsheesh, &c., set out for Tiyari, only to discover on their arrival that the walnuts were not, and never had been, in Nimrud's power to dispose of, and that the agreement which they had made with him was absolutely valueless. A letter from Mar Shimun, warning them that the trees were Church property, and as such inalienable, was accompanied by another addressed to the Chaldeans, expressly forbidding them to allow a single Armenian to set foot in the country.

Nimrud was at his wit's end. His former patrons had withdrawn their subsidies, being heavily in debt themselves, and realising that he could no longer be the convenient stepping-stone they once hoped towards the fulfilment of their propagandist ambitions. In his desperation he turned to the maliks, who a few years previously had sided with him in his attempt to raise the standard of rebellion against his brother, begging them to send him at least a portion of the revenue from the taxes of Tiyari. They not only met his entreaty with a flat refusal, but actually invited Mar Shimun to send down his own servants to receive the tribute, promising at the same time to collect an additional sum as a proof of their unswerving loyalty to himself and to the Turkish government.

Like all Orientals they had only needed strong leadership, and would probably never have wavered in their allegiance but for the apathy of their spiritual chief. With all his personal charm and plausibility, Nimrud could never have retained a permanent hold on their affections, and his foreign sympathies ran counter to their most cherished traditions and prejudices. Intensely and jealously proud of their individuality as a Church and as a nation, which they owe mainly to their identification for centuries with the Eastern See in its triumphant protest against the arrogant pretensions of the West, they know full well that, for them, emancipation from Turkish rule means political and ecclesiastical extinction. It is this knowledge which, affording in their case a surer guarantee of fidelity to the existing régime than any supplied by faith or fatalism in the case of the Mussulman, places it in the power of the Turkish government to create, by a wiser and more sympathetic policy, a stronghold of unalterable devotion and loyalty in the mountain fastnesses of Hakkiari.

The recent action of the Sultan has put new heart into this people. It has encouraged them to look to him for the redress of their grievances, the vindication of justice, and the condemnation of official rascality. It has done more to bridle the insolence and license of the Kurds, the spoilt children of avaricious and irresponsible governors, than the despatch of an army corps could have effected. But intervention of this kind, however well-timed, can produce no lasting effect. The Christians, outnumbered by their enemies, often shut out during a large part of the year from all communication with the outside world, and ignorant of any language but their own, must remain powerless

to defend themselves, or to refute the calumnies of
their traducers, unless they are allowed direct access
to some nearer tribunal than that of the Vali at Van.
What is required is constant and immediate supervision by some one charged with suspensory powers,
pending the Sultan's decision, in all cases where a
governor transgresses the strict limits of his authority.
A country like Hakkiari cannot be governed effectively so long as it is treated merely as an insignificant
district of huge vilayets like those of Van or Mosul;
and the situation is rapidly becoming so acute that,
unless a serious attempt is made before long to grapple
with the problem, it may at any moment become, like
the Armenian question, the unhappy sport and victim
of the bungling diplomacy of Europe !

There has been no symptom, for many years past,
so ominous of the spread of anarchy in this region as
the attack by a party of Kurds[1] upon Her Majesty's
Consul, Major Maunsell, in August 1900.   Fortunately
he was one too many for them.   His dragoman slightly
wounded, his baggage captured, and his zaptiehs disarmed, he yet succeeded by his courage and presence
of mind in driving back his cowardly assailants, and
forcing a passage under cover of the darkness, which
afforded them an opportunity to effect their own escape.
But so dastardly an outrage on the representative of a
friendly Power in a country where every Englishman
has a treaty-right to travel unmolested, cannot without
grave danger be allowed to pass unnoticed and unpunished.[2]   Had the victim been a Russian instead of

---

[1] Probably the Zheriknaii (Jerik) Kurds, a sub-tribe of the Artoushi.
A year and a half ago they killed eighteen native Christians and drove off
9000 sheep from Lizan and Ashitha, a crime for which no reparation was
ever exacted.

[2] It is only fair to state that since this was written full retribution for
the outrage has been inflicted upon the offenders by the local authority. But

a British consul—nay, had he been but the humblest subject of the Czar—the insult would have been followed within twenty-four hours by such a vigorous ultimatum, backed with the threat of military force, as has more than once under far less provocation wrested from the Persian government the vindication of Muscovite prestige at Tabriz.

Therein lies the secret, alike of Russia's success and of the growing paralysis and impotence of Great Britain in the East. It is a hard saying, but a true one. We know, and so does Russia, how to govern; but we have never learnt, like her, the art of persuasion. We expect by an artificial and laborious diplomacy to outwit the most highly trained intellects in a nation of born diplomatists, and when we fail, as we are bound to fail, it is not on Downing Street but on the legations and consulates that we cast the whole blame. The truth is, that neither with regard to Turkey nor Persia have we any policy worthy of the name. By choice or necessity deducing, it would almost seem, from the impossibility of omniscience the futility of foresight we have adopted as the cardinal article of our creed the identity of statesmanship with opportunism. Lord Beaconsfield is dead, his policy in a state of suspended animation. Like the bare forms of an ancient ritual no longer inspired by the living spirit of its author, it has nevertheless maintained for thirty years, and still maintains, the essential

---

an insult offered to a British consul calls for sterner measures than would suffice in the case of a private individual, and advantage ought to be taken of such an occurrence to bring home to the minds of the Central Government the imperative necessity of strengthening their control over the tribes. Remedies, not palliatives, are required, and if we shrink from the task of enforcing them it were better instead of reducing the number of our consuls where they are most required, to withdraw them from the country altogether.

objects for which it was originally designed. We, who have deliberately discarded his methods, and neglected our opportunities, may condemn as a failure what we have never tried to make a success; we may criticise where we are powerless to suggest, and destroy where we cannot construct. But it was not by such methods that we built up our Empire in the East and obtained a hold on the imagination and respect of neighbouring races which constitute to this hour our strongest bulwark against the flowing tide of foreign aggression.

Once let Arab, Kurd, or Persian suspect that your arm is shortened, that you cannot strike where Russia can, that you will no longer draw the sword to enforce retribution for any slight, however small, to one of your own countrymen, and his suspicion will to-morrow become the belief of every Baluch and Afghan, of every hill-tribe from Quetta to Gilgit. It is not by a tame acquiescence in the decrease of our influence and prestige in the East that we shall avoid the calamity of an increase in our territorial responsibilities, for the desire to "save face" is the surest incentive to rash annexation. When the disaffected subject of Sultan, Amir, or Shah, returning from the opulent bazaars of Hindustan, asks himself why we do not extend our authority beyond the limits of the Gulf, the deserts of Seistan, or the barrier of the Hindu Kush, he will convict us of timidity if he does not credit us with fidelity to our engagements. His answer will be governed largely by his experience of our position in the country he knows. Accustom him to rank Englishmen below Firenghis of another nationality, to see their representatives less deferentially treated, less magnificently equipped or attended, less influential, be it by fear or favour, in the councils of the state, and his awe and liking for us as individuals will be outweighed by his contempt for the nation whose star appears to be no longer in the ascendant.

It is the peculiar misfortune of our relations with Turkey that, in order to assert our own prestige, we can hardly avoid assuming in the eyes of her government the invidious rôle of religious partisans. The Christian has no more claim, politically or morally, upon our good offices than the Mussulman, but the very fact that we happen to be Christians ourselves renders it inevitable that outrages perpetrated with impunity on Chaldeans will eventually lead to the perpetration of similar outrages on British subjects. If the Kurd is allowed to rob and murder *giaours* with the tacit approval or connivance of the local authorities, he will soon cease to care whether his victim wears a pigtail and knickerbockers, or short hair and the consular uniform. Yet during the whole course of the last twenty years I doubt whether there have been more than one or two instances, at most, of the punishment of a Kurdish tribe for assassination and looting in the Ashirets. The country which Layard roamed in unquestioned security has been within the past twelve months the theatre of two successive attacks upon inoffensive missionaries,[1] and a third upon a British consul travelling in the discharge of his official duties. Isolated robberies may at any moment be succeeded by organised massacre or by some daring infringement of international rights, which will rouse a storm of passionate indignation in Europe.

The decision rests with the Sultan, and upon his

---

[1] One was the attack upon Mr. Browne, which I have related; another, the robbery of Mr. Coan, an American missionary from Urmi, by the petty Kurdish chieftain Calash Agha in the district of Albeg, near Bashkala.

decision depends not merely the future of Hakkiari, but the ultimate fate of the Ottoman Empire in Asia. When the armies of invasion march by the southern shores of Lake Van down the river-gorge which echoed centuries ago to the tramp of the Ten Thousand, will they find in the grim fastnesses upon their flank an array of sturdy, warlike highlanders—Christian Janissaries, bound to their suzerain no less by the ties of gratitude than by those of pride in their own national life; or a motley rabble of untamed Kurdish Ishmaelites, inured to no discipline, torn by internal factions, and loyal only to their own sordid personal interests? Armenia has not, never could have, any semblance of national unity.   Yet the mere suspicion that an attempt might be made to form one was sufficient to draw from Prince Lobanoff his famous protest against the creation of another Bulgaria in the heart of Kurdistan. "*Fas et ab hoste doceri*": the history of the advance of Mussulman power supplies more than one instance of triumphs won by the aid of Christian swords. The history of its retreat may yet be a record of disasters averted and failures retrieved by the desperate heroism of those whose ecclesiastical autonomy is bound up with the civil supremacy of an alien faith.

What justice and good government have prevailed to accomplish in India, where around the same banner the soldiers of the Crescent and the Cross are rallied by a patriotism that knows no distinction of race or religion, it is still possible for Turkey to accomplish in the land which she holds as we hold India, by the power of the sword. But "*lakirdi ili pilaf olmaz.*" Talking will never make *pilaf,* and the miserable hashes produced by the concert of European cooks do not encourage a repetition of similar culinary experiments. Turkey must work out her own salvation. She must judge for herself of the disinterestedness of those who vie with one another in their proffers of patronage and advice. She may baffle their selfish designs for the moment by playing upon their mutual jealousies, but the real peril that threatens her existence is not assault from without, but the canker of misgovernment that is devouring her within. If the hour of her dissolution and the partition of her inheritance is at hand, it is not by the accumulation of hostile armaments on her border, but by the exhaustion of her internal resources; not by the inrush of the sea of nations on her shores, but by the drying up of her own river Euphrates, that the "way of the kings of the East" is being prepared.

CHAPTER XIII

BORDER FEUDS

WE remained to dinner with the governor, who gave us his photograph and informed us that he had just received notice of promotion from Constantinople. He did not appear to be sorry to leave Bashkala, but remarked with pride that he should at least leave behind him one useful memorial of his tenure of office in that place in the shape of a new road over the Chukh pass to Van. At parting he earnestly reiterated his assurance that he would take every precaution to prevent bloodshed in Tiyari, gave orders for a fresh escort of men to accompany us as far as Neri, and sent word to Moussa Bey, the Kurdish chief of Khumaroo, that we proposed to pay him a visit on our way.

Mr. Browne, though anxious to return to Kochanes, very kindly consented to accompany us as far as the matran's village. Leaving Diza, the road runs northward, skirting the edge of the plain and thereby avoiding the villages, which are for the most part perched on the lower spurs. The only human habitations visible were a house belonging to the chief of the Dereni [1] Kurds and the small church of Mar Gerwergis (St. George), situated in the vicinity of sulphur springs which are famed as a remedy for the itch.

---

[1] A valley of the same name in Persia contains three monasteries, and the word is variously derived from *dere* (a valley) and *deir* (a monastery).

The valley, as it narrows to the southern extremity, is covered with long rank grass, affording pasture for numerous herds of buffalo; and green plovers, ravens, and buzzards abound. At the end of three hours a low col is crossed to the valley of Khumaroo, in which, ten miles lower down, the castle of Moussa Beg stands on the summit of a low rounded hill. A picturesque group of horsemen had ridden out to greet us, headed by the chief's son, a ,boy of ten (he began to learn rifle-shooting at the age of four), superbly mounted and accoutred. Dressed in a white frilled shirt and wide, baggy trousers, and wearing a plum-coloured turban on his head, he put his fine and perfectly-trained Arab through a series of curvets and caracoles which elicited loud and reiterated plaudits from his armed retainers. Small-built, but soldierly-looking men, they were all provided with Sniders, while their diminutive leader carried a Martini, which he brandished about his charger's ears to the accompaniment of the shrill *hou-has* by which his countrymen always work themselves up to the requisite pitch of martial excitement.

Close to the chief's house, on the very edge of the declivity, stands a sort of martello tower roofed with thatch, which, projecting about a foot from the sides, gives the whole edifice the appearance of a big thick-stalked fungus. The house itself, built of mud and stone with a staircase of solid masonry, is provided with walls of enormous thickness, and two sides of the large room in which Moussa Beg receives his guests are pierced with loopholes for defence. Consequently the draught was appalling, and the only means of defying the cold was to turn oneself like a leg of mutton in front of a small Persian stove which stood in the centre of the carpeted floor.

Our host was dressed in tight-fitting trousers and a long frockcoat of light blue, and having motioned us to the fire, he resumed the cross-legged posture in which we had surprised him on our entrance. Never have I seen any one of so grave and dignified a demeanour. Every word he spoke was low and deliberate, and his nearest approach to hilarity was a melancholy half-apologetic smile. Typically Persian in type, and remarkably slim in figure, his fair olive complexion, jet black eyes and hair, small and carefully-trimmed moustache, high cheek bones, and somewhat sunken cheeks, would have given him a strikingly handsome and attractive appearance had it not been for the abuormally large ears, which had been flattened at the top by the ungainly habit of wearing the turban low down on the forehead. One could not help feeling that if many of the old Begs were like Moussa, their almost total extinction has been a disaster for the country ; and while the part which he had played in recent incidents confirms the favourable estimate of character which his expression would lead one to form, it also explains the absence of that lighter vein which is ordinarily the most distinguishing characteristic of his countrymen.

In order to understand the present situation in the district, it is necessary to revert to the events of three years ago. The most powerful chieftain at that time, as now, was Sheikh Sadiq of Shemsdin, the younger son of the famous Sheikh Obeidullah, who in 1880 raised the standard of rebellion against the Turkish government, crossed into Persia, and actually laid siege to the town of Urmi, which was only saved by the action of the missionaries, who kept the invader parleying until the Shah's troops arrived from Tabriz. On the suppression of the revolt the Sheikh was exiled to Mecca, where he was joined not long after by his eldest son, Sheikh Hadr, formerly a colonel in the Turkish army. His successor, Sadiq, determined to repair the broken fortunes of his house, spared no effort to convince the government of his loyalty, and in contrast to his only rival, Moussa Beg of Khumaroo, cherished secretly feelings of the greatest antipathy to the Chaldean Christians of the neighbourhood. For some time, however, he refrained from overt action against them, and when at last he threw aside the disguise of friendliness which he had thought it politic to assume, it was to perpetrate a deed of wanton perfidy and cruelty for which even in the East it would be difficult to find a parallel.

Hearing that Mar Gauriel, the Bishop of Urmi and Solduz, was staying close by, on a visit to the Matran Mar Khnanishu at Mar Ishu, he sent him a pressing invitation to accept the hospitality of his own palace at Neri. The bishop, unsuspicious of treachery, availed himself of the offer, but had scarcely crossed the threshold when he was recognised and accosted by a Chaldean woman who had lately become a convert to Islam.

"Would to God," she whispered, "that you had not come, for you will never leave this place alive."

Accordingly, as soon as night fell the bishop and a deacon who had accompanied him were taken out to the hillside by the sheikh's orders, and decapitated. The murder was witnessed by a Herki Kurd and his wife, who happened to be returning to their village and had concealed themselves on the approach of the party. Every possible effort was made to bring the sheikh to justice, and a commissioner was sent out to hold an inquiry ; but the case was declared not proven, and nothing further was done.

The matran himself would almost certainly have
shared the bishop's fate, for the sheikh had despatched
soldiers to keep watch in front of his house and to
beset all the paths affording egress from the valley.
But, knowing the sympathy of Moussa Beg for the
Christians and his antagonism to the chief of
Shemsdin, he lost no time in forwarding a message
imploring his assistance. The Beg, on hearing the
facts, promptly sent a superior force, which rescued
the matran without opposition and brought him in
safety to the castle at Khumaroo. Here he was
lodged in tents with a number of other Christians,
and carefully guarded until an opportunity presented
itself of conveying him to Kochanes, where he remained until the British consul at Van paid a visit
to Mar Shimun, and on his return journey through
Persia took the refugee back with him to Urmi.

Since that time, although the house of the Bishop
Mar Dinkha, half-way between Neri and Khumaroo,
has been pillaged, and he can never go about with
an escort of less than thirty men, the sheikh and
the matran have, outwardly at all events, been on
friendly terms, and the quarrel between the former
and Moussa Beg has been patched up. But the
immunity from punishment which Sadiq has enjoyed,
and his rapidly growing power on the frontier, are
of ill-omen alike to the security of the Christians, to
the authority of the government, and to the prestige
of those chieftains who, like Moussa Beg, have,
regardless of consequences to themselves, boldly stood
up to protect their humbler neighbours from tyranny
and oppression. For them the outlook is dark, almost
desperate, and few spectacles could be imagined at once
so heroic and so tragic as the struggle of these knight-
errants of Moslem chivalry to defend the right against

apparently overwhelming odds, in the hope and belie
which underlies the fatalism of Islam no less than th
confidence of Christianity, that, "though the mills o
God grind slowly, yet they grind exceeding small."

We passed a chilly night round the stove, whil
the servants slept in a confused heap on the ston
staircase outside; and in the morning set out witl
our small friend and a number of the clansmen, oi
the road to the matran's house. Before startin
Moussa Beg had insisted on our taking photograph
which, unfortunately, proved failures, of himself an
his son, of whom he was inordinately proud, both oi
account of his skill with the rifle, and his educationa
acquirements, which enabled him to read his father'
letters.

The valley of Khumaroo contains several Christia
villages, all of which rely on the Kurdish chief fo
protection. Formerly they looked to the Sheikh o
Shemsdin to defend their interests, for Obeidullah
although disloyal to the government, was not incline
to oppress his Christian dependants, and alway
shielded them from the attacks of the Herki Kurds
Sheikh Sadiq, however, succeeding his father befor
Moussa Beg had come to Khumaroo or built th
present fort, devastated the whole valley, and the in
habitants had only recently summoned courage to
return to their abandoned homes and occupations.

I have before alluded to the relations which existed
up to a very recent date between the old miras and
their Christian subjects, and which still subsist between the Moslem chiefs and the Syrian Jacobites in
the district between Mardin and Mosul. The quarrels
and faction fights in former times took place not
between Christian and Moslem, but between the
adherents of rival chiefs, and it was by no means un-

usual to find the Chaldean Ashirets leagued against each other under Mussulman leadership. The organisation of the various tribes of the frontier districts was elaborate and exceedingly curious. The Mira of Hakkiari, who had his summer and winter quarters at Julamerk and Bashkala respectively, divided his people into two Bazikki[1] or wings; the Left comprising the Christians of Tiyari and Baz, with the Kurds of Astousha and Dereni (the valley lying between Diza and Urmi, including Marbishu); and the Right, the Christians of Tkhoma, Jelu, and Diz (Deezen), with the Kurdish Ashirets, the Dustik, the Oramar, and the Apneanish (or Apenshai). Shemsdin, which was not included in Hakkiari, was under the jurisdiction of the Mira of Suren, the district lying between Neri and Ushnu, and extending to the south of Rowanduz.

We stopped for lunch at a small Chaldean village, where the staple food of the inhabitants seemed to be acorn bread, eggs, and walnuts. The weather became steadily worse as the day wore on, and during the two hours which we spent in crossing the range (8000 feet) above Mar Ishu, we could see nothing for the mist which shrouded the hills and the sleet and hail driving in our faces. The matran's house stands on a terrace half-way down the mountain-side, surrounded by a few fine mulberry trees, and as we rode up to the entrance we were met by his father and brother, wearing magnificent silver sheathed khanjas in their sashes, and their *loandis* or long pointed sleeves, unwound and dangling, in the fashion prevalent among both Kurds and Chaldeans on great occasions, about a foot and a half below the hands.

They led us through the courtyard, two sides of which are occupied by the old church and the matran's

---

[1] Bazikki (Bazikka = "pipe stick ").

private apartments, into a large room on the right, so badly roofed that the rain-water stood in a pool in the centre of the floor. A large log-fire blazed at the farther end ; and we had hardly taken off our riding-boots and warmed ourselves beside it, before our host walked in. A bulky middle-aged man, with a bushy black beard and hair, and a kindly, but decidedly unintelligent, face, he is regarded by the Chaldeans themselves as the weakest of their ecclesiastical dignitaries, always prone to be deceived by the last speaker, and so indolent, that he is content to leave his flock in Azerbaijan to go their own way to the Russian Church without making any strenuous effort to retain them in the fold of their ancient communion. Decision, it must be admitted, is not a quality very common among any of the spiritual leaders of the Christian Ashirets, and the problems involved in the administration of the frontier diocese would tax the capacity and nerve of the strongest. Deserted by many of his own people, menaced by the animosity of his powerful neighbour and overlord, Sheikh Sadiq, through whom he pays his taxes to the government, and tempted to throw in his lot with the rising fortunes of Nimrud, it is not surprising if, while remaining loyal to his superiors, he shares the same defects of weakness and infirmity of purpose as the Catholicos himself.

The most signal display of firmness on his part is said to have been his persistent refusal to marry, when a young man, although his prospects of appointment as matran being at that time by no means assured, he was strongly urged to the step in order to avert the possible extinction of the elder branch of the family. Candidates for the office of metropolitan, as for that of the Catholicate and the subordinate grades of the episcopate, though not for the priesthood, must satisfy the two conditions of celibacy and abstention from animal food. This rule has been introduced within the last three or four hundred years, and the original custom of leaving the choice of a successor to the laity has been supplanted by the practice of confining it

MAR KHNANISHU

wherever possible to the nearest relative of the deceased, who, as we have seen in the case of the diocese of Jelu, is sometimes a mere child. The new metropolitan, when selected, receives his ordination from the Catholicos, to whom, it may be, he has himself administered the same rite on his appointment to the patriarchal chair, and thereafter shares with him the privilege of admitting others to the episcopal office.

In contrast to the majority of his brethren, who are, as a rule, deplorably ignorant, Mar Khnanishu is a well-read man, and takes a genuine interest in the traditions and ancient records of his Church. In the course of a rambling conversation upon this subject, he imparted to us various items of desultory information, as, for instance, that Melchizedek was believed by the Chaldean commentators to have been a descendant of Shem, that the words of our Lord on the Cross, " Eli, Eli, lama sabachthani," should be pronounced " El, El, lama bshthwakni," and that the word "Maranatha" in I Cor. xxii. signifies "The Lord is coming," or "The Lord is come," a translation which has been inserted in a footnote by the authors of the Revised Version, though for some reason or other they have refrained from introducing it into the text. Then, taking us into his own study, a long comfortless room, containing only a few divans and a small stove, he showed us an ancient and bulky manuscript, which, together with a history of early monastic institutions, is ordinarily kept in the church. It contains a lengthy commentary on the books of the Old Testament, dating from the first half of the fourteenth century, and annotated with copious marginal scholia, being the only copy extant, with the exception of one which, I believe, is now in the possession of the American missionaries at Urmi. The first page, which he read and translated for our benefit, commences with a long invocation to the Blessed Trinity to bless the work of the writer, and proceeds to describe how at the time of the Babylonish captivity the sacred books were all destroyed by fire, and were rewritten in their present form under direct inspiration by Ezra.

The church of Mar Ishu, which is entered from the courtyard, is not particularly interesting. Its plan and arrangement are of the usual type, the roof very high, and the light almost entirely excluded. The sanctuary is closed by a heavy curtain and wooden folding-doors, but these are not adorned with carving like the doors at Zerani, and the only peculiarity of the interior is the baldachino above the altar, supported on four lofty stone pillars.

We now took our leave of Mr. Browne, who was going back by the direct road, which reaches Kochanes in eleven hours, and set out ourselves for the neighbouring town of Neri. From the matran's house the road descends into the valley, and passing a small Chaldean village ascends the opposite range by toilsome curves till it reaches a ridge 7300 feet in height, from which the white front of Sheikh Sadiq's house [1] is visible far below in the hollow, while in front an irregular line of snow peaks cuts the northern horizon, dominated by the magnificent pyramid-cone of Shahatan. At the konak we found the kaimakam, a new arrival, with the members of the medjliss, among whom I recognised several old acquaintances, and after a preliminary refreshment in the shape of iced sherbet (fruit-syrup) they conducted us to a house which had been hastily made ready, one of several built in a tiny square overlooking and enclosing the *charshi* or market-place, and containing no fittings or screens to the windows except a loose paper-covered framework.

We were chatting with the kadi or judge, a dear old gentleman, wearing a voluminous white turban, when a messenger from the sheikh arrived to inform

[1] Neri, 4800 feet.

us that he had postponed his departure for Katoona on hearing from the mutessarif at Diza of our intended visit, and that while he hoped to have the pleasure of calling upon us next day, he would be gratified if we would honour him by taking a cup of coffee at his house after lunch. The new palace was not yet completed, but his temporary quarters, although of mean exterior, were furnished inside with extraordinary luxury and extravagance. He was seated, in the company of his servants, in a large room strewn with costly carpets, and adorned with what appeared to be a number of iron safes in the corner, and fine cabinets of inlaid tortoise-shell. Dressed in an absurd garment, like a loose coarse bath towel, and wearing a white turban on his head, a style of costume adopted by only one other equally saintly and portly personage of my acquaintance, the Sherif of Wazan in Morocco, our host possessed the most unattractive and even repulsive physiognomy it has ever been my lot to behold. A fat, puffy countenance fringed with a short ragged beard, eyes of a soft and luminous black, and a thick-lipped sensuous mouth, combined to form an expression of cruelty and treachery masked by a more than cat-like serenity and politeness. He talked smoothly and pleasantly (except that his observations were interrupted by loud and frequent hiccoughs), asked us to accompany him to his palace at Katoona, inquired about our intended route, and strongly dissuaded us from adopting that from Neri to Ushnu, which I had been half inclined to take. In spite of his overwhelming prestige and authority he was, he said, quite unable even to protect his own caravans from frequent pillage by marauding tribes on the Persian side of the frontier. Up to that point we could of course travel in safety under a Turkish escort, but beyond it there was an extensive tract of country which was notoriously insecure, and over which the government of the Shah exercised no effective control. He advised us, therefore, to follow the route southward through Rowanduz and the Bradost valley, an advice which seems extraordinary in the light of what we afterwards saw there, but which we decided to adopt, not merely because the risks involved in taking the alternative route seemed hardly worth running, but also because we had no one with us who could speak a word of Persian, and if difficulties arose with the authorities at a distance from any telegraph station we should be placed in a very awkward situation, and subjected at all events to considerable delay.

On taking our leave of the sheikh, the kaimakam proposed that we should make the round of the town in company with the architect of the new palace. I remarked on the unwonted absence of pariah dogs in the streets, which he explained by saying that, as the sheikh's followers belonged to the Shaffi sect, the introduction of these animals had been sternly prohibited, any stray one that might find its way into the place being immediately killed.

The district, in addition to its Kurdish and Nestorian population, contains three villages occupied by Jews, and governed by a rabbi from Bagdad. Although the exact date of their immigration is unknown, it is certain that they have resided in the country from a very early period, and having adopted the local dress and even the language of their Mussulman neighbours, are now, except in features, practically indistinguishable from the Kurds. In the majority of the great towns of the interior the Jews are conspicuous by their absence, and the fact that they are to be found in considerable numbers not only in Mosul, but in pastoral villages like Diza, Neri, Girdi, and Bashkala, may indicate an origin derived from one of the numerous Israelitish colonies which the kings of Assyria planted in distant portions of their empire after the fall of Samaria.

The sheikh's new palace stands in a fine position, on rising ground at the lower end of the town, and is designed on so ornate and extensive a scale that, although its erection has already occupied four years, it is still only half completed. Of its three stories little more than the first has been finished, each of the flanking walls being pierced with seven windows, while that on the entrance side is of immense thickness, and the doorway broadens out towards the inner courtyard. Built entirely of white porous stone taken from a quarry close by, and timber from the surrounding hills, the amount spent on its construction must be very large. The sheikh is commonly reported to possess an income of 300,000 piastres, a large fortune for this country, and the neighbourhood may be almost said to depend for its existence on his expenditure. Nominally he receives, like Mar Shimun, a subsidy from the government, but for some years past this is believed to have been withheld, and the bulk of his revenues is probably now derived from his monopoly of the cultivation of the famous Shemsdinan tobacco, for which he paid £500 to prevent the introduction of the Regie. By far the strongest of the quasi-independent chieftains, and governing practically as he pleases in the large tract of territory which extends from Mar Ishu to Girdi, he derives additional influence from the religious character of his office. According to information which I afterwards received, he can in an emergency command the services of more than 2000 men, and though the troops of Moussa Beg make up, to some extent, by their superior bravery for their decided numerical inferiority, they are far less well armed and equipped. Many of the sheikh's followers are provided with rifles of the latest pattern, which can be easily procured from Persia, and, like the tribesmen of the Kohat pass in India, who turn out Lee-Metfords of tolerable precision at short range, they are said to manufacture rifles and ammunition of their own in the small village of Garar, near the frontier, at about three hours distance from their chief summer quarters at Katoona. None of these men enlist as Hamidiehs, and though more than once an attempt has been made to press them into government service, they have always successfully evaded it by migrating into Persian territory.

There can be little doubt that the authorities are at present biding their time, and that sooner or later the sheikh or his successor will meet the same fate as that which overtook Sheikh Hadr and Obeidullah. They grossly overrate his power, and imagine he can reckon on too many adherents to render it safe for them to attack him openly. Stranger things too have happened than an alliance between the Christians and even so red-handed a persecutor as Sadiq; and though I am convinced that overtures on his part would be rejected by them as scornfully as the advances of the Herki or Artousha chiefs, yet his own conduct, if report speaks true, seems to indicate that he does not regard the contingency as an impossible one. It was affirmed by many that he had only recently refused a request from the mutessarif for a loan of troops to assist the government in settling matters with the Chaldeans of Tiyari, and though Mohammed Pasha had spoken in high terms of him to me, he would probably do so in any case from motives of policy.

Owing to the numerous cross-currents which govern the political situation on the frontier, the conduct of the sheikh or of the Turkish authorities in any given emergency is extremely difficult to forecast. The main desire of the latter is to maintain friendly relatious, if possible, both with the Herki Kurds and with their powerful neighbour at Shemsdin. But it so happens that, next to Moussa Beg of Khumaroo, the most dreaded antagonist of the sheikh is Piru, the chief of that section of the Herki which occupies the Persian side of the borderland; and the only Christian Ashirets with whom Piru is not on good terms are the Chaldeans of Tiyari and Berwer, in whose coercion the mutessarif had invited Sadiq to co-operate. Such a battle of cross-purposes, in which the government are invariably and necessarily the losers, cannot be waged indefinitely. The occasional extortion of a few hundred pounds from a handful of Christians by means of an expensive military occupation is a poor compensation for an annual loss of thousands to the imperial exchequer. The intolerable rapacity and cruelty of the sheikh, and the imprudent ostentation, by which he betrays his inordinate wealth and ambition, are the surest precursors of his downfall; and I should not be at all surprised if a traveller to Neri in the near future were to find himself quartered in the spacious apartments of the new palace as the honoured guest not of Sheikh Sadiq, but of the Turkish governor.

A little path runs down below the walls, past pretty grottoes hung with ferns and creepers, to the quarries near the banks of the stream, the current of which is utilised to work a powerful saw-mill, constructed on the spot, of three blades ranged in a row, the stone being kept in position by means of thick ropes. We passed several groups of more than thirty men each, carrying entire poplar trunks up to the house, and indeed the greater part of the population seemed to be employed in building. The town has no native industry, and the diminutive bazaars are furnished principally with goods imported from Persia. The kaimakam himself complained most pathetically of the loneliness of his position. He evidently felt himself quite overshadowed by the sheikh, and remarked to me that the task of governing efficiently a country in which the great majority of the people were Kurds, and in which there were no *mukhtars* or village headmen who could be held responsible for wrong-doing or for the punctual payment of taxes, was one of which, for his part, he almost despaired.

CHAPTER XIV

THE PLAINS OF THE TIGRIS

THE morning of our departure from Neri commenced with a three hours' bargaining for mules, with the united assistance of the kaimakam and the colonel of the zaptiehs. There was no lack of animals in the town, and the demand for them appeared to be slight ; but one and all the katirjis refused to hire them out except at an extortionate charge of four medjidiehs (nearly a pound) per mule per day, and it was whispered that this combination was due to the forethought of the sheikh, who commanded all the means of transport, and had, before leaving for Katoona, impressed upon his people the desirability of fleecing us as much as possible. So it was past midday before our caravan got under weigh and we started down the wooded glen to the south-east.

A little below the town a small stream runs in from the Persian hills to join the Saralla Chai, which, flowing through the centre of the valley, ultimately turns south-west, and probably unites its waters with those of the Zab somewhere near Rezan. Crossing by a newly-built bridge of stone, and riding along shady spurs, we met long strings of labourers carrying poplar trunks to Neri, and for many miles the green sward was littered with newly-felled trees. A small, clear spring, bubbling out from under the roots of a gigantic plane, afforded a pleasant halting-place for lunch, where, through chequered glades and vistas of oak and hawthorn, the snow ranges glimmered hazily across the tremulous mist of the valley. Another hour and a half's ride and we turned up a side ravine, running north-east and south-west to the Kurdish village of Aulliol[1] (or Avliol), lying low down by a trickle of water in a thicket of gold and tawny poplars, and crowned by a beautiful peak of the purest white. The houses, all of stone, are built in one long row, like those of a northern colliery village, and so indescribably filthy, that it was only after a thorough sweeping that we succeeded in making one of them tolerable for a night's lodging.

Continuing southward the track crosses a prettily wooded valley, through which a second stream flows in the direction of the Zab, and close to its banks stands the house of Bedr Khan, a Kurdish chief, said to be a relation of the famous Beg of Bohtan, who in the early forties made his name infamous by a ruthless massacre of the Chaldeans of Lizan, Tkhoma, and other villages of Hakkiari. Through a dense growth of trees—walnut, apple, plane, beech, willow, and Spanish chestnut—we climbed to the top of the ridge above Girdi (6200 feet), whence a lovely prospect unfolds itself of rolling dun-coloured downs sparsely covered with tufts of gum tragacanth and a species of bog myrtle, and melting away to westward in the pale pink hues of the hills of Gavar, Serdasht, and Michmich. Behind us the snow pyramid of Shabatan marked the limit of the lofty highlands we had left, while south and east, like billows of a shoreward setting sea, range on range, in low and dwindling undulations, the wooded hills swept down to the verge of the Assyrian plains.

Girdi is a small settlement surrounded by smooth

[1] Avliol, 4300 feet.

grassy lawns, and containing a mixed population of Jews, Christians, and Kurds. The road leaves it on the right, and passing out of the sheikh's territory continues eastward by a gradual descent until it reaches, at the end of five hours, the tiny military outpost of Bigijni, a few houses clustering round the base of two mud forts with round towers, on the right bank of a burn flowing from the frontier hills. From this point, as from Neri, a track branches off to Ushnu, a caravan march of about seven hours, but the pass is said to be a difficult one, though not absolutely impracticable for troops. The Turkish garrison consists of thirty-six soldiers, brought together from the most distant parts of the empire. Of the five men told off to escort us through the Bradost valley, one hailed from Baiburt, near Erzerum, a second from Dara, between Nisilis and Mosul, while the bimbashi was a native of Bulgaria.

We forded the stream a little lower down, where another village occupies the summit of a remarkable outcrop of steep cliffs, and struck up through the oak copses that clothe the intervening ridge. Suddenly the soldiers raised a cry of "robbers," and dashed off in hot pursuit; but coming up with them, we saw nothing more formidable than two eminently peaceable-looking muleteers wending their way up the hill, while a third sat calmly on a stone in the middle of a brook, washing his feet. The bimbashi thought his appearance suspicious, but after a severe cross-examination consented to let him go, and we proceeded without any further alarm.

From the watershed a magnificent view opens out, far to westward, of the Zab valley, where the eye is caught by one of the most striking features of the landscape, as seen from Amadiyah, a long even ridge

of barren rock marked with perpendicular lines of
strata and crowning the gentle slope of the mountain
side.   At the end of two hours we ascended into the
Bradost valley, which lies almost due east and west,
and made our way to the village of Gonirash (or
Kaniresh = Kara Su, "Black Water"), perched on an
eminence overlooking the plain and the snowy Persian
range that forms the background of Rowanduz.

To our great surprise not a soul was to be seen.
The streets were empty, the houses all deserted, and
the only sound that broke the weird silence was the
wailing of a deserted pariah puppy.   The nearest village was some miles off, and even if we had felt
inclined to force our animals over another stage, our
baggage was already far behind, and the men were
strongly averse to travelling in the dark.   We were
discussing the problem, the difficulty of which was
aggravated by the fact that we had brought no provisions with us, when we caught sight of a small group
of figures on a housetop silhouetted against the red
flush of the evening sky.   Joining their party, we
found that it consisted of three Turkish commissioners
and their servants, who had arrived a short while before
us, and were in much the same plight as ourselves,
without either food or bedding for the night.

They explained that they had been appointed by
the government to conduct an official inquiry into the
cause of certain recent disturbances, and, if possible,
to arrange a settlement.   Apparently the Sheikh of
Shemsdin, being involved in a quarrel with the Kurds
of the Bradost valley, who lie outside the sphere of his
own jurisdiction, had made common cause with the
chiefs of the Herki Kurds, and the latter, swooping
down upon their unsuspecting victims, had massacred
every inhabitant and looted every house in Gonirash,

as well as in other neighbouring villages. It is said that when news of this outrage was brought to the Mutessarif of Bashkala he prepared at once to send a body of troops to restore order, but that the sheikh despatched a telegram to Constantinople saying that there was no occasion for action on the part of the government, as he intended himself to adopt measures identical with those proposed by their local representatives. The necessity, however, for some investigation was apparent, and in Turkey, as in England, the appointment of a commission suggests itself as a convenient mode of displaying sympathetic interest in a problem, while deferring its solution and remaining unpledged with regard to any recommendations which may be made. In the present instance, the task of inquiry was surrounded with difficulties of a peculiarly baffling character. It was impossible to examine any witness of the massacre, for the Kurds had taken very good care to leave none alive, and while the obvious course was to arrest and question the chiefs themselves, the commissioners seemed entirely in the dark as to who these gentlemen were, and how or where they could be found.

But for the moment these doubts and perplexities were quite overshadowed in importance by the gloomy prospect of having to go to bed supperless. They had brought with them a canister of tea, and squatting in a disconsolate row round a brass samovar on the very edge of the flat mud roof, they extended to us a cordial invitation to share their humble repast. One of them, a fat, good-natured, but incompetent-looking gentleman, informed me that he was a native of Van, and had come to the conclusion that life was hardly worth living. He never had a moment's rest. At one time he was sent off to arrange matters with the turbulent Haideranlis in the district of Adeljivas, north of the lake, at another to settle disputes among the Artousha in the valley of Berwari, and now to perform an even more hopeless duty in a part of the country which lay altogether outside the borders of his own vilayet. The stream at Bigijni forms the northern boundary of the province of Van, and accordingly the Vali of Mosul was represented on the inquiry by a

THE THREE COMMISSIONERS

member of his medjliss, while the military element was supplied by the third commissioner, an officer of the regiment quartered at Bashkala. Their depression was happily somewhat lightened by the announcement that one of the soldiers had succeeded in effecting the capture of two stray chickens, and they despatched their servants to see if there was any sign of the approach of our caravan. By dinner-time it was

R

obvious that all hope of its arrival that night must be abandoned, and indeed our friends kindly reminded us that it was not impossible that the muleteers would decline to come on at all, since they were themselves servants of the sheikh, and would naturally be averse to entering the valley where any Bradost Kurd who might happen to have escaped the massacre would be only too pleased to knock them on the head. So we made the best of a bad situation, shook down a quantity of straw in one of the rooms, and having lit a roaring fire in the centre, to counteract the cold wind that swept through the gaping crevices of the walls, slept very comfortably with our saddles for pillows. The commissioners, although they had brought few provisions with them, had, with curious perversity, supplied themselves with ample material for a pyrotechnic display, and as soon as the last rosy tinge had faded from the Rowanduz snows, amused themselves, far into the night, by letting off red squibs and crackers from the roof.

At sunrise we all sat down for our morning cup of tea, in which slices of bitter tamarind supplied the place of sugar, and the commissioners reviewed the situation. They were by no means disposed to remain in this deserted spot, and, as they very pertinently remarked, it was not easy to see how they could arrange matters in a place where there was no one with whom to arrange them. In fact they admitted that a settlement was, in their opinion, impossible, a view in which I was the more inclined to concur, as one of their own servants had, to my knowledge, just informed our sowars that his master was himself in the pay of the sheikh! They knew that the Herki had four chiefs, Sadr Agha and three others, all of equal authority; but it was impossible to discover the whereabouts of.any of the four, since the Herki, like their neighbours, the Ben Agee, the Artousha, and the Oramar, move southward to the Mosul plain as soon as winter sets in: The government has learnt by bitter experience the danger of making themselves the catspaw of these Kurdish chiefs, and would now infinitely prefer if they could to leave them to exterminate each other. An amusing story is told in this connection of Hadji Agha, the chief of the Artousha. He had just reached the edge of the Tigris plain when news was brought to him of an intended attack by his inveterate enemies the Dikran Kurds. Thereupon, having divided his forces and placed a large body of men in ambush, he sent word to the Vali of Mosul explaining the situation, affirming that he desired to avert a breach of the peace, and asking for reinforcements. On the following day Hadji Agha deliberately forced an encounter, the two tribes met in combat, and the Dikran Kurds, falling into the trap which had been so skilfully prepared for them, were completely worsted and fled, leaving forty of their number dead on the field. Shortly after the engagement the government troops arrived on the scene and found the Artousha women wailing over the corpses of their enemies, which Hadji Agha astutely declared to be the pitiful remains of his own followers. The commanding officer, having no means of testing its truth, accepted this version of the story, and the Herki, besides inflicting a handsome thrashing upon their opponents, reaped the whole credit of having been the aggrieved party in the matter.

The commissioners had just dismissed this topic of the Kurds, and were discussing with infinite gravity the probable truth of a German professor's prediction, of which they had lately heard, that the world was to come to an end on the 12th instant, and of a report

contained in a letter from the Patriarch of Babylon to
the Patriarch of Mosul, that the throne of Nebuchad-
nezzar had been unearthed from a well near Babylon,
when the caravan with our baggage appeared on the
scene. The muleteers, fearing an attack under cover
of the darkness, had decided that it was safer to turn
back to Bigijni and pass the night there. We sent
them forward at once with the soldiers, and following
later in the day, found them, to our disgust, sitting
contentedly under a tree not half a mile off. As the
commissioners had predicted, they had no sooner
realised, from the deserted aspect of Gonirash, the
perils of their own situation, than they began at once
to talk of returning to Neri. And to make matters
worse, the soldiers themselves had suddenly bethought
them that they had no orders to proceed as far as
Rowanduz. Threats and expostulations proving alike
useless, we sent a mounted zaptieh back to the village
to inform the commissioners of what had happened.
He stayed so long that I feared he must have availed
himself of his opportunity to slip off to Bigijni, and, as
a last resource, I made a proposal to the sergeant that
he should consent to accompany us, on condition that
as soon as we reached Rowanduz we would send a
telegram to his commanding officer explaining matters
and exonerating him from all responsibility. He hesitated for some time, saying that his period of military
service had nearly expired, and that he feared it might
be extended if he was convicted of acting beyond the
letter of his instructions. However, he at last consented to waive his scruples, and two of his men agreeing to come on the same understanding, we once more
resumed our march. The zaptieh caught us up soon
afterwards, bringing instructions from the Bashkala
colonel that the soldiers should go on, but they ap-

peared to attach very little weight to his authority, and more than once during the afternoon their scruples returned, and they were on the point of turning back.

Traversing a strip of the flat and fertile plain, the average level of which is only 2500 feet, we crossed a shallow stream and rode over two low wooded ranges, where most of the tree-roots bore witness to the ravages of wild boar. A third and higher ridge (4500 feet) brought us to the outskirts of the Rowanduz plain, and looking back from the crest we saw the long line of precipitous cliffs to the north-east, reflecting the radiant splendours of the west, change slowly from a glorious magenta colour to the deepest tints of hyacinth and iris against a pale saffron sky. A thousand feet lower down, fronting a wall of bare, whitish scarped hills south of the valley, lies the village of Sheitner, occupied by a most Hebraic-looking lot of Kurds. This valley stretches from south-east to north-west, to meet the Bradost valley, and Rowanduz itself, lying at the far end, below a conspicuous-peaked hill, is, I believe, rather east of Neri than, as indicated in most maps of the district, almost due south and a little west of that town.

The house assigned to us contained a single and very dirty room. In the centre of the floor, which was littered over with a carpet of dead oak leaves and branches used as fuel, was a circular pit for the fire, and along the walls stood a row of tall mud cylinders, which served as a kind of oven for baking the coarse bread-napkins that are plastered round the outside. The necessary cleansing process took some time, and the dictatorial manners of the soldiers very nearly brought them to blows with the owner and his friends. The sheep dogs, too, were more than usually fierce and famished, and it was impossible to walk out

than a few yards from the door without being attacked
by a howling pack of them.

From Sheitner the track, after following the hill
slope for a short distance,. crosses the stream at its
foot, and running over a stony spur dips down to the
Rowanduz Su at the Kurdish village of Balachan,
where there is an old half-ruined bridge of masonry
resting on fourteen piers. A short cut over another
ridge on the left bank brings the traveller to the headquarters of the Kaza, a small town lying, as it appears
from a distance, on a platform in the hollow, but in
reality on the projecting foot of a steep promontory
that runs out between the deep gorges of the Rowanduz and Nalkevan streams, with the tall range of the
Beni Handarin for a background on the south-east.
Both streams are spanned by bridges, and entering by
the Neri road you pass under a low archway and find
yourself in the steep, uneven street that leads up to
the konak. On the hill above, overlooking the ravine,
are the barracks, and from the opposite side of the
stream, at no great distance, rises a low hummock
crowned by a fort apparently modern, and behind it a
higher eminence topped by ruins of a fine old Kurdish
castle. The Kaimakam, a snuffy old gentleman and
nearly blind, at first seemed disposed to raise difficulties,
like the Kaimakam at Julamerk, but was dissuaded by
the colonel of the troops, who not only promised to
provide us with fresh mules and an escort, but found
us a vacant house pleasantly situated in a garden above
the town.

To the south-west the mountain of Gejjan, wooded
but terribly stony, rises to a height of 5800 feet. A
little way down the farther slope stands another
Kurdish castle on a round grassy knoll, and, a few
miles below, the Oudel Agha river is forded near a mill

surrounded by dense thickets of blackberry. Stretching almost due south between the naked cliffs of Serazi on the left and the parallel range of the Beni Harid to the right, the valley contains several curious flat-topped mounds, though the ruins at their base appear to be remains of quite recent settlements. Only one halting-place—the miserable Kurd hovels of Tarow—intervenes between Rowanduz and the large village of Balassan,

ROWANDUZ

in a dense grove of poplar and mulberry, where the southern exit to the valley is blocked by an oak-clad range of 4000 feet. On the farther side the road winds along a pretty ravine, thickly planted with orchards, to the Kurdish village of Sikhteh, and here we found a sergeant sent by the Kaimakam of Keui Sanjak to offer us his compliments and to escort us next morning to a village a little farther on, whither the colonel of the local troops had come out to meet us.

We found him seated with about fifteen men round a blazing wood-fire, near the banks of the Djel Su, facing a little village of the same name on the opposite hillside. He insisted that we should dismount and take a second breakfast of tea and bread and cheese, an operation which necessitated our waiting a whole hour, half-roasted between the fierce rays of the sun on our back and the furnace in front, since the samovar, like the buckets of the water-carriers in Hades, leaked so much that the contents ran out almost as fast as they were poured in. Even when we were once more in the saddle we could only proceed at a foot's pace, for our new friends, who were splendidly mounted, insisted on giving us an exhibition of " powder play," careering madly backwards and forwards across the path in pursuit of one another, and firing their rifles into the air. The commanding officer performed the same antics with a pistol, which he held so unsteadily as he lowered himself to the horse's girths in mid-gallop, that we expected every moment to feel a stray bullet through our brains. At last, however, after the course had been cleared for a breakneck race between two of the soldiers, over ground which would have knocked any English horse's feet to bits, the animals were fairly done up, and we settled down to a steady trot.

One more rugged ridge lay between us and Keui Sanjak, and at the end of six hours we found ourselves winding down the ravine, bordered by pink flowering oleander and gardens of fig, pomegranate, and myrtle, which forms the picturesque approach to the town. Lying almost at the foot of the hills, it overlooks a wide expanse of brown and arid plain, bounded by a long low chain that marks the course of the Lesser Zab, while in the far distance to the south-east rises

the striking peak of Pir Omar Gudrun above Sulei-
manieh. A dirty collection of clay-built houses, it
contains no fine mosque or buildings of any kind,
except the large barracks, in which a battalion is
quartered, and the Government konak. Here we were
warmly received by the Kaimakam, who had formerly
held the governorship of Basrah for nine years, and
was a great friend of an old acquaintance of mine,
Abdul Raffur, once the librarian at Yildiz, and now
president of the municipality at Mardin. He invited
us to spend the afternoon with him in the little adjoin-
ing gardens planted with fig, roses, and gum-trees,
and discuss the route we should take to Bagdad with
a friend of his who had performed the journey by raft,
a sallow-faced Kurd with large black eyes, that looked
all the larger and blacker for the inky lines of kohl
painted round them. In the spring, when the snows
are melting, it is possible to start the expedition down
stream at Taktah, not four miles away, but just now
the water was so low that we were advised to take the
mules as far as Altun Keupri, a town about two days'
ride to the south-west.

The intervening country is dreary and monotonous
in the extreme, a sea of brown bluffs and hummocks
broken by deep nullahs and covered with coarse grass,
that stretches south and east towards the flats of Mosul
and the Tigris, unrelieved by any animal life except a
few pigeons near the crumbling mud villages, innumerable lizards, and solitary flights of great bustard winding their way eastward towards the Rania plains. At
noon on the first day we struck the Shirwazan river
(1500 feet) near the ruined castle of Hanilala, which
occupies a commanding position on a big bluff near
the stream, and shortly after came in sight of the
Lesser Zab. The road keeps at a distance from the

river, following the hillocks past the villages of Seh-konak and Seh-khane (three houses), where we found tolerable quarters for the night in a room divided by mud partitions, the family sleeping in one section, their guests in the other, and the horses and soldiers in the stables opening out at right angles from the sleeping apartment. The whole district is covered with ancient and unexplored mounds, from which the natives said that they sometimes extracted "written stones," and the numerous villages lying on or near the river are called by Assyrian-sounding names, like Khorkhor, Ashka, and Chomer-zer-de-lar. The almost total absence of cultivation is due not to any lack of fertility in the soil, but to the extreme paucity of the population, and I have little doubt that if ever a branch railroad were laid from the Persian side down the valley of the Lesser Zab, communicating with a main line along the Tigris to the Gulf, it would, before many years were past, restore to the country much of the prosperity which the vestiges of a former civilisation prove it to have originally possessed.

Altun Keupri (the Golden Bridge) stands on an island in the centre of the sluggish current, which, to judge by the broad belt of stony margin on either side, must in winter become a considerable torrent. Each arm of the river is spanned by a magnificent bridge with high-pitched arches, erected by Sultan Murad IV., that on the right bank having a small turret built across the roadway, while the other is adorned with two tall pillars over the apex of the arch. The name of the town has been commonly, but erroneously, derived by travellers from the ruddy colour of one of these bridges. This is curious, because, as a matter of fact, both are plain white, and local tradition is probably at least as near the mark in ascribing the origin

of the word to the fact that at the time when the
bridges were commenced several mule-loads of gold
pieces were deposited under the masonry. Most of the
houses are built in two storeys, and the inhabitants
sleep in the upper one, or on the roof itself, to avoid
the malarial mists that rise after sunset or in the early
morning. The level of the plain is only a thousand
feet above the sea, and although snow has been known
to fall in exceptionally severe winters, the climate
during the greater part of the year is exceptionally
feverish. The bazaars, roofed over with matting, are
insignificant, and the natives mostly Kurds and Jebour
Arabs.

The Mudir was absent from the town, and with
great difficulty we hunted out his vekil or represeu-
tative from one of the neighbouring cafés, of which
there seemed to be an inordinate number in the
bazaars. To our inquiries about rafts and an escort,
he informed us that he could easily procure a raft of
one hundred skins, which would take us and our
baggage comfortably as far as Bagdad, but that there
was only one zaptieh left in the place, and he could
not be spared. So we had to telegraph to the Mutessarif of Kirkuk, who replied that he could not send
any men from that town, but that we might take on
with us two of the soldiers who had accompanied us
from Keui Sanjak. It was all the same to us, but
they were much disgusted, and not unnaturally, for the
rafts are broken up as soon as they arrive at their
destination, and the return journey meant for them a
weary tramp across long miles of desert on foot.

The stony beach upon which the kelekjis were
hastily putting together the framework of the raft presented a gay and animated appearance. A hundred
inflated skins arranged with their mouths uppermost,

so that they could be untied and blown out again in case of necessity by means of a long hollow cane, were being covered over with several layers of bamboo, screened from the sun by awnings of muslin, and divided into two compartments for ourselves and our servants.   The whole population, dressed in their striped abbas, had flocked down to watch the proceedings, and one could hardly make oneself heard for

BUILDING THE RAFT

the babel of voices.   The vekil and other notables squatted solemnly on their haunches, alternately encouraging and abusing the raftsmen, who would every now and then pause in their efforts to bargain for an increase of pay or additional baksheesh, while the bystanders joined eagerly and vociferously in the discussion.   The only people who seemed able to pursue their ordinary avocations with complete indifference to the prevailing excitement were a few fishermen, who stood up to their knees in the water, casting their six-feet circular nets, weighted at the bottom with stones, and hauling them in with hardly a moment's delay, capturing at least two fish at every cast. These are big brutes, not unlike cod, and fairly good eating, except for the murderous three-pronged bones that stick out through the flesh in every direction.

At last the raft was completed, and dragging it down to the water's edge, we pushed off, and drifted down stream, leaving the crowd shrieking and dancing like maniacs on shore. For two whole days we floated lazily with the current, amusing ourselves by occasional shots at rock-pigeons and cormorants, which were fished out by the kelekjis, who swam and dived splendidly, and devoured by them with every appearance of relish. The temperature during the daytime measured over 90 degrees in the shade, and though it never sank below 50 degrees at night, the cold seemed very great by contrast, and the dew fell so heavily between the meshes of the thin awning that it soaked through everything but mackintoshes. For the first night after leaving Altun Keupri we were obliged to anchor off the village of Sinnagha, as the kelekjis were not sure of being able to steer in the darkness, and if the raft were to drift on the numerous shallows or sunken rocks its skins might be irreparably damaged. The scenery became gradually flatter as we advanced, and the only prominent features that broke its desolate monotony on the second day were the artificial mounds near the villages of Tel Ur, Mahrouz, and Tel Alee. The current, however, had increased in volume and rapidity, and nothing could be more delightful than the almost imperceptible motion of the raft on the broad smooth reaches, and its strange swaying undulations as it shot down the long shelving cataracts. The kelekjis, becoming bolder, started for a short spin at three the next morning, with the result that we were soon roused from our slumbers by a sharp shock, which told that we had run aground and split four of the skins. This was rather serious, as Tekrit, the nearest town of any size in which we could repair the damage, was still some way off, and a few more accidents of the kind might necessitate our covering the remaining distance on foot. Even during the daytime the navigation of the cataracts, which at this season of the year are extraordinarily shallow, requires considerable skill and attention, and the Tigris itself can in many places be forded by men and animals on foot. Of this we had an amusing experience after reaching the junction of the two rivers the next day, near the sulphur springs at Howindeh. We had swept round a rocky bend, and were standing up to take an unsteady aim at the pigeons that darted from the honeycombed face of the cliffs, when suddenly we found ourselves charging headlong through a caravan which stretched in single file across an apparently deep and raging swirl of water. The long oar paddles, formed of poplar poles with blades of thin transverse strips of wood fastened across them, proved quite powerless to arrest our course, and the next minute we had nearly capsized, while a storm of spluttering curses arose from the confused and floundering heap of mules and Arabs whom we had scattered to right and left. In company with half-a-dozen naked boys, propelling themselves on skins and racing each other for the wounded teal that had afforded easy shots at our approach, we at length drifted under the high mud ramparts of Tekrit, and halted for a few hours in order to procure a change of raftsmen.

Founded, it is said, by Alexander the Great, the

birthplace of Saladin, and the seat of an early
Christian bishopric, it is now little more than a
crumbling mass of round turrets, latticed mud bal-
conies, and old brick-faced bastions, breaking the
sharp outline of the sandy cliff that overhangs the
river. The moon being at the full, and the current
broad and deep, we travelled all night, and at dawn
passed the tomb of Imam Mohammed Dur, a lofty

SWIMMING ON SKINS

conical structure like the tomb of Zobeide at Bagdad,
marking the supposed site of the passage of Julian's
army after their leader's death, where the ignominious
treaty with Sapor was subsequently concluded by the
Emperor Jovian. A strong southerly breeze springing
up soon after made further progress impossible, and
beaching the raft on the left bank a few miles above
the town of Samara, we proceeded on foot to visit the
so-called *medresseh*, dating from the times of the

Abbaside Khalifs, whose ruined outline formed a prominent landmark on the horizon.

A huge oblong shell of mud and brick, 810 feet long by 490 broad, the entrance facing towards Mecca, and the lofty walls broken at regular intervals by semicircular bastions, its inner court is dominated on the north by a remarkable spiral tower of brick, the Malwiyeh, which rises to a height of 163 feet. Of the palace of Motassem, the eighth Caliph, who first transferred the seat of government from Bagdad to Samara,[1] owing to a conflict between the soldiery and the civilian population, there are now scarcely any traces left. The turbulence of the inhabitants, resulting in the violent death of no less than three out of the seven rulers who, for the brief space of eighteen years, ruled the empire from the northern centre, compelled Muhamed to revert to the original capital of Mansur, and after the successive inroads of conquerors like Zenghis Khan and Tamerlane, the old city of Samara fell into the same condition of utter desolation as the ancient Sassanian palace of Ctesiphon. Its remaining inhabitants moved a little farther to the south, and in 1848 Commander James Felix Jones[2] computed their number at no more than two hundred and fifty households, of which the large majority belonged to the Sunnis. Whatever prosperity the town enjoyed was mainly derived from the enormous annual influx of 10,000 pilgrims from Persia, for although no tax was levied upon them, the proprietors of the various caravanserais and houses received a subsidy of about fivepence per head from

[1] Samara was built by Khalif el Motasun, son of the famous Harun el Rashed.

[2] Memoirs of Commander James Felix Jones, I.N., Bombay Government Records, xliii.

the Government for each lodger whom he entertained. Among these pilgrims were a certain number of Shiahs from India, and as the town was entirely undefended and exposed to constant attacks from the surrounding Beduin tribes, who were in the habit of extorting money by threats of pillage, the richer

MEDRESSEH AND MALWIYEH, SAMARA

devotees combined to defray the cost of erecting the massive square wall which now surrounds it, flanked on each side by four round towers.

At the present time the Shiahs outnumber the Sunnis by more than four to one, and the great domed cupola of the tomb of Imam Hussein Askar, which forms the principal object of their veneration, has been

s

plated over with gold, like those of the more celebrated shrines of Kazimin, Kerbela, and Nejef. The
glint of the sun upon its polished surface, flashing
through the whirling drifts of a sandstorm, produces a
strange and weird contrast to the barren savagery of
the surrounding desert, which for many miles is strewn
with crumbling skeletons and brilliant-coloured fragments of glazed pottery. Around its base runs a
beautiful band of inscription in enamelled tilework,
and close beside it, decorated with yellow and white
flowers on a ground of bluish - green, arranged in
diamond-shaped perpendicular lines, rise the smaller
dome and minarets of the mosque, on the site of
which Imam Mohammed el Mahdi is said to have
disappeared, to return with Christ at His second
advent in the end of the dispensation.

With a strange disregard for convenience, the town
has been built at a distance of nearly a mile from the
river, and consequently all the water that is required
has to be conveyed thither by means of an aqueduct.
A little backwater provides safe anchorage for the
rafts, many of them carrying as much as forty tons
weight of bales or stone for building, which would
otherwise be exposed to the risk of serious damage in
rough weather from the sharp edges of the black rocks
that line the main stream's banks. Here, too, are
moored a number of round "guffas," the ordinary ferry-
boats of Bagdad, which are never seen on the upper
reaches of the Tigris. It was with considerable difficulty that we eventually succeeded in gaining this
shelter by laboriously towing and poling our raft down-
stream in the teeth of the hot wind, which had now
acquired the force of a hurricane, and did not abate
until long after midnight.

A mile and a half below Samara the river is spanned

TOMB OF IMAM HUSSEIN ASKARI, SAMARA.

by a bridge of boats, and the villagers take toll of the larger craft before swinging back the central barges to allow of their passing through.   Having attached ourselves to one of the largest rafts, bound for the same destination, we relieved our kelekjis of any further need for paddling, and employed them in retrieving the pelican and ruddy sheldrake which crowded the sandbanks and shallows, or the sandgrouse that from

GUFFA, BAGDAD

time to time passed in flocks over our heads.   Jackals and foxes would often come down to drink in the evening, and once, as dusk was falling, two large wild boars plunged from the low banks and swam across within a few yards of our raft.   On the second day after leaving Samara we reached the first belt of palms at the Arab village of Hawesh, and were again driven ashore for several hours by contrary winds.   On the whole, however, we had suffered singularly little from such interruptions ; and when at last we came in sight of the minarets of Bagdad, and, sliding between the broad brown-sailed " baggalas" under the lee of the tall house fronts with their staircases descending to the water's edge, stepped ashore at the crowded custom-house, we found that just one hundred and thirty hours had elapsed since we first pushed off our floating tent from the Golden Bridge on the Lesser Zab.

CHAPTER XV

"TO BE, OR NOT TO BE.?"

Is Turkey moribund, or is she still capable of resuscitation ? Are the phenomena of her present condition merely those of arrested development or of hopeless, senile decay ?

It is an old, a familiar question, the answer to which will always determine, as it has determined in the past, the policy of Great Britain in the Near East. Twenty years ago the question was the same : to-day, it is to be feared, the answer is different. Whatever their private doubts upon the subject may have been, the statesmen who controlled our policy up to the time of the Berlin Treaty and the Cyprus Convention, professed in public their belief in Turkey's powers of recuperation and reform. And they acted accordingly. They interposed to save her from the consequences of defeat : they pledged the whole resources of their country to maintain the integrity of her possessions against attack from outside, on the sole condition that she would remedy the abuses of misgovernment within. She has not done so. We may find excuses for her ; we may even confess that our own action has been liable to misconstruction. We may recognise that to demand of a Government little more than four hundred years old,[1] that within the space

[1] Some of the provinces of the Turkish Empire were not acquired until a century after the fall of Constantinople. The greater part of Armenia, Mesopotamia and Kurdistan were added by Selim I. and Suleiman the Magnificent, 1512-1566.

of a single century it should suddenly transform and adapt its methods to the standard of Western ideas and requirements, was as unreasonable as it would have been to expect in the England of the Tudors or Stuarts the religious tolerance or the purity of public life which are almost coeval with the Victorian era.   We may acknowledge that the Power which holds Egypt and Cyprus, and which cannot send its ships over the Taurus, is no loser at any rate by conduct on the part of Turkey which enables us to enjoy the fruits of our bargain while it relieves us from any inconvenient obligations attaching to it.   But whatever the explanation or apology, the fact remains indisputable.   The system of administration in 1900 is little if at all better—in the opinion of many competent judges it is decidedly worse—than it was in 1878.   Trade is hampered by petty exactions and needless restrictions.   Justice is perverted.   Crime, often unpunished, is not uncommonly encouraged and rewarded.   Corruption, peculation, and extortion are rife ; the Treasury is bankrupt ; the army and police unpaid.   The potential wealth of the country remains undeveloped ; its actual resources are exhausted by mismanagement or squandered in favouritism.   Yet, in face of these evils, Turkey maintains a stolid indifference, an imperturbable composure.   She will neither listen to advice or warning from others, nor make a serious effort to initiate reforms herself.   What must be must be ; it were impiety to anticipate the decrees of Allah ; and her best friends in England, however incurable their optimism, can no longer pretend that it is justified by appearances, or blame their political leaders if they profess their inability to share it.

Hope has been succeeded by doubt, if not by

despair; and it is that scepticism which has destroyed our purpose, that indecision which has condemned us to inaction. The "forward" policy, which was inspired and energised by faith in the future of Turkey, has been abandoned with the abandonment of that belief; the policy of "masterly inactivity," which has been substituted for it, is the natural corollary of suspended judgment. The question of to-day is not how we may best confirm and extend our authority with a powerful ally, whose interests are, in many respects, identical with our own, but how, without committing ourselves irretrievably to the support of a tottering cause, we may most effectually shield it from external pressure on the part of ourselves or others which might impair or destroy its precarious equilibrium.

To those of us, therefore, who desire that Great Britain should once more assert herself in the Near East, and who believe that her influence, if it does not advance, must recede before the steady encroachment of more active and ambitious Powers, the question of the future destiny of Turkey is of paramount importance. If her hold upon Anatolia and the Tigris and Euphrates valleys is assured, it is worth our while to safeguard our interests in those regions by fostering and promoting our influence at Constantinople. If it must inevitably be superseded, sooner or later, by the control and suzerainty of European Powers, we may, by arresting, actively or passively, the process of transition, only imperil those ultimate advantages which it is in our power now to secure by a timely understanding with the rival claimants for Asiatic dominion. Immediate "moral or material damage" is not the only consequence that may result from our neglect of present opportunities. Another and more serious one is the forfeiture or diminution of our legitimate claim to a preponderating voice in the determination of the future settlement.

But is there any conceivable settlement which, in the event of Turkey's collapse, would secure to us the essential objects which we have in view? A "condominium" of all the great Powers being a manifest impossibility, the only alternative would be a partition in which we might or might not be sharers. In either case, the result, from our point of view, would, I think, be disastrous. Assume, for the sake of argument, a fourfold division of the Sultan's Asiatic territories, by virtue of which Anatolia would be assigned to Germany, Syria to France, the north-eastern provinces between the Black Sea and Lake Van to Russia, and to ourselves the valley of the Tigris and Shat el Arab, which command the approaches to the Persian Gulf. Such a compromise, even were it desirable in our own interests, could scarcely be achieved by pacific means, for our presence in the southern estuary would constitute a fresh check upon Russia's advance, and a death-blow to the cherished dreams of German colonisation. The former, indeed, might still attain her goal through Central or Eastern Persia, and there is good reason to believe that in the course of her private negotiations with Teheran she has already pegged out her claim to the future usufruct of a port at Bunder Abbas or Chahbar; but no compensation in Anatolia would reconcile Germany to the loss of that rich alluvial basin upon which she has long cast covetous eyes, and where she is even now seeking to lay the foundations of a commercial, if not political, supremacy, that will enable her to restore to the land of Chaldea, as we have restored to the land of the Pharaohs, a prosperity unknown since the days of the Arab Caliphate.

But supposing these difficulties to have been surmounted and the partition effected, what prospect of permanence would such an arrangement afford? Our territorial responsibilities are already sufficiently large and formidable to tax our military and financial resources to the utmost. The annexation of a new province, unprotected from invasion by any natural barrier, and coterminous with the same powerful empire which menaces India, would be an act of suicidal insanity. The mountain gorges of the Upper Tigris might, it is true, be rendered almost impregnable; but any force, relying on its defensive position in the passes north of Mosul, would find its communications exposed to a flank attack from the east by way of the Rania plain and the Lesser Zab, from the west by way of Diarbekr and Mardin. Apart from the teaching of history, it is pretty safe to prophesy that in these days no Power except Russia can hope to retain a lasting hold on the Mesopotamian valley which is not prepared to maintain there a vast army of occupation, or which does not, at the same time, control practically the whole line of the Euphrates and the greater portion of Southern Persia. The second of those conditions is never likely to be realised by Germany. The first can assuredly never be satisfied by ourselves. The more we consider the problem, the more irresistibly are we forced to conclude that the almost certain result of the expulsion of the Osmanlis from Asia would be the substitution of the Persian Gulf littoral for the shores of the Euxine as the southern boundary of the Muscovite empire.

"And why not?" say some; "why must we for ever entertain this morbid and selfish jealousy of Russia's legitimate expansion in regions which we can never hope to occupy ourselves?"

The love of contradiction and the love of fair-play are qualities so deeply ingrained in the English character that the narrow and aggressive prejudice peculiarly characteristic of Russophobe oratory would alone be sufficient to ensure a measure of popularity for the more plausible, if equally unreasoning, creed of the Russophil. But impatience of the traditional antagonism between ourselves and the Slavonic people, a desire for some friendly understanding which shall remove the more dangerous causes of dispute, are feelings shared by many who distrust and reject all extremes, who neither love Russia nor fear her, neither underrate nor exaggerate her power; but endorse the opinion expressed more than fifty years ago by the Czar Nicholas, that there is ample room for both empires in Asia.

And indeed, if the question were merely one of empire, it would present but little difficulty. The gigantic expansion of our colonial possessions in Africa, accomplished with an ease and rapidity, hardly less astounding than that which has marked the triumphal progress of Russia through Central Asia, renders it impossible for us, even were we so inclined, to transgress the bounds of a sane and unaggressive Imperialism in the East. Indeed, paradoxical as the statement may appear, it is just this impossibility which constitutes the chief danger of a conflict between Russia and ourselves. In Africa there has been the fiercest rivalry for territorial acquisition, yet the ownership of the Dark Continent has been practically decided without bloodshed between the competitors, and without the necessity for any concerted action on their part in order to avoid it. Very different has been their attitude in regard to the vast, turbulent, and undeveloped kingdoms of the Orient. Every disturbance that takes place between the Yellow Sea and the Levant—a revolution in Crete, a massacre in Kurdistan, a native rising in China, a frontier war in Thessaly—all alike compel European intervention, and an intervention directed not to resettling the affairs of those countries on a permanent basis, but to keeping them unsettled as long as possible, in order to avoid an even more disastrous unsettlement of the affairs of Europe itself.

What is the explanation of this remarkable difference of policy in regard to the two continents? Why is it that in the one case an exchange of views between Germany, France, Belgium, and Great Britain is directed to the delimitation of their respective spheres of authority or to the preservation of their mutual rights of commerce and navigation, while in the other the collective wisdom and forbearance of all the Western powers is invoked to frame or sanction a self-denying ordinance for maintaining the integrity of Turkey and the independence of China?

The very fact that such an understanding is necessary proves that it is not the greater power of resistance possessed by a Sultan, Emperor, or Shah, as compared with the barbarian potentates of the South, that has preserved the Euphrates, the Karun, or the Yangtze Kiang from the foreign control already established on the Nile, the Congo, the Niger, and the Zambesi. Nor is it that the territories in their possession offer less inducement to the cupidity of the conqueror. The dense forests of Mazanderan and the fertile tracts of Khorassan are worth all the blood and treasure expended by Russia on the acquisition of desolate steppes and deserts beyond the Caspian; and no province of Africa except Egypt possesses a tithe of the vast potential wealth which lies dormant

in the populous highlands of Szechuan or the alluvial
plains of Jezireh and Arabistan. The value of the
prize and the growing weakness of its defenders
alike invite attack ; yet the vultures gathered together
around the carcase have bound themselves by mutual
compact to rein in their voracious appetites, and allow
a free course to the natural processes of corruption.

In face of so peculiar a phenomenon, we may
well ask whether it is not a significant coincidence
that, while Russia is a competitor, almost the only
competitor on a large scale except ourselves, for
Asiatic Empire, she has no concern in the partition
of Africa ? There we may paint the map red from
Alexandria to the Cape of Good Hope, and our
action is regarded with comparative equanimity by
the owners of the Congo jungles, the Sahara deserts,
or the infructuous tracts of Damaraland.   In Asia
the advance of Russia is watched with as jealous a
suspicion by Powers that have scarcely more than a
foothold on the sea-board as by the lords of India
and the possessors of two-thirds of the commerce of
China.   And the reason is not far to seek.   It is not
because we enjoy greater popularity on the Continent
than Russia, but because, in one sense at all events,
we are less feared.   It is not because other nations
are less jealous of our world-empire and commercial
supremacy, but because our success offers' fewer
obstacles than does the success of Russia to the
free play of their own energies and the development
of their own resources.   Among the many benefits
conferred upon Great Britain by her policy of free
trade, none has been greater, none perhaps would
have been less welcomed, could they have foreseen
it, by the Abolitionists of the Manchester School,
than the indirect support which it has afforded to

the policy of imperial expansion. It has compelled her rivals, not, as Cobden prophesied, to abandon the heresy of protection themselves, but to resist the establishment of political control by any but a free-trade power over markets to which they desire free access for their own manufactures. And the Russo-phobia, which on the Continent is mainly actuated by commercial motives, is of course reinforced in our own case by the instinct of self-defence. The independence of Turkey, Persia, or Afghanistan is, we think, as necessary to our security in India as the independence of China to the maintenance of international rights and privileges under the Treaty of Tientsin. If our motto in the Far East is "The open door," in the Near East it is "British supremacy in the Persian Gulf."

This is the real, in fact the only answer to those who advocate an agreement with Russia on the basis of partition. Commercially, such an agreement is impossible, because it would entail the loss of valuable markets : politically, it is impossible, because it would threaten our hitherto undisputed mastery of the Southern Seas. Possession by Russia of Southern Persia and the Euphrates valley must carry with it possession of commercial emporiums and outlets on the Gulf, which, in the course of time, will become naval bases and coaling stations ; and having surrendered our monopoly, we shall have to content ourselves, as in the Gulf of Pechili, with a balance of power. At Bushire or Bunder Abbas will arise a second Port Arthur: at Muscat, Kishm, or Koweit, another Wei hei Wei. But the balance will at best be a temporary one. As Sweden retained her naval power in the Baltic so long, and only so long, as she held the provinces of Isthia, Livonia, and Esthonia, so shall we retain ours in the

Persian Gulf only so long as its shores are governed by a Power whose policy we can control or whose hostility we can afford to despise. Few Englishmen would contend that the possession of Aden enabled us to regard with indifference the establishment of Continental control over the shores of the Red Sea ; and what the Suez Canal is to the Erythrean, the Euphrates Valley Railway may one day be to the Persian Gulf. It is by no means impossible that the old highway, followed for three centuries[1] by the merchants of Genoa and Antwerp, should, under German auspices, again become the main artery of commerce with India, or that the Levant and the Persian Gulf should recover, through the enterprise of modern engineers, the trade that was ruined by the nautical discoveries of Vasco da Gama. The same considerations which led Sir John Drummond Hay and Nelson to regret the impossibility of exchanging for Ceuta, with its rich Moorish hinterland, our isolated position at Gibraltar, would apply with tenfold force to any stronghold which we could obtain on the barren coast of Arabia as a counterpoise to a Russian *place d'armes* fed by the inexhaustible resources of Southern Irak.

Nearly four hundred years have elapsed since Albuquerque first attempted to lay, at Muscat and Ormuzd, the foundations of Portuguese supremacy in the Persian Gulf. Within a century that supremacy was overthrown ; its solitary relics are a few mouldering cannon perched on the volcanic rocks of the Muscat harbour, and the Power which holds undisputed command of the whole stretch of waters from Aden to Bussorah, from Bussorah to Kurrachi, is represented by a single gunboat in the bay. We care not who may be the nominal owners of the ports at which we touch, pro-

[1] From the thirteenth to the sixteenth.

vided only that their strength is weak. "I have little
doubt," says Lord Curzon, "that the time will come
when the Union Jack will be seen flying from the
castles of Muscat." It may be so. But of more importance than his prediction is the emphatic declaration
which follows it:—

"I should regard the concession of a port upon the
Persian Gulf to Russia by any Power as a deliberate
insult to Great Britain, as a wanton rupture of the
status quo, and as an international provocation to war;
and I should impeach the British Minister who was
guilty of acquiescing in such surrender as a traitor to
his country."

In the seventeenth century Persia was still a naval
power. In the twentieth her whole armament consists of a decrepit battle-ship, which she has happily
christened by the name of the noblest ruins of her own
departed greatness, *Persepolis*. But if the fleets of
Russia ever ride at anchor where the *Persepolis* rides
now, Her Majesty's ship *Pigeon* may yet share with
the cannon of Portugal the honour of a prominent
place among the antiquities of Muscat.

"But," it may be urged, "the perpetuation of corrupt despotisms in the fairest regions of the globe,
however desirable in our own selfish interests, is neither
justifiable in theory nor possible in practice." And
certainly, if we admit the premises, it is difficult to
dispute the conclusion. No contrivance of human
statesmanship will avert the collapse of empires,
civilised or uncivilised, which have lost the will and
power to battle with evil habits that are slowly but
surely corroding their constitution. Reform of some
kind is imperative. Do we sincerely desire its adoption? Have we adequate grounds for the confident
assertion that it will never, or can never be adopted?

Ever since the Reform Act of 1832 there has been a growing disposition among Englishmen of all classes to test the principles of foreign policy by what may be termed an abstract standard of morality, such as a former generation would never have dreamed of applying. The sentiment of Imperialism, which has gradually permeated every rank of society, is marked by a feature which at once distinguishes it from the vulgar spirit of aggressive militarism characteristic of all democracies, and affords a promise of stability which in their case was lacking. That feature is the belief in a civilising mission so clearly designed for the Anglo-Saxon race that it almost appears to have been forced upon us in spite of ourselves. Foreign nations may indicate it as the smug conviction of the Pharisee : " It has pleased Providence that I should be fat." Sceptics at home may compare it to the proud boast of the Roman city, which pampered itself on the treasure of its defenceless provinces, or to the fervid creed of the Jacobins, which deluged Europe in blood. But of no other empires in the history of the world can it as truly be said that they governed not in their own interests, but in the interests of their subjects, or that the mere suspicion of the injustice of a forward policy, however profitable to themselves, had been the chief obstacle to their continuous growth and expansion. And it is this deep-rooted sense of responsibility which experiences a kind of moral shock when it contemplates the traditional policy of England in the East. There alone are we lending our direct or indirect support to nations of a distinctly lower type of civilisation than that of their would-be assailants ; we content ourselves with unavailing protests against massacre and misrule in Turkey, and, paying no heed to the atrocities which are of daily occurrence in Cabul, we arm and subsidise

its Mussulman rulers that they may be our allies against
the Christian power of the North. The Concert of
Europe, which seven centuries ago sought to wrest
Jerusalem from the hands of the Saracens, now seeks
to confirm their successors in the control of the holy
places and the worship of the Prophet in the great
Church of Justinian. Is it possible to reconcile such
a policy with the conscientious discharge of the high
mission to which we lay claim?

I confess that I think it is. If the spirit of the
Crusades no longer animates us, it is partly because
the conditions are changed. Mahomedanism, which,
be it remembered, even in its most militant days, conferred upon Christianity a benefit greater than any
injury it inflicted by exterminating the most formidable heresy ever encountered by the infant Church, is
now impotent for purposes of aggression. Internal
apostasy and schism, not the sword of the infidel, are
the foes by which in these days the faith of Europe
is menaced, and which, far more than the stubborn
loyalty of the Mussulman to his monotheistic creed,
impede or baffle the efforts of its most zealous propagandists. Politically, at all events, the religious
beliefs of Turk, Persian, or Afghan are no concern of
ours, and, were it not for the missionary question, which
continually obtrudes itself upon the attention of distracted statesmen and ambassadors, we might ignore
it altogether. That the State should hold itself aloof
from all connection with the missionaries, and having
warned them that they prosecute their enterprise at their
own peril, should regard with indifference attacks upon
their lives and property, is a view which, however
defensible in principle, cannot be translated into practice. British citizenship, like the *civitas* of ancient
Rome, is a privilege upon the sacrosanct character of

which we are compelled, in the interests of our own prestige, at all hazards to insist. Nor would the difficulty be obviated if, as some have suggested, every herald of the gospel were obliged, on entering the sphere of his labours, as it were, to denationalise himself and so renounce his claim to the protection of any particular Government. The spread of Christianity might or might not be facilitated by such a course, but the political effect would be none the less calamitous. Could the missionary disguise his origin by assuming the physical attributes of the people among whom he ministers, the case would, no doubt, be different. But so long as every native can recognise him at the first glance as a European, they will make no distinction between him and any other white man, and disrespect or outrage offered with impunity to one will inevitably be extended sooner or later to all.

On the other hand, it may fairly be questioned whether, having once provided for the personal security of missionaries, the State ought not more rigidly to preserve an attitude of strict neutrality in regard to the work which they are carrying on. Were the Turkish authorities, for instance, allowed complete freedom of action, there can be little doubt that they would not only prohibit active proselytism, of which even now, so far as the Mussulmans are concerned, there is practically none, but they would also close every school and college in which Armenians or other native Christians receive education of a Western type. Ought they to be prevented from doing so by the intervention of the Christian States? Even if the divine commission, intrusted in the first century to a specially chosen band, and sanctioned and attested by miraculous powers, which have long since been in abeyance, be admitted as the marching orders of a divided Church nearly two thousand years afterwards; even if it be held to constitute a claim to some extent on the support of the civil authority, yet no legitimate construction of the terms of that commission can be supposed to authorise of itself the dissemination of secular education.

I do not in the least wish to disparage the importance of such teaching or to deny that, on general grounds, a duty may rest upon us to extend if we can to others all the benefits of civilisation which we have ourselves received. I yield to none in my admiration of the courage displayed by those who recognise and endeavour to discharge this obligation, and it is possible that such work supplies a means of exerting influence which could never be obtained by the methods of religions persuasion. But I see in this no justification whatever for compelling a foreign state against its will to sanction the propagation of knowledge or principles which it believes to be prejudicial to its own interests. The rights and advantages of free thought, free inquiry, and free speech are not universally recognised in Europe; they are energetically repudiated in the East. Russia asserts for herself in the Caucasus the fullest liberty to close the schools of the Armenians, to regulate their curriculum, and to exercise a most rigorous censorship of the vernacular press at Echmiadzin. Why is the same liberty to be withheld from Turkey? She believes, as Russia does, that the ideas and theories imbibed at the seminaries by Greeks and Armenians are of a distinctly subversive and revolutionary character; nor can any one converse with them without perceiving that the hopes and aspirations awakened in their minds are absurdly out of keeping with the actual conditions by which they are surrounded. The missionaries do not desire such a result of their teaching.

Many of them do their utmost to guard against it, and to discourage it in their pupils. But they are attempting the impossible. They may not educate the Turk or the Kurd; by educating the Armenian they are only adding to the racial cleavage, which already exists, an ever-increasing disparity of intellectual attainment. The question is not whether they are justified in endeavouring to promote what they believe to be the

KELEK

cause of progress, be the immediate consequences what they may, but whether we are justified in affording political support to their efforts by putting pressure upon the Turkish Government to respect what, in its view, is the cause, not of progress, but of disintegration? To improve the social condition of the whole people, instead of intensifying the discontent of a class by educating them to appreciate and desire advantages

which are beyond their reach ; to persuade the rulers
to initiate practical reforms in their own interests
instead of rousing vague ambitions in the minds of a
minority among their subjects, should be the one aim
of all those Powers which honestly desire the regene-
ration of the Turkish Empire.

CHAPTER XVI

WANTED, A POLICY

IN the course of the preceding chapters I have briefly indicated one or two reforms without which no real improvement in the present system of administration is possible.

First and foremost of these, an indispensable condition of and preliminary to any other, is reform of the finances : a material reduction of expenditure by the abolition of sinecures, and an equitable readjustment of imperial and provincial revenues. Secondly, administrative reform : the full and punctual payment of all salaries, and the regulation of official appointments to the more important posts in the vilayets, possibly by means of a Board of Judges and Ministers sitting at Constantinople, to advise the Sultan upon the qualifications of candidates for institution or preferment, and to conduct a public inquiry into all petitions charging a governor with malpractice or abuse of his authority. Thirdly, judicial reform : comprising direct nomination of judges from headquarters, and the substitution for the Napoleonic Code of a system more readily adaptable to the peculiar conditions and habits of the people.[1]

---

[1] The question of the military administration also requires investigation. At present, the military commanders are believed to exercise more influence with the Palace than the valis, and the two do not always co-operate as they should. My own belief is that the military training in Turkey produces, on the whole, a better class of administrator than does the

Such are the main objects to which the Powers should direct the attention of Turkey, while carefully abstaining from making any recommendations calculated to infringe the royal prerogative or to excite the religious prejudices of the dominant caste. To obtain for the governors greater security of tenure, and, in some respects, a wider discretion, is not more imperative than to preserve undiminished the controlling and supervisory powers of the central authority. No good can be achieved by weakening the latter, and thereby lessening respect for the autocratic principle upon which the cohesion of the whole Empire depends. Local autonomy will best be reconciled with the claims of despotism, not by transferring to foreign Powers or dividing with them the responsibility for working the administrative machine, but by bringing the exercise of that responsibility under the sobering influence of publicity. The mistaken and mischievous idea of forcing upon a Mussulman power the admission of Christians to civil or semi-military offices must also be abandoned,[1] and the efforts of diplomacy directed to

civil service ; and that where, as sometimes happens, the local ferik performs the duties of administration in the temporary absence of the vali, the province is generally the gainer. It is possible that in the more unsettled vilayets, such as Van, Bitlis, Diarbekr, and Erzerum, a combination of the two offices would lead to better results than are obtainable under the existing system.

[1] The policy adopted by Turkey towards her Christian subjects is not unlike, but even more liberal, than that adopted by Russia towards the natives of Central Asia. *Cf.* the remarks on this subject by Lieut.-Col. C. E. Yate in his recently published work on Khurasan and Sistan (p. 263) : " Except for the Turkoman militia, there is no military service whatever open to the natives of Central Asia ; there is little or no education and no civil employment for them. Hardly a single one is employed, and almost every appointment there, down to the lowest clerkship, is held by a Russian. This is the case not only with the administrative offices in Central Asia, but the customs, postal, telegraph, railway, and every other

persuading Turkey, if possible, to avail herself of
external assistance in improving the material condition
of the entire community, rather than in removing the
social disabilities, such as they are, of a comparatively
insignificant minority.

It must be admitted that, of her own initiative, she
cannot do very much. Any change that threatens
their monopolies and emoluments will be strenuously
resisted by the bureaucratic clique at the capital ; and
the peculiar traditions of court life deprive the occupant
of Yildiz of those opportunities of judging character,
or of forming independent opinions upon public affairs,
which European sovereigns acquire from their earliest
youth by close contact and intercourse with their subjects. A Commission of Inquiry composed of natives
can possess neither the experience, the integrity, nor
the impartiality requisite to invest its conclusions and
recommendations with the least semblance of weight
and authority ; and before reform can be seriously
attempted by any Sultan, the necessary evidence must
first be collected and sifted by European inspectors
conversant with the details of those systems of finance,
administration, and jurisprudence which have been
successfully applied to native races under conditions
similar to those which prevail in Anatolia and Kurdistan. We are scarcely warranted as yet in assuming
that Turkey will never consent to avail herself of such
counsellors, or that, if she did, she would reject their
conclusions and advice. During the last twenty years

sort of official is a Russian, and in Russian Central Asia the native has
practically no share in the administration of his country. In the whole
of Transcaspia, I have only heard of one or two natives who have been
given civil employment, and that only as interpreters on small pay. The
Turkoman interpreter to the Governor-General, and one or two more
with other officers, and a few Kadis for the administration of Mohammedan law, are the only native officials that I know of."

she has enlisted the service of both British and German officers and instructors for her army, and a wiser diplomacy on our part might have induced her to accept the same loyal assistance in purifying her judicial and administrative systems. The impulse towards reform which was checked by the reaction that followed upon Sultan Mahmoud's well-meant but too precipitate innovations is by no means extinct, even among the governing classes. The Consular Reports testify to much sporadic activity and public spirit displayed by individual governors, which, if encouraged and allowed free scope, would soon effect a sensible amelioration in the condition of the provinces. Both in the Trebizond and the Aleppo vilayets large sums have been annually expended of late years, in addition to the unpaid labour of the peasantry, on the construction or repair of roads, culverts, and bridges, and I have myself mentioned more than one instance in which valis have interposed to repress the extortion of tithefarmers or to exempt the more poverty-stricken families from taxation.

The comparative rarity of such cases is due, not so much to lack of good intentions on the part of governors as to the instability of their position, the want of sufficient funds at their disposal, and the limitations placed upon their authority. If money is devoted to local purposes, the budget accounts have probably been manipulated so as to conceal the existence of a surplus which would otherwise be instantly appropriated by the imperial exchequer. If the collection of tithes or taxes, in the nature, imposition, and amount of which the local authority has no voice, be conducted with due discrimination and regard for circumstances of exceptional hardship, it is at the risk of calumny and misrepresentation, which the victim may never have the opportunity of refuting before he is suddenly dismissed or transferred from the scene of his labours. A searching investigation should be instituted into the resources of the various Asiatic provinces; the produce of certain definite taxes, assessed in proportion to the relative taxable capacity of each, should be assigned to imperial purposes; and a wide discretion should then be permitted to each governor with respect to his financial expedients and methods of raising the revenue necessary to defray the ordinary charges of administration, and provide a reasonable surplus for expenditure of a remunerative character. He should be compelled to forward to Constantinople at the beginning of each financial year a detailed statement of his proposals, of the revenue he anticipates, and of the manner in which he intends to allocate it. At the same time, a small body of carefully selected and well paid European experts should be appointed to check these estimates, to advise upon the most suitable and economical methods of developing the resources of each province, and to supervise the execution of the various public works. All farming of taxes should be absolutely prohibited,[1] the laws against extortionate usury should be strictly enforced,[2] and vilayets comprising tribal districts should be encouraged to subsidise the nomad

---

[1] The value of the tithe for the past five years should be ascertained, and the owner, who now pays on an average 15½ per cent., should be assessed for a fixed sum annually, subject to quinquennial revaluations. Tax collectors, of course, should be paid a regular salary independent of the amount they collect.

[2] The legal rate is limited to 9 per cent., but the usurer still exacts with impunity his interest of 100 per cent. (*vide* Consular Report for 1897, Trebizond, 2069). If alienation of title-deeds to foreigners were made a penal offence, a most salutary check would be placed upon improper use of relief funds for purposes of religious proselytism.

chieftains, on condition that they kept the roads open and protected traffic.[1]

By such measures confidence would be speedily and universally restored, and it might truly be said of every province between Bagdad and Stamboul, as Mr. Longworth says[2] of one which has but recently been the scene of violent disorder, and where the government still confine themselves mainly to the duty of collecting the taxes: "Peace and security reign to an unparalleled degree." The growing wealth of the vilayets would of course justify a periodic readjustment of their imperial contribution, and the central government would thus be supplied with a direct and tangible incentive to choose as their administrators men of tried energy, probity, and capacity.

No one can read the records of the vast revenues, amounting, it is said, to 272 million dirhems and 4½ million dinars,[3] annually raised in the Mosul and Bagdad districts during the second century after the Hegira, and contrast it with the miserable yield of taxation—less than £250,000 in the Bagdad budget for 1891, or scarcely more than double the salary of Harun el Rashid's principal physician[4]—without marvelling at the short-sighted policy of the present régime. All that has been effected by English and French engineers in Egypt in increasing the acreage of cultivation, and thereby enormously increasing the

---

[1] The nomad Kurds will not take voluntarily to a settled pastoral life, although those that have done so, as in the Taurus, soon lose their lawless instincts. It might be worth Turkey's while to imitate, in some cases, the policy adopted by Russia when she brought colonists compulsorily from the Black Sea to cultivate the Amur regions, giving them grants of land and money, and exempting them from military service and taxation.

[2] Consular Report, Trebizond, 1897.

[3] A dirhem is roughly equivalent to 4½d., a dinar to 10s. 8d.

[4] See General Chesney's Survey of the Euphrates and Tigris.

total revenue while diminishing the actual pressure of taxation, could as easily and quickly be achieved in Mesopotamia by competent and trained men, who would probably be able in some cases to reopen the ancient canal-cuttings, and to restore the massive aqueducts which have been allowed to fall into disuse and disrepair. The blame for this neglect cannot be justly attributed altogether to the Turks, certainly not to the paralysing effects of Mussulman rule. Historical causes had changed the face of the country before the Turks became its masters, and the greatest prosperity it ever enjoyed was enjoyed under a Mussulman dynasty. Arabia Irak, east of the Tigris, which furnished the Sassanians with a large portion of their revenues, owed its marvellous fertility to the water of the Diala River and the Nahr-wan Canal, constructed by the Persians, for defensive as well as for economic reasons, from Dur to Kut el Amara, and rescued by the Abbaside Khalifs, after the battle of Quadesiyeh, from the long neglect which had followed on the victories of the Roman Heraclius. Long before the Osmanli occupation, however, the ravages of Timur and Zenghis Khan had completed what the apathy of the Seljuks began, and the task of clearing out the accumulated deposits of silt would now involve an initial outlay which, without financial assistance from Europe, the impecunious treasury certainly could not afford.[1] Such assistance, however, would be readily procurable were precautions taken against the misappropriation

---

[1] *Cf.* Chesney, "Survey of the Euphrates and Tigris." The Dujail Canal, west of the Tigris, on the road between Bagdad and Tekrit, is still used for irrigation. The Mahmudieh, between the Euphrates and Ctesiphon, and the Isa, formerly navigable for big ships, between Bagdad and Anbar, the capital of the first two Abbaside Khalifs on the Euphrates, are now quite neglected. The Hindiyeh, south of Hillah and west of the Euphrates, and the Shat el Hai, are both practicable for sailing vessels.

of public funds so as to afford reasonable security for investments.

A more serious difficulty presents itself in the extreme paucity of population over the whole area of Jezireh, and indeed throughout the Asiatic provinces, which renders problematical the prospect of any large or immediate return on expenditure. The similar problem which confronted the Government of India when they set themselves to provide, by adequate canalisation and storage, against the losses entailed by recurring droughts and wholesale remissions of rent, was rendered easier of solution by the fact that, although extensive tracts of country were almost deserted, others were overcharged with a teeming population. On the completion of the Chenab Canal more than half a million acres of land were distributed among cultivators drawn from the crowded districts of the Punjab, and so rapid has been the growth of competition and increase of land values, that a capital expenditure of sixteen lacs of rupees is now yielding a return of 7½ per cent.; or, in other words, the value of the total crop in a single year equals the capital cost of the entire works.[1] The same may be said of the Orissa works, which cost 2½ millions; and an interest of from 7 to 9 per cent. represents the average profit to the State on the whole outlay which has been incurred during the past twenty years in restoring to cultivation an area of more than fifty million acres. No such result could be hoped for at present from an equally lavish disbursement in Asiatic Turkey, where misrule, famine, massacre, and disease have for centuries arrested the growth of a naturally prolific race. In the Trebizond vilayet, the next in density of population to Constantinople, the Lebanon, and Crete, the inhabitants

[1] Speech of Lord Curzon at Lyallpur, October 1899.

number only 89 to the square mile, and with 6½ million acres of arable and pastoral land, import from abroad [1] half the cereals required for their own consumption. If public works are to be undertaken at all it should be on a methodical system, with due regard for their relative urgency and importance and the varying needs of the different provinces; nor could the Turkish Government do better than take as its model the admirable organisation which has been elaborated in India. There a substantial sum of money for necessary works is set aside every year, and a public office is charged with the responsibility of framing the programme of construction, after full consideration of the recommendations which have been drawn up, in consultation with the local engineers and revenue departments, by its officials in the various districts. The chief engineer, besides weighing the respective claims of each locality, is bound to satisfy himself of the utility and financial soundness of every project before submitting his completed estimate for the sanction of the executive, and having obtained their approval, he then proceeds, with the assistance of the sub-engineers on the spot, to supervise the execution of the contracts and the expenditure of the moneys assigned.

Much of the forced labour and expense which, for lack of any central control, is now frittered away in the Anatolian provinces upon public works of questionable value, such as palatial konaks and municipal buildings, might be utilised to far better advantage if there were at Constantinople a State bureau under European superintendence, capable of revising and co-ordinating the improvement schemes suggested by the Valis and their trained engineer advisers.   Foreign loans, con-

[1] Consular Reports for 1897, 2069.

tracted in order to meet the initial cost of construction, might be secured on one or other of the normal sources of revenue rather than on the prospective profits of the works themselves, so as to avoid any pretext for European interference in the internal administration, the efficiency and purity of which would become a matter of vital interest to the central government, were it the only means of recouping the treasury for the temporary sacrifice of other valuable assets. It is true that the resources of Turkey are already deeply pledged, but in many cases their yield could easily be increased tenfold by a stricter management, similar to that which has been recently applied under Belgian auspices to the customs revenues of Persia. The Shah's government, having been apprised of the inordinate fortunes amassed by the farmers of these revenues, applied for the services of a Belgian commission of experts to visit the ports, investigate the methods of administration, and report on the profits accruing to the concessionaires. The immediate result of their inquiry was that the government found themselves in a position to bargain with the lessees for an advance of more than £40,000 upon the sums they had previously received.

There is scarcely any department of Turkish administration which would not benefit by a spring cleaning of the same kind. The management of the *Wakfs*, the property assigned or bequeathed to religious or educational objects, is notoriously corrupt, and a number of petty exactions from the peasantry are required to make good the losses sustained through official peculation. The magnificent forests of the Black Sea range, the Zigana, and the Anti-Taurus, which in the sixteenth century supplied Sultan Suleiman with material for his navy, and in the nineteenth inspired Napoleon with his wild dream of descending the Euphrates in a flotilla constructed of Cilician timber and seizing Bussorah as a fortified *place d'armes*,[1] are either left uncared for, exposed to the merciless ravages of Circassian and Avshar charcoal-burners, or protected by an army of officials, on whose maintenance alone nearly half of the total proceeds are exhausted.[2] A country which possesses, on a rough calculation, no less than seventeen and a half million acres of woodland, and inexhaustible mineral wealth of every kind, prefers to see the exploitation of its metals abandoned rather than develop its coal stores or reduce the prohibitive cost of wood fuel by facilitating transport.[3] Capital and mining enterprise, which it would almost pay Turkey to attract by concessions of land at prairie value, are discouraged by exorbitant demands for baksheesh, and the exaction of a 20 per cent. royalty on all output exported. In order that the farmer, by delaying his visit of inspection, may wring a few extra piastres from the peasantry, grain lies rotting on the threshing floors of the Angora and Sivas vilayets, while famine rages at Bitlis or Van; and it is more profitable to send abroad, to the United Kingdom or India, the produce of a harvest which more than suffices to feed the whole population of the interior, than to incur the heavy double expenses of transit dues and wheeled transport.[4]

Everywhere the excess of imports over exports is

---

[1] Chesney, "Survey of the Euphrates and Tigris."

[2] In the Trebizond vilayet £1935 out of a total yearly income of £4563. Consular Report, 1897, 2069.

[3] *Cf.* Consular Report, Samsun, 1898, for the cessation at Tokat of the smelting of copper from the Arghana mines.

[4] In 1899, £254,742 worth of barley and doriseed were exported from Bussorah. *Vide* Consular Reports.

increasing; the purchasing power of the population is proportionately diminishing; consideration of price rather than of quality rules the markets; the credit system of the agricultural banks, which might go far to encourage a revival of rural prosperity, is hampered by needless formalities; and the transference of business, once transacted by great European houses, to small and insufficiently capitalised native merchants, has increased the number of middlemen and enhanced the cost of articles to the consumer. The system of taxation, light and merciful in theory, is antiquated and abused. Crown lands, including, it is said, large tracts of the most fertile land iu Mesopotamia, for which the original proprietors were compelled to accept any offer the commissioners of the privy purse chose to make, are altogether exempted. Hereditary lands, granted in the first instance to the old feudal troops in addition to their one-fifth share of the spoils of war and their claim on the State revenues, still enjoy the same relief from public burdens, although their liability to service is shared by the whole non-Christian manhood of the nation, and their exclusion from agricultural pursuits has long been a thing of the past. Kurds who refuse to enlist either as regulars or as Hamidiehs are allowed to escape the contribution which is levied on their Christian neighbours; the civilians are plundered by the police and the soldiery, and these in their turn are robbed by their commanding officers.

With all her free-trade orthodoxy in matters of tariff, Turkey has yet to learn that the object of taxation is to encourage industry, not to depress it, and that that which is spread over the widest area is not necessarily the least onerous or the most productive. Nor is she likely to learn it until an exhausted exchequer compels her to seek in the development of untried resources the means of repaying her foreign creditors.

Nevertheless, signs of awakening are apparent in her diminished reluctance to sanction railway enterprise, and her tentative experiments in the construction of permanent improvements. I have already alluded to the great engineering project of irrigating the Konia plain with water brought from the Beyshehr Lake, and within the last few years a French engineer has been entrusted with the erection of a barrage on the Euphrates above Hillah, which will prevent the waste hitherto occasioned by the overflow of the river into the Hindiyeh Canal.[1] Similar precautions are urgently needed on the lower reaches of the Tigris, where the main stream, as well as the large cuttings that radiate from it, are rapidly becoming exhausted by the absurd system of drainage employed by the Arab cultivators along the banks. Freed from all supervision, and too indolent, or too heavily taxed, to care about raising more crops than are absolutely necessary for their own wants, they are constantly tapping the supply with trenches of their own, cut on no regular plan; while the high floods are allowed to disperse among the marshes the rich alluvial deposit which should fertilise vast tracks of unreclaimed land.

When I reached the town of Kut, the canal connecting it with the Shat el Hai was so low that not even a sailing boat could proceed up it, and the unhappy *mektubji* (secretary) whom we put ashore, and who had no camping requisites with him, told

---

[1] The soil, as in Upper Egypt, is extremely porous. At Bagdad the water-line on the walls of the subterranean *serdabs* shows ten feet below ground level, while outside the city newly-made graves are often flooded before the coffin can be placed *in situ*.

me that he might have to wait some weeks before
he could proceed to his destination at Sheikh es Shinkh.
Not long ago complaints were, I believe, made of the
alarming shrinkage of water in the bed of the Tigris,
and the Sultan gave orders that one of the main canals
should be closed, and the riparian owners compensated
out of moneys forwarded from Constantinople. The
canal, however, remained open, and the funds were
gratefully appropriated by the local officials.

As far back as 1848 Commander Jones[1] drew
attention to the extreme gravity of the situation.
"Until recently," he writes, "the tribes were compelled to keep the waters within their due bounds,
whereas now the rivers and canals, uncontrolled and
unrepaired, are annually committing such ravages as
a profuse expenditure will not redeem, and the fine
streams are becoming less navigable every year, although our interests are thereby directly threatened,
since the Tigris is the single navigable highway for
our Indian commerce." And again: "Within quite
recent years the Euphrates was navigable from Basra
as far as Diwanieh, but this is no longer the case
owing to the dilapidation of the embankment which
formerly restrained the river within its channel."

At the present time, the river during the low
season is scarcely broad enough in many of the reaches
below Amara to allow of the steamer lying broadside
to the current, although extensive marshes stretch
for miles on each side, covered with high bulrushes
and bamboo-cane, among which the Muntafik Arabs
conceal themselves and issue forth at intervals to
plunder passing craft. Few sights on the Tigris
are more picturesque than the league-long gleam at

[1] Memoirs of Commander James Felix Jones, I.N., Bombay Govern-
ments Records, No. xliii., April 1848.

night of the marsh-fires, lit by these piratical husband-
men to burn off the coarse tops, that their cattle may
browse on the tender shoots of the undergrowth.
Forts have been erected at the mouth of many canals
as a means of checking their lawlessness, with what
success may be judged from the fact that it is not
so very long since one of Messrs. Lynch's passenger
steamers was attacked on its way up the river, and
subjected for an hour to a hot rifle· fire from the banks.

This energetic firm, which for many years past
has divided with an incompetent and obstructive
Turkish company a monopoly of the carrying trade
between Bussorah and Bagdad, is to be congratulated
on having at length obtained, after persistent agitation,
the removal or abatement of one at least of the many
irritating obstacles that seemed to have been deliberately designed to impede the successful prosecution
of their business. Some idea of the utter inadequacy of
the present means of transport to cope with the rapidly
increasing export and import trade of the lower port
may be gained from Mr. Wratislaw's testimony, which
every visitor will corroborate, that to this cause alone is
due a normal accumulation of merchandise amounting
to several thousand tons.[1] Yet, despite the manifest
injury which all this delay and risk of damage en-
tails upon producer and consumer alike,[2] the Turkish
Government, fearful of increasing the profits of the

---

[1] *Cf.* Consular Report on Samsun, 1898, for similar complaints of insufficient warehouse accommodation at that port.

[2] Of the increased value of the import trade by £450,000 in 1898, Mr.
Wratislaw estimates that two-thirds were due to Manchester goods alone.
The export trade is equally affected, and the wild liquorice which flourishes
over a vast area of Mesopotamia can only be utilised in the neighbourhood
of the river where water transport is available, and even there the trade
is ruined by the dishonesty and carelessness of the native lightermen.
(Consular Report, Bussorah, 1898.)

English company at the expense of its native rivals, whose steamers occupy nearly double the time in transit, and are so cranky that they have to go into dock for repairs at the end of every trip, not only forbad them to run more than two boats, the *Khalifa* and *Medjidieh*, both necessarily of light draught,[1] and consequently of limited cargo capacity, but has persistently refused to allow them even the modest privilege of towing a barge alongside. This senseless restriction, however, has at last been withdrawn, and we may hope that it will also be found possible before long to modify, to some extent, the absurd quarantine regulations, which add gratuitously to the delay and cost of transhipment. Last year the whole navigation of the river had been thrown out of gear by the imposition of a double quarantine of ten days against plague at Bussorah for vessels coming from India and Persia, and another seven against cholera at Kut el Amara for vessels arriving from Bussorah. Needless to say, the Persian Government, eager to be quits with Turkey, had retaliated by instituting at Mohammerah a twenty days' quarantine against Bussorah, and yet all the while no impediment whatever had been placed in the way of land traffic between the two countries, and that most prolific source of infection, the annual pilgrimage from the Shah's dominions to the Shiite shrines of Kerbela and Nejef, continued its uninterrupted discharge of ragged "hadjis" and ill-coffined corpses across the border at Khanikin. When, in 1843, the Sunnites first asserted direct administrative control over the holy cities, the Shah marked his displeasure by temporarily discouraging the "hadj," and thereby inflicting a serious loss of revenue on the Bagdad vilayet. For their own sakes, therefore, the

---

[1] About three feet.

Turks would think twice before they blocked the caravan route, and although thousands of intending visitors
from India must have been excluded in 1899 by the
virtual closing of the Shat el Arab, yet so vast was
the influx that during our ride back from Hillah we
passed, on an average computation, over forty persons
per minute.

Personally, I have little doubt that the coming
century will witness a great accession of foreign influence and enterprise both in Persia and Turkey.
For the moment it has been retarded, owing partly
to the idiosyncrasies of individual rulers, partly to
the reactionary tendencies aroused by the very rapidity
of those changes which are inexorably intertwining
the destinies of East and West, of Progress and Conservatism.   "Turkey for the Turks" may be, probably
is, the only principle which has consistently determined the policy of Stamboul during the reign of
Abdul Hamid, and in theory it is an eminently laud-
able and patriotic sentiment.   Only it is no longer a
practicable one.   "Ghiumlek kaftandan yakinder"—
"The shirt is nearer than the waistcoat."   But if the
shirt is falling to pieces, the wearer, even though he
spurns a foreign-made waistcoat, will do wisely to have
his beloved nether garment patched up betimes by the
best workman he can find.   If, as some think, it is
because foreign enterprise has tended to concentrate
wealth and power throughout the maritime provinces in
the hands of Greeks and Armenians, that the Government dreads lest a continuance of the process may
eventually make these Uitlanders the lords of the
country, it will also be because foreign assistance
can alone preserve the nation from foreign control
that the attempt to avert both will be abandoned as
hopeless.

It is being abandoned now; tentatively, grudgingly, it is true, but still abandoned. There is the "open door," and though visitors are not encouraged to enter, and every obstacle is invented to deter them from doing so, they can enter if they please. Their attitude at present is most interesting. Russia stays at home, contenting herself with occasional remonstrances upon the unruly conduct of her neighbour, and warnings against the exhibition on her part of any undue partiality for people who might display a selfish or disinterested inclination to raise her in the social scale. Great Britain stands on the doorstep, uncertain whether she ought to have any dealings at all with a person of such antecedents; while Germany bustles inside, with profuse assurances of friendship and a lusty appreciation of the material advantages to be reaped from her new connection.

Strangely enough, Turkey respects and likes us best of the three. But we cannot remain on the doorstep for ever. We must make up our mind. Shall we cast our influence on the side of Germany and the open door, or on the side of Russia and the boycott? In either case our action will be decisive. With Russia we can keep Turkey isolated and accelerate her ruin. With Germany we can make her strong and prosperous. Last year the two rivals showed their hands. One chance remains of a brighter future for Asiatic Turkey—the speedy opening of roads and railways, which will introduce money into the country, and bring crime and outrage within striking distance of the law. Germany asked and obtained permission to run a line across the whole length of the continent; Russia offered nothing herself, and extorted a pledge that no one else should be allowed to place the means of civilisation within reach of the population that inhabits the provinces bordering on the southern shores of the Black Sea.[1]

Did we protest? Did we even make an effort to induce our co-signatories of the Berlin Treaty to do so? Of course not. We had no *locus standi* for complaint! We, who go out of our way to lecture Turkey on the way in which she should govern her Christian subjects, who solemnly pledged ourselves to watch over the introduction of reforms into the Armenian provinces when we tore up the Treaty of San Stephano, have, forsooth, no ground for remonstrance if the authors of that treaty now interpose to veto the introduction into these same provinces of the one reform which must infallibly benefit Mussulman and non-Mussulman alike. Members in plenty will get up in the House of Commons to call for vengeance on Turkey at the slightest whisper of riot or massacre. Not a word of protest is breathed when Russia sets herself to perpetuate the conditions which make riot and massacre inevitable. Yet if judgment ever falls upon us, as a nation, for neglect of that responsibility which we voluntarily took upon ourselves, it will not be because we were unable to punish Turkey for her crimes, but because we are too timorous to prevent others from depriving her of the opportunity to amend.

There is no need to insult Russia. She has her own policy, and its morality is no concern of ours. Let us have a policy ourselves. She placed her veto on the armed intervention of Europe against Turkey

---

[1] The effect of this arrangement may be judged by the following instance. Railway communication is urgently needed between Sivas and Samsun. The prolongation of the Angora line will not meet the case, as the cost of carriage from Sivas to Haidar Pasha would still be almost prohibitive. Yet under the recent Russo-Turkish agreement, the German company having carried the railway as far as Sivas, would be prohibited from connecting it with any seaport on the northern coast.

in 1895, and we acquiesced. If she intends to prevent the friendly co-operation of Europe with Turkey, at all events in the north-eastern provinces during the coming years, we are bound by every consideration of honour and humanity to defeat that intention. Before relinquishing the seals of the Foreign Office Lord Salisbury has taken a step which has long seemed to many people the only means of securing the objects of Great Britain in China—an agreement between Germany and ourselves. It is the policy of Lord Beaconsfield, decried in the Near East, resuscitated in the Far East— the policy of integrity, re-christened the policy of the " open door," and guaranteed by the only two Powers whose interests both in Asiatic Turkey and China are practically identical. " Blood is thicker than water," wrote the German Emperor to Lord Curzon in forwarding the Berlin contribution to the Indian famine fund, and the new agreement is sanctioned by a community of interests even more binding than any tie of blood relationship. Let us give the compact a wider application, and extend it to the empires of the Sultan and the Shah ; if possible before " spheres of influence " or "interest" have been created in either. It will save us from much trouble and danger in the future. Those who look askance at such a policy do so for two reasons. They say that it gives Germany everything and ourselves nothing ; that it perpetuates mistrust between the Cabinets of London and St. Petersburg, and makes the colonial policy of Great Britain a pawn in the European game of the Triple Alliance. Germany, they point out, has already her sphere of influence in Shantung ; she does not recognise ours in the Yangtze Kiang valley. She is between two fires in Europe, and, however absorbed to all appearance in her new " welt-politik," will not prosecute her own colonial ambitions, much less ours, at the risk of a rupture with Russia. At the same moment that she is signing a treaty of alliance with Great Britain, she is secretly assuring Russia of her support, and by embittering the relations of the two Asiatic Powers she hopes to force us into a thorough-going offensive and defensive alliance with herself and Italy in view of the impending break-up of the Austrian Empire.

All this may be perfectly true, although it is improbable that the policy of Continental nations any more than our own is animated by these deep-laid Machiavellian designs. Germany's expansion, like ours, is due mainly to the astonishing increase of her population and industrial activity. The acquisition of fresh markets and territory, and the creation of a navy adequate for their defence, which, for America or Russia, is still a luxury, is for her a necessity of existence; and curiously enough, both in the Near East and in the Far East, she has managed to place herself in the direct line of a Russian advance. It is idle to suppose that she will voluntarily relinquish her position in Shantung and Mesopotamia without a struggle, or that she believes in her ability to retain it unaided; and although she would no doubt be glad of our effective support in Europe, she is not likely to underrate its value in Asia. Nor is it quite fair to say that she offers us no *quid pro quo* for that support. If she declines to recognise our exclusive right to the Yangtze Kiang valley, it must be remembered that we have ostentatiously disowned any territorial designs in China. On the other hand, she has claimed in Shantung no commercial privileges in the way of tariff for herself, and if she has demanded preferential consideration for the applications of her own concessionaries in that province, we have done the same in what we regard as our sphere.

The important question to us is, not whether we or Germany are likely to build most railways or work most mines, but whether we both consent to trade on equal terms. If we do, the expansion of Germany in China and her enterprise in Asiatic Turkey is an unmitigated boon to us, and it is worth our while to back her for all we are worth, in order to keep our access to markets which we cannot annex ourselves, but which may very likely be annexed by those who will turn them into close preserves.

If Russia would frankly adopt the policy of a " fair field and no favour," we might back her on the same principle, were it not for her geographical position, which places it in her power at any moment to close the markets of China as she closed the treaty port of Batum. A great deal of superfluous indignation has been vented on the ʿfaithlessness of Russia to her engagements. The truth is that our relations with any Power in regard to matters of this kind are determined, not by its willingness to play fair, but by its ability to play false. From a military point of view, Germany and Great Britain in China stand at least upon an equal footing; Great Britain and Russia do not and never can. An agreement between the first two Powers to maintain the *status quo* may be sufficient to deter any third Power from attempting to disturb it. An agreement between the last two for the same purpose would offer no guarantee whatever which does not already exist without it.

There is therefore every reason why we should co-operate heartily with Germany in the Near East, and it is to be hoped that no petty commercial jealousy will prevent us from doing so. So far as we are concerned, the more railways she can run through the country, the greater will be our chance of preserving trade which is even now seriously threatened, and of pushing it in quarters where no opening has hitherto existed.   On the other hand, while we need not grudge her the concessions which she has obtained, there are many considerations which render it expedient that we should come to a mutual arrangement with regard to them. In the first place, it is doubtful whether a German company can raise sufficient capital for railway undertakings which do not promise an immediate and substantial return, without some artificial stimulus in the shape of a guarantee which must impose a burdensome liability on the Turkish Exchequer.   An English company might be able and willing to do so, but joint action would be preferable, both as avoiding friction between the two nations, and offering no ground for the suspicion that either aimed at the creation of a political sphere of influence.   Such a suspicion, which is abundantly justified by recent events in China, will only tend to strengthen the conservatism of the Turks, and provoke demands for compensation elsewhere by Russia and other interested Powers.

In the second place, considerations which I have already discussed make it difficult, if not impossible, for us to acquiesce in the possession by the Germans. or any other Europeans, of a terminus on the shores of the Persian Gulf.   If the Euphrates railway is carried to Bagdad, its prolongation to Bussorah or Koweit would naturally be assigned to ourselves, and might some day form at the latter place a junction with the much-talked-of all-British line, which, starting from Suez and the head of the Akaba Gulf, would pass along the thirtieth parallel through the peninsula of Arabia, and the coast-line of Persia and the Mekran to India.

Lastly, the railway question in Asiatic Turkey is

not merely a commercial, it is also a strategic one. The defence of the Eastern frontier, hitherto almost wholly neglected, is becoming increasingly urgent with the advance of the Russian line from the Caucasus, and the overwhelming predominance of Russian influence in North-Western Persia. But no adequate military preparations will be made without foreign assistance, and no one Power can give that assistance without thereby placing itself in an invidious attitude of hostility to Russia. Trouble in Manchuria and lack of funds have temporarily tied her hands nearer home and strengthened the peace party, whose chief desire is to attract foreign capital to Siberia and the Caucasus. But as soon as she finds herself once more disengaged, the Alexandropol-Kars railway will be pushed forward across the Julfa ferry to Khoi, and thence eastward to Tabriz and Teheran, and southwards in the direction of Suj Balak. The completion of the latter section will enable her to dominate the entire length of ill-defined frontier between the plains of Ararat and the Lesser Zab, and, almost immediately after the declaration of war, to deliver a simultaneous attack on Erzerum, Bayazid, Van, and Mosul. Neither of the two northern fortresses, with their existing provisions for defence, would be likely to offer a prolonged resistance ; but their capture would not necessarily be a fatal blow to the Turkish cause if there was any force capable of making a successful stand along the road leading from Van to the Tigris. At present there is no such force, no transport vessels on the lake, and no means of bringing up reinforcements from Erzingjian in time to prevent the enemy's advance, much less to carry the war into his country by striking north and east across his lines of communication. The establishment of railway communication with Bitlis and Van is

therefore the obvious and the only effective answer to
the Russian line; and it would be rendered still more
effective by the construction of another line in the
south, for the conveyance of troops from Bagdad and
the Gulf to the upper plains of the Tigris and the Zab.
Until this is done, there can be no sense of security
in Mesopotamia, and all foreign enterprise there will
remain at the mercy of the invader.

Now, for ourselves, no less than for Germany, the
security of this region is a matter of vital and increasing importance.   Our future trade, both with Turkey
and Persia, is certain to become more and more rigidly
confined within a line drawn roughly from Bagdad,
through Dizful, Isfahan, Yezd, and Kerman, to the
north-western corner of Baluchistan.   Already the import of British goods for Tabriz and Meshed, by the
Trebizond-Erzerum-Bayezid route, the safeguarding of
which was one of the main objects of the authors of
the settlement of 1878,[1] shows a tendency to decrease,[2] and will cease altogether with the practical
absorption of Azerbaijan by Russia.   The Caucasian
and Transcaspian lines will engross the trade of Tabriz,
Teheran, and Meshed, and our only hope of retaining
any hold at all upon the northern markets will lie in
the opening up of communications from the south,
where, if we act with energy, our commercial and
political influence should continue unassailable.   A
concession has already been granted to the Germans
to make a road from Teheran *via* Hamadan and Kermanshah to Bagdad; another, practicable for caravans,

---

[1] By the Treaty of San Stephano, Bayazid, as well as Kars Ardahan
and Batum, was to be ceded to Russia.

[2] In 1898 they were valued at close upon £300,000.   The imports into
Khorassan from India by the long caravan route through Bunder Abbas
and Meshed were in 1897 worth £89,000, as against £92,000 from Russia.

is in process of construction, under the auspices of
Messrs. Lynch, from Isfahan *via* Naghun to Ahwaz;
and a third should be commenced, with as little delay
as possible, between Dizful and Kum,[1] through Kho-
remmabad, Burujird, and Sultanabad. On the western
side communication might profitably be opened up by
the short cross-route from Dizful to Amara if the
tribesmen of the Pusht-i-Kuh and the Beni Lam Arabs
were brought under proper control; while on the
eastern or Beluch frontier a regular dak service was
instituted three years ago by the Indian Government
between Quetta and Seistan *via* Nushki, Chagai, and
Kuh Malek Siah. This has taken the place of the old
trade-route to Meshed through Ghazni, which was
practically closed by the Amir's fiscal policy, and has
also diverted much of the traffic which formerly passed
through Bunder Abbas and Kerman, the value of the
transit trade in the first year after the road was opened
increasing by more than 3½ lakhs of rupees. The
Russians having successfully strangled British trade
with Transcaspia by forbidding the importation of
manufactured goods and subjecting raw articles to
prohibitive duties, did their utmost in 1897 to kill the
new trade with Seistan. Under pretence of plague
precautions they stationed Cossack posts along the
whole Perso-Afghan border from Zulfikar to Turbat-i-
Haidari to prevent all traffic between Persia and
Afghanistan or Baluchistan; and the Afghan and
Indian trade with Meshed was diverted into Russian
territory through Panjdeh, where caravans were subjected to only three days' quarantine instead of ten.

---

[1] Between Ahwaz and Shuster, or rather Shellalieh, goods can be
carried by steamer, and thence by road to Dizful. Kum and Teheran are
already connected by a good carriage road, made by the Imperial Bank of
Persia.

This outrageous abuse of her influence at Teheran in order to infringe the treaty rights of Great Britain in Persia is a warning of what may be expected if Russia ever obtains political control of Khorassan or the western provinces along the shores of the Caspian and the Black Sea.   Her policy in regard to all of them is the same.   It is she who has made the road from Resht to Teheran, she who will build the railway to Tabriz, she who alone is to have the right of constructing any line that may traverse the vilayets of Kastamouni, Sivas, or Trebizond.   The latter are perhaps the least likely to be constructed, for Turkey realises, as Persia apparently does not, that her independence is incompatible with the realisation of Russia's ambitions for commercial monopoly, and she will probably prefer to let her estates lie fallow rather than give a lien upon them to so grasping a neighbour. But unless the commercial impartiality and territorial integrity of Persia is, at all costs, insisted upon by Great Britain and Germany, they will have hard work to protect even the southern markets when Meshed and Teheran have become links in the Caucasus-Transcaspian Railway, and the Shah, like the Khan of Bokhara, a puppet in the hands of Russia.

Apart from this contingency, however, they may trust by their own enterprise and free-trade policy gradually to shift the centre of Persian trade, and revive at Dizful or Ispahan a mercantile supremacy that will rival the political predominance of the ancient capitals at Susa and Persepolis.   Similarly, in Asiatic Turkey the effect of Russia's latest move may ultimately be to throw the bulk even of the trade with such markets as those of Sivas and Erzerum into the hands of the companies which own railway lines starting from Konia, Angora, or Bussorah ; in which case the value of our interest in Turkish trade would be susceptible of almost indefinite expansion, the mass of the population of the interior conducting their exchange of commodities through the Gulf or the Levant instead of the Black Sea.

As it is, although our trade does not increase in the same ratio as Germany's, and in some respects may even be said to be losing ground,[1] yet on the whole we hold our own, and are still by far the best customers both of Turkey and Persia. In the case of the former we take, on an average, about half her total exports, and supply one-third of her total imports: in the case of the latter, more than half the aggregate yearly trade is in our hands.[2] On the other hand, if we compare our trade with Russia, we find that whereas in 1896 we sent £4,000,000 worth of cotton goods, yarn, and woollens to Turkey, we sold in 1898 only £1,000,000 of the same goods to Russia. It is true that Russia took from us £5,500,000 worth more of iron, copper, and machinery, but then these are precisely the articles which she is rapidly becoming able to produce for herself, whereas the demand for them in Turkey must necessarily be an increasing one. Already a greater disposition is shown, especially in Western Anatolia, where the government has instituted model farms, to import agricultural implements from England and Germany, and a fresh impetus will be

[1] Principally in the case of Austrian and Swedish ironware and German cutlery.

[2] The total value of the Persian Gulf trade, exclusive of the Shat el Arab, in 1898 was £5,500,000, of which £3,000,000 was with Great Britain and India. The figures of the shipping trade are even more significant. Of the shipping entered and cleared at Constantinople in 1896, Great Britain owned a fourth of the vessels and more than half the total tonnage. Of the steamers that entered Basrah in the same year, 101 out of 106 were under the British flag. Of the interport trade between Mohammerah and Shuster more than half is Indian.

given to the trade in iron, coal, and machinery by the
development of railway and mining enterprise. Manchester goods may be depended upon to make their
way wherever the requisite facilities for transport are
provided, and sugar is another article for which there
is a large and growing market, hitherto almost mono-
polised by French and Russian producers.[1] Persia
and Turkey, on their side, would equally benefit by
giving us in exchange many raw materials, such as
wool, tobacco, gall-nuts, and madder-root, which are
now raised only in comparatively small quantities, but
for the production of which the soil and climate of
Kurdistan and Ardilan are as admirably adapted as
the warmer southern plains for the breeding of horses,[2]
and the raising of cotton, cereals, liquorice, and
indigo.

There are no markets in the world so near to our
doors which have received less attention from our
manufacturers, and few that would repay it more. The
natural resources are greater than those of Africa, the
population is more industrious, and though infinitely
smaller is also infinitely less fanatical than the population of China. Had there been a Sir Robert Hart
during the last thirty years at Constantinople or Teheran,

---

[1] Out of £648,926 worth of goods imported to Tabriz *via* Erzerum in
1898, £100,000 are ascribed to Russian sugar (*vide* Consular Reports).
Mr. Wratislaw also notes the importation of sugar from Marseilles into
the Basrah vilayets. But the Egyptian product is making way in the
Karun markets, and if Sir William Hudson's estimate, presented to the
Indian Government in connection with the new scheme for the cultivation of cane sugar on the estates of the Behar indigo planters, that it will
be possible to produce sugar at little more than a farthing per pound, be
correct, Indian sugar, like Indian coffee, ought to be able to compete successfully in these regions with the foreign grown article.

[2] At present the Turks levy a tax of £4 10s. on every horse exported.
Many are smuggled into Persia and shipped at Mohammerah, paying an
ad valorem duty of 5 per cent.

or a Gordon to train the Kurdish mountaineers, as
Russia has trained the far less hopeful rabble out of
which she has evolved an efficient Cossack brigade at
the Persian capital, progress in the Near East would,
I believe, have been relatively far more rapid and continuous than it has been in the Far East. For all the
labour, advice, and assistance that have been lavished
on the Celestials, their military organisation is in as
backward a condition as ever; railway development has
scarcely begun; commercial enterprise, except within
a short radius of the coast, is baffled by the rapacity
and obstructiveness of provincial officials. The much-
abused Turk, left to his own devices, or bullied about
matters with which his mentors have no direct concern,
has made of his army at least a creditable fighting
machine, has half opened his one great navigable river
to commerce, and not only allowed, but pledged foreign
concessionaires to connect his most distant possessions
by rail with the capital. What recognition or encouragement has he received? Granted that he has
many of the worst vices of his predecessors, the corruption of the Roman *publicani*, the venality and
profligacy of the Byzantine Court; he has at least the
excuse of poverty, which the Powers have done their
utmost to increase by denuding him of his richest
provinces. Prevented by them from taking the pre-
cautionary measures which he thinks necessary to
guard against sedition, he is denounced for the
severity of the methods by which he seeks to repress
it; and although naturally more humane, less stained
by love of torture than any Oriental nation, he is held
up, as the Chinese, with all their innate savagery,
have never been, to the execration of civilised man-
kind.

Two ideas, equally erroneous, seem to have rooted themselves in the public mind at home—that Europe alone knows what is best for Turkey, and that her salvation depends upon European coercion. As a matter of fact, it is impossible to mention one single administrative improvement in the provinces remaining under her effective control which has resulted from the repeated interference of Europe, and every practical reform which has been conceived or carried out in the course of the present century has been due to the initiative of her own rulers and statesmen. It was Selim III. who first attempted to create an army modelled on European lines. Mahmoud II. who suppressed the Janissaries and abolished the authority of the Dere Beys. The Hatti Sherif of Gulkhaneh and the Hatti Humayun, the two great charters which guarantee protection to life and property, equality before the law, uniformity of taxation and religious liberty, were the work of Abdul Mejjid and Reshed Pasha; and no more practical pledges of reform could have been given by Abdul Aziz and Fuad Pasha than the construction of highroads through the heart of the remotest provinces, the encouragement of European enterprise in the shape of banks, railways, and schools, and the appointment of a European Commission to reorganise the financial and judicial systems of the Empire. In every case but the last it was external trouble that cut short internal reform. It was the outbreak of war with England and Russia in 1806 that provoked the Janissary rising and the deposition of Selim. Mahmoud had hardly punished the insubordination of his army before his fleet was destroyed at Navarino; and a more daring than Abdul Mejjid might well have hesitated to try experiments at home

with Mehemet Ali in revolt and the Russians knock-
ing at his gates.   Abdul Aziz alone, during his brief
reign, maintained friendly, and even intimate, relations
with Europe, and he fell a victim to the disaffection of
his own subjects.   Whatever mistakes the present
Sultan may have made, his inveterate hostility to
Midhat Pasha and the Young Turkish party was not,
I think, one of them.   They failed to see that although
Turkey might get on well enough without the intervention of the foreigner, she could not get on without
his assistance ; and by deposing Abdul Aziz and
Murad, and extorting from the Sultan a Parliamentary
constitution framed on Western principles, they struck
the greatest blow ever levelled at the cause of Turkish
reform.

The only period during which Turkey has enjoyed
a real though transient measure of good government
and prosperity was the interval of twenty years between the Crimean war and 1878, during which
foreign influence was strongest and foreign capital
poured into the country.   Then was the time when
England, supported by the Young Turkish party,
might have made use of her unbounded popularity
in Turkey to obtain pledges of financial reform as a
condition of financial assistance.   Instead, the native
reformers wasted their energy in futile agitation for
popular institutions, and England looked on while vast
loans were recklessly squandered, and a period of depression set in, which even the subsequent increase of
investments in railways and the reduction of the
interest on the public debt after the Russian war
proved powerless to arrest.   The Young Turkish
party saw that what was needed was some guarantee
for economy.   They chose the wrong method to obtain

it. Parliamentary control of supplies was, and always must be, an ideal incompatible with the fundamental principles upon which the whole fabric of government in a Mussulman country rests. You may destroy the belief in the divine right of kingship in Europe and yet preserve a limited monarchy. You may deprive a Pope of his temporal power without touching his ecclesiastical prerogatives. But the spiritual authority of a Padishah is derived from his civil authority as Sultan, and you cannot limit the one without at the same time endangering or destroying the other.

So long as Turkey retains her independence, reform must emanate from the ruler, but it can only be carried out through the agency of Europeans. Either of his own free will or driven to it by his financial embarrassments, he must consent to employ foreigners who will overhaul the entire administration and insist upon efficiency and economy in every department. This does not necessarily mean that bribery or the " spoils system " must be altogether abolished : only that it must be confined within definite limits. The civil list assigned to the Sultan may be as large, his right to dispose of it as untrammelled, his assignment of public posts as irresponsible as it is at present, provided that full security is taken against the dissipation or misappropriation of other public funds, and against malversation and peculation in the various ranks of the official hierarchy. The Sultan would not thereby lose a particle of his authority or prestige, while he would gain the confidence of those Powers which alone command the means of restoring the commercial credit of his country. The real obstacle to any such reform would be the desperate opposition of the bureaucracy, which would strain every nerve to defend its cherished privileges, and endeavour by alarming the fears of the priesthood to raise the cry of "Islam in danger," which has more than once hounded the populace to revolution as well as to massacre. To what extent there exists among the Mullahs and religious orders a party which could be depended upon to support the policy of a progressive ruler it is impossible to say. Men of broad and enlightened views are to be found in some of the highest ecclesiastical offices, but they are probably a small minority, and might be unable or unwilling to exert their influence actively in a crisis. Care must therefore be taken not unnecessarily to offend and alienate the leaders of religious opinion, and for that reason, if for no other, reforms for the Christians are the last that should be prominently put forward. But if Abdul Hamid or any of his successors wish to earn for themselves the title of "Saviour of their country," it is to the army that they must look for support. There is no more staunch and devoted soldiery in the world than the Turkish : none which have more cause for disaffection. The assurance of adequate and regular pay in future for men and officers of all ranks would of itself create a sentiment of enthusiastic loyalty for the person of the sovereign which would enable him to defy the combined forces of reaction and to carry any measure he pleased. So long as his motto is "Isolation," distrust of every section of his subjects, and suspicion of every foreign Power, he will find it impossible to retrieve that position and influence which Turkey alone of Oriental countries once exercised in the councils of Europe. Do what he will, his Empire will be torn piecemeal from his grasp ; his exchequer will become more and more depleted by the system of bribery and espionage with which he seeks to buttress his throne. There are but two courses by which he may still safeguard the dynasty and avert national bankruptcy—a frank appeal to the loyalty of the army, and hearty co-operation with one or other of the European Powers.

SUNRISE ON THE PERSIAN GULF

APPENDIX

Translations of Two Documents issued by the Bishops and Village-Headmen of the Chaldeans in connection with Recent Events in Hakkiari.

I.

"Be it known to all faithful Christians in our Lord in every land, concerning the state of us Chaldean Christians of the East in the government of the city of Van, the county of Hakkiari.

"Perchance some of you heard the story of five or six years ago. There was distress and hunger through locusts and other mischances that occurred ; as in many former times in different places, so they happened amongst us   And we heard that merciful men of the kingdoms of Europe were giving alms of money according to their merciful habit who enlarge the needy. and distressed, as cometh forth from their merciful hand.[1]   And because of this we are grateful to them, and God will repay them, doers of good, a thousand for one.   So also we heard about one whose name is Priest ——, who lodgeth in the city of Van, capital of the province of Van.   This man caused word to go forth in our lands, as that he was giving money in alms to assist distrest, needy, and poor persons. Therefore we also, because of our distress and need and poverty, went to him in that name,[2] that he might give us alms.   And he showed unto us for each soul four or five piastres[3] apiece, and this amount he considered fitting for us, as if it would suffice us for all the period of our need and distress.   And when we knew that this is the assistance and alms that he doeth, we were greatly ashamed.   But from our distress and need, though it was but little, yet we took it with un-suspecting hearts according to the necessity of the day.   But in secret and covertly he inscribed us as purchased by him.   But we

---

[1] i.e., as they are able.
[2] i.e., in the name of the charity he had professed.
[3] i.e., from tenpence to a shilling.

knew not that this was his intention, and even at the time when he gave to us he did not inform us. Afterwards we heard of it from a distance—men saying of us on this account, 'You have joined yourselves unto —— in respect of religion by that sum of money which you received from him.' And this report grieved us exceedingly, for he played a cunning trick upon us, luring us in the name of almsgiving. And this is a story unheard of in the ages of the world, buying religion in the name of almsgiving.

"And now be it known unto the sympathy of all faithful Christians! By the blood of our necks we will not sell our religion.

"And now we, six villages of the neighbourhood of Van, men of us who took that false alms, have returned from after him, and have informed the Government and our chief men of our story. And now there are not any men in the province of Hakkiari who adhere to ——, except five or six, and they also will return. But they are looking to receive a little more money, after which they will return. And now we are learning that even as there is a trickiness in their giving of these moneys in the name of alms, so also there is a trickiness in their collection of the same.

"This letter was drawn up and written by the counsel and concordant opinion of all the chief men of the nation, and our seals are hereto set, establishing it without doubt or discussion. Amen."

Here follow the four seals and signatures of the eight Maliks of the Syrian Ashirets.

II.

J A II.

"Notification given to all the newspapers of all orthodox Churches in Christ our Lord. Amen.

"Now be it known unto the dignity of all of you. In the year 1898, in the month of July, came —— here with a sum of money of alms in his hand. And poor people heard the report of alms, and came unto him, according to the custom which merciful people make, with a clear conscience and with a pure heart to receive from him alms according to the necessities of the time, which befell them from locusts and smallness of harvest and the like. And —— within himself had other thoughts. He disbursed money to poor people with the condition that they should adhere to Popery. And those who received moneys with a simple heart, in that self-same year were all sorry and returned from after him. And some few who remained, they too are saying unto those who returned, ' We also shall return, but at present we are eating in the name of alms.' And they who returned paid him back the moneys they received from him, and went back unto their former religion.

" And now ——— is calling himself Catholic and is putting a blemish on us Nestorians.[1] And this is evident unto all the orthodox Churches. Until a period of a hundred years after the Synod,[2] we were called Eastern Chaldeans. And Nestorius came unto St. John of Antioch and was accepted by him, and assented to us Easterns, not we to him.[3] But we, our name beareth witness, in our own kingdom also, from the time of Mar Shimun Bar Sabaï until now, are called Millet d'Nasara (the Nazarene people), that is, Eastern Chaldeans. But we are greatly astonished at this almsgiving of the Papists. Thereby it is becoming apparent to us that the name of almsgiving is being lost, and there is happening the buying of souls for the Church of Popery by money and the like. Now far be it from us. We are not hindering goodnesses and favours from merciful Christians who are giving for the needy and straightened. But our whole purpose is this : Let not men be bought in regard to religion. This is a thing above nature."

> Here follow the two seals and signatures of "The feeble Shimun, Patriarch of the East," and "The feeble Mar Khnanishu, Matran."

[1] i.e., is blemishing us by calling us Nestorians.
[2] The first Synod of Nicæa.
[3] This is curious, as showing that the Chaldeans regard Nestorius as their follower, not their teacher.

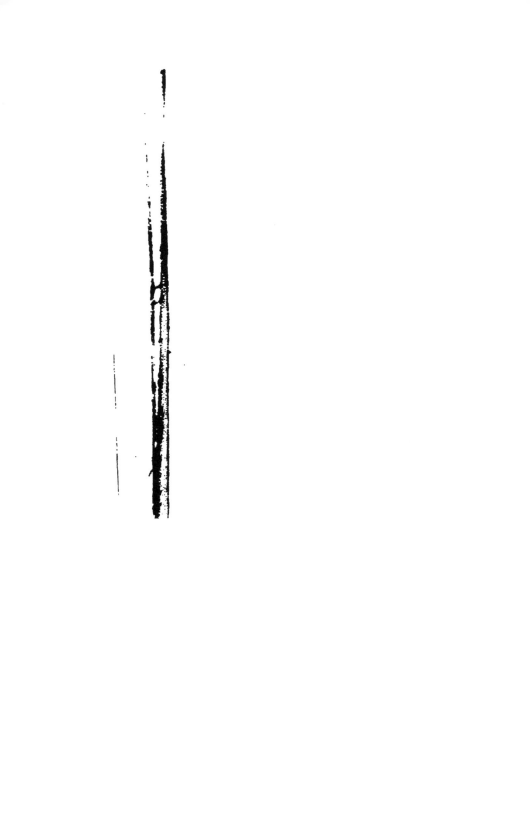

INDEX

333

THE END

Printed by BALLANTYNE, HANSON & Co.
Edinburgh & London

Books on Turkey and the Near East

TURKEY IN EUROPE. By Odysseus. Demy 8vo,
with Maps, 16s.

Spectator.—"Odysseus's book is far too brilliant to need the peculiar charm of the disowned. No one, however distinguished, need be ashamed to put his name to a study of modern Turkey at once so accurate and penetrating, and set forth with such exceptional literary talent, as the work before us. We cannot recall any recent book on the subject, and scarcely any of the older authorities, of equal or even approximate merit."

ENGLAND 'IN EGYPT. By Sir Alfred Milner,
G.C.M.G., Governor of the Transvaal and Orange River Colonies, and High Commissioner for South Africa. Popular Edition. With Maps. Crown 8vo, 6s.

Times.—"An admirable book, which should be read by those who have at heart the honour of England."

Morning Post.—" Full of brilliant writing, of picturesque touches, and of sustained interest.'

FIRE AND SWORD IN THE SUDAN. By Sir
Rudolf Slatin Pasha, K.C.M.G. Translated and Edited by Sir F. R. Wingate, K.C.M.G., Sirdar of the Egyptian Army. Fully Illustrated. Popular Edition. 6s. Also a few copies of the Original Edition. Demy 8vo, 21s. net.

Times.—"Whether Slatin's work is more important and attractive as a powerful exhortation on a subject of the greatest political importance and of special rational significance from the noble English blood spilt in the Sudan, or as a chapter of human experience wherein truth far surpassed fiction in hair-breadth escapes and deeds of daring beyond what seemed possible, it would be difficult to decide ; but the whole result is one that places this volume on a shelf of its own, not merely as the book of the day, but as the authority for all time on the great Mohammedan upheaval in the Sudan, which was accompanied by an amount of human slaughter and suffering that defies calculation."

WITH THE BRITISH MISSION TO MENELIK,
1897. By Count Gleichen, Grenadier Guards, Intelligence Officer to the Mission. With numerous Illustrations by the Author and a Map. Demy 8vo, 16s.

Times.—"Count Gleichen has produced a book which deserves to be read by every one who cares for good tales of travel, for the record of a considerable English achievement, and for a first-hand account of an almost unknown and very interesting country."

THE EXPLORATION OF THE CAUCASUS. By
Douglas W. Freshfield, F.R.G.S., lately President of the Alpine Club. Illustrated with Photogravures and Maps. 2 vols., 4to, £3, 3s. net.

Daily Chronicle.—"We can only say, in a word, that a more interesting, more vivid, more conscientious, more exhaustive, and in parts more thrilling, account of a region as yet comparatively unknown has never come before us. No record of exploration has ever been published in this country in so splendid a material form, and, beyond contradiction, no pictures of mountains to illustrate the exploits of climbers have approached the very numerous photographs of Signor Sella."

THROUGH UNKNOWN AFRICAN COUNTRIES.
By A. Donaldson Smith, M.D., F.R.G.S. With Illustrations by A. D. McCormick and Charles Whymper. Super royal 8vo. One Guinea net.

Pall Mall Gazette.—"Will be of the greatest interest to sportsman, traveller, and man of science."

Standard.—"Tells in clear, succinct, and well-chosen language the tale of a very adventurous journey."

N MOORISH CAPTIVITY. An Account of the
"Tourmaline" Expedition to Sus, 1897-98. By H. M. Grey. Illustrated. Demy 8vo, 16s.

Athenæum.—". . . Altogether his book commends itself as of great human interest, and as one of the very few good books about Moorish life."

Truth.—"A singularly graphic picture of a country and people almost absolutely unknown."

LONDON : EDWARD ARNOLD, 37 BEDFORD STREET, STRAND

Mr. Edward Arnold's
New and Popular Books.

Telegrams :
'Scholarly, London.'

37 Bedford Street,
Strand, London.

THE WORK OF THE NINTH DIVISION.

By Major-General SIR HENRY COLVILE, K.C.M.G., C.B.

With 8 Maps. Demy 8vo., 10s. 6d. net.

General Colvile in this important work includes a brief account of the operations under Lord Methuen for the relief of Kimberley, in which he was engaged prior to the formation of the Ninth Division, while subsequent chapters deal with the capture of Cronje at Paardeberg, Sanna's Post, and the Lindley affair, and the numerous engagements in which the Division took part.

TROOPER 8008 I.Y.

By the Hon. SIDNEY PEEL, Barrister-at-Law,
Late Fellow of Trinity College, Oxford.

With numerous Illustrations from Photographs. Demy 8vo., 7s. 6d.

Mr. Peel was among the first to enlist in the Imperial Yeomanry on its formation early in 1900, and his volume gives a very amusing and outspoken account of life on the march, in camp, and in hospital, as viewed from the ranks.

HIGHLANDS OF ASIATIC TURKEY.

By the EARL PERCY, M.P.

With 40 Illustrations from photographs taken by the Author and two Maps, demy 8vo., 14s. net.

'A thoughtful, statesmanlike, and deeply interesting book.'—*Illustrated London News.*
'It is an exceedingly able production, interesting for its facts and information, and valuable for its opinions and suggestions.'—*Glasgow Herald.*
'Lord Percy in this fascinating volume introduces many new subjects to our study. Geographer, ethnologist, antiquarian and historian all alike will find pleasant companionship with him. It is the finest and most instructive book of travel that has this season appeared.'—*Irish Times.*

THE KHAKI ALPHABET.

By L. D. POWLES.

With 26 full-page Illustrations and cover in colour, by Tom Browne, foolscap 4to., 1s. net.

DICKENS AS AN EDUCATOR.

By JAMES L. HUGHES,

INSPECTOR OF SCHOOLS, TORONTO ; AUTHOR OF 'FROEBEL'S EDUCATIONAL LAWS,' ETC.

A New Volume.   Crown 8vo., cloth, 6s.

FINLAND AND THE TSARS.

By JOSEPH R. FISHER, B.A.,

A NEW EDITION, WITH SUPPLEMENTARY CHAPTER ON THE EVENTS OF 1900.

Demy 8vo., 12s. 6d.

'In this book for the first time a mass of matter, previously only accessible to specialists, has been collected and condensed ; and we have a really adequate statement of the Finnish case, enforced by quotations from State documents.'—*Pall Mall Gazette.*
'A powerful and illuminating book.'—*Speaker.*

THE JOURNAL OF MRS. FENTON

In India and the Colonies, 1826-1830.

One volume, octavo, 8s. 6d. net.

Seventy-five years ago the writer of this journal married Captain Campbell, and accompanied him to India. Within a year Captain Campbell died, and his widow, after an interval, the greater part of which was spent in Calcutta, became the wife of Captain Fenton. Shortly afterwards Captain Fenton decided to quit the army and settle in Tasmania, and with this object they left India and sailed to the Mauritius. Here Mrs. Fenton spent several months, and a daughter was born to her. She then followed her husband to Tasmania, where they settled permanently. Such in dry outline is the story of this journal. It chronicles no great events, but the writer has the true Boswellian turn for vivid presentation of everyday scenes and incidents, for artless portraiture, and naïve self-revelation. She has a keen eye for scenery, but is more interested in persons than things. In her wanderings she is thrown in contact with many, and expresses a decided opinion on the merits and demerits of most of them. Altogether it is a lively glimpse into ordinary life under many skies in the time of our great-grandparents. The gossip of 1827 is history in 1901.

MEMORIES OF THE MONTHS
(FIRST SERIES).

By the RIGHT HON. SIR HERBERT MAXWELL, BART., M.P.

A new edition, large crown 8vo., with additional plates, 7s. 6d.

The demand for this volume (which has been out of print for some years) has been so persistent that a new edition has been prepared, in deference to the wishes of many readers of the Second Series (issued in 1900), who were desirous of purchasing the First. Advantage has been taken of the necessity of resetting the type to give the volume a more handsome appearance, and to make it uniform with the Second Series. Two additional plates have been included, making seven in all.

THE LONDON SCHOOL ATLAS.

Edited by H. O. ARNOLD-FORSTER, M.P.

WITH AN EXPLANATORY INTRODUCTION

By DR. A. J. HERBERTSON,
HON. SECRETARY OF THE GEOGRAPHICAL ASSOCIATION.

Paper cover, cloth back, 1s. 6d. *; paper boards, cloth back,* 2s. *; cloth boards, cut flush,* 2s. 6d. *; cloth limp,* 3s. *; cloth, bevelled boards,* 3s. 6d.

'The London School Atlas' is an atlas of general geography, specially prepared on scientific educational principles, for use in colleges, schools, and for home work. It has been approved by members of the Geographical Association, the College of Preceptors, the Teachers' Guild, and by teachers in all parts of the kingdom. The work contains forty-eight pages of beautifully coloured maps and diagrams (130 in all) and eight pages of useful explanatory text.

TRAVERSE TABLES.

WITH AN INTRODUCTORY CHAPTER ON CO-ORDINATE SURVEYING.

By HENRY LOUIS, M.A., A.R.S.M., F.I.C., F.G.S., etc.,
PROFESSOR OF MINING AND LECTURER ON SURVEYING, DURHAM COLLEGE, NEWCASTLE-ON-TYNE ;

And G. W. CAUNT, M.A.,
LECTURER IN MATHEMATICS, DURHAM COLLEGE OF SCIENCE, NEWCASTLE-ON-TYNE.

Demy 8vo., 4s. 6d. *net.*

The publication of this little work is due to the writer's conviction, gained in many years of miscellaneous surveying practice, as well as in some spent in the teaching of surveying, that the co-ordinate method of plotting traverses is far preferable to any others, on the score of both accuracy and expedition. It is hoped that the publication of these tables, which have been checked in all possible ways, may serve to popularize this most convenient method of working out traverse surveys in this country.

THE PHYSIOLOGICAL ACTION OF DRUGS.

AN INTRODUCTION TO PRACTICAL PHARMACOLOGY.

By M. S. PEMBREY, M.A., M.D., Joint Lecturer in Physiology in
Guy's Hospital Medical School, and C. D. F. PHILLIPS, M.D., LL.D., late Lecturer in Materia Medica and Therapeutics in the Westminster Hospital Medical School.

Demy 8vo., 4s. 6d. *net.*

TALKS WITH MR. GLADSTONE.

By the Hon. L. A. TOLLEMACHE,
AUTHOR OF 'BENJAMIN JOWETT,' ETC.

With a Portrait of Mr. Gladstone. Large crown 8vo., 6s.

A new and revised edition, with an additional chapter containing further talk with Mr. Gladstone.

'An extremely agreeable volume, in the production of which Mr. Tollemache's rare talents for the difficult art which he practises claim a creditably large and important share.'—*Literature.*

'Reams have been written about Mr. Gladstone within the last few weeks, but no sketch of him can approach in vividness and veracity such records as Mr. Tollemache preserves to us of his casual conversations upon everything under the sun.'—*Daily Chronicle.*

ENGLAND IN THE NINETEENTH CENTURY.

By C. W. OMAN,
DEPUTY CHICHELE PROFESSOR OF HISTORY IN THE UNIVERSITY OF OXFORD; AUTHOR OF 'HISTORY OF ENGLAND,' 'THE ART OF WAR IN THE MIDDLE AGES,' ETC.

One vol., crown 8vo., 3s. 6d.;

'Mr. Oman's book satisfies every requirement. From every point of view this work strikes us as a masterly production. The facts are chosen with consummate judgment and presented with tact; the relation of cause to effect is kept well in mind; and such is the author's literary skill and teaching power that he is able to make even the dry record of bygone party strife and changes of Ministry intelligible and interesting to the merest schoolboy. The whole work calls for unqualified praise.'—*Guardian.*

'One finds clearness of statement, simplicity of style, general soundness of historical judgment, impartiality, as well as a notable spirit of patriotism, which loves to dwell on the greatness and glory of our Empire at home and abroad.'—*Morning Post.*

POULTRY-KEEPING
AS AN INDUSTRY FOR FARMERS AND COTTAGERS.

By EDWARD BROWN, F.L.S.,
SECRETARY OF THE NATIONAL POULTRY ORGANIZATION SOCIETY.

A new Edition (the Fourth). Crown 4to., illustrated, 6s.

The popularity of Mr. Brown's works on Poultry-keeping, a list of which is given on page 25, is now fully established. In the present volume all the statistics have been carefully revised and brought up to date, and the latest developments and improvements in the industry are described in a new Appendix.

FRANCIS:
The Little Poor Man of Assisi.

A SHORT STORY OF THE FOUNDER OF THE BROTHERS MINOR.

By JAMES ADDERLEY,
AUTHOR OF 'STEPHEN REMARX,' 'PAUL MERCER,' ETC.

With Photogravure Frontispiece. Second Edition. Crown 8vo., 3s. 6d.

' Mr. Adderley has written a pleasant, sympathetic, graphic account of the most fascinating of mediæval saints. We can heartily recommend Mr. Adderley's book. It is thoroughly up to modern knowledge, and contains references to works as recent as M. Sabatier's publication of the "Tractatus de Indulgentia S. Mariæ in Portiuncula." A useful abridged translation of the Franciscan rule is appended.'—*Guardian.*

' Admirers of St. Francis will gladly welcome this little book. The story of his life is told clearly and in beautiful language.'—*Ave Maria.*

TURKEY IN EUROPE.
By ODYSSEUS.

One vol., demy 8vo., with Maps, 16s.

' "Odysseus's" book is far too brilliant to need the peculiar charm of the disowned. No one, however distinguished, need be ashamed to put his name to a study of modern Turkey at once so accurate and penetrating, and set forth with such exceptional literary talent, as the work before us. We cannot recall any recent book on the subject, and scarcely any of the older authorities, of equal or even approximate merit.'—*Spectator.*

' Whoever "Odysseus" may be, his knowledge of a most baffling and difficult subject is both wide and deep. This book is an illuminating contribution to the understanding of the history of Turkey in Europe and the character of the Turk. From cover to cover it is full of sound judgment, humour, and political wisdom, and no student of the Eastern Question can afford to leave it unread.'—*Daily Telegraph.*

' Of the many books that deal with the politics and history of South-Eastern Europe, there are but a few which can be regarded as altogether trustworthy and impartial, and the present volume is a notable addition to the number. This book is a solid and valuable contribution to the literature of European politics, and will rank among standard works on what is still the " Eastern Question." '—*Standard.*

A SHORT HISTORY OF BRITISH COMMERCE
AND INDUSTRY. By L. L. PRICE, M.A., Fellow of Oriel College, Oxford. One volume, crown 8vo., 3s. 6d.

' It is well adapted to the needs of students. It is, moreover, in the best sense popular, and should be read by all who would gain a knowledge of the subject.'—*Sheffield Daily Telegraph.*

SHADOWS OF THE WAR.

By DOSIA BAGOT.

With Illustrations from Photographs by the Author.
Second Edition. Demy 8vo., 10s. 6d.

'This is a war-book which should be read even by those who have only time to read a few of the war-books. It not only tells us what the war was like from the point of view of a hospital nurse, but it actually draws the pictures so that we see them.'—*Literature.*

'Here we have a war-book for which there is every excuse, for it deals with life in hospital—a subject on which comparatively little has as yet been written. The book is sure to be widely read.'—*Globe.*

'An able and interesting book. It is full of graphic little touches, which contribute to bring the kaleidoscope of her experience vividly before the reader in all its changing shapes and colours.'—*World.*

'No man's South African war library can be complete without this volume, which will finish off the education of him who has studied the books that deal with the march and the fight.'—*Pall Mall Gazette.*

'Among the many books inspired by the war in South Africa, few are more deeply interesting than these "Shadows."'—*Westminster Gazette.*

THE STORY OF MY CAPTIVITY DURING THE TRANSVAAL WAR, 1899-1900.

By ADRIAN HOFMEYR.

With Portrait. One volume, crown 8vo., 6s.

'A narrative full of interest, and one which will arouse sympathy, not unmixed with admiration, for a patriotic and brave Cape Colonist who has suffered much for his loyalty to the Mother Country.'—*Manchester Courier.*

'We do not know whether to recommend the book more for its entertaining or for its instructive qualities.'—*Pall Mall Gazette.*

'The book is one that is quickly read, and that is well worth reading by any man who wishes to get at the truth behind the Transvaal War. Little Englanders will do well to avoid it.'—*Daily Graphic.*

A MEMOIR OF
ADMIRAL SIR T. S. PASLEY, Bart.

By LOUISA M. SABINE PASLEY.

With Frontispiece. Demy 8vo., cloth, 14s.

'Its pictures of naval life—1819-1857—including the Black Sea operations, must have a value for scholars and historians in time to come, and are even now of absorbing interest.'—*Yorkshire Post.*

PICTURES AND PROBLEMS FROM LONDON POLICE-COURTS.

By THOMAS HOLMES.

One vol., large crown 8vo., with Portrait, 10s. 6d.

'This is a very remarkable book. We trust that it will be very widely read. It will take a stronger grip of many people than a fascinating work of fiction, for it is a "human document" of a singularly vivid and engrossing character.'—*Westminster Gazette.*

'This book contains many amusing pages, and the author is ready to see the humorous side of a situation even if the laugh be against himself.'—*Literature.*

'This is an absorbing and a thrilling book. It should be read by every observer of life and every student of social problems. Mr. Holmes has been for years the missionary at the North London Police Court, and to the admiration we feel for the work he has done there we must add our appreciation of the ability and literary faculty which have enabled him to present the result of his experiences so powerfully and yet with such good sense and restraint and absolute freedom from sensationalism. The pictures are drawn with extraordinary vividness, and the problems presented with great knowledge and treated with great judgment and good sense.'—*Saturday Review.*

MILTON.

By WALTER RALEIGH,

PROFESSOR OF ENGLISH LITERATURE IN THE UNIVERSITY OF GLASGOW,
AUTHOR OF 'STYLE,' 'THE ENGLISH NOVEL,' ETC.

Crown 8vo., cloth, 6s.

'Admirably written. We congratulate Prof. Raleigh upon what we do not hesitate to call a beautiful as well as a stimulating book, one which suggests high hopes for the future of English criticism.'—*Athenæum.*

'Prof. Raleigh's study of Milton is marked by sensitive and supple judgment, and by an uncommon sense of poetic workmanship no less than of poetic imagination.'—*Literature.*

'A notable piece of criticism. A book which it is a pleasure to read and to applaud.'—*Saturday Review.*

'Prof. Raleigh's study is decidedly the most important deliverance on Milton since Pattison.'—*Manchester Guardian.*

THE LIFE AND LETTERS OF ZACHARY MACAULAY.

By the VISCOUNTESS KNUTSFORD.

With Portrait. Demy 8vo., 16s.

'By judicious selections from Zachary Macaulay's correspondence, with no more commentary or supplement than serves to elucidate the story, Lady Knutsford has done justice to his memory, and made a welcome addition to the records of the famous group of philanthopists.'—*Athenæum.*

'Full justice is now done by his granddaughter, Lady Knutsford, to his great philanthropic activity, and it is to be hoped that her volume, which has been neatly put together, will have a considerable vogue.'—*Globe.*

FOOD AND THE PRINCIPLES OF DIETETICS.

By ROBERT HUTCHISON, M.D. Edin., M.R.C.P.,

ASSISTANT PHYSICIAN TO THE LONDON HOSPITAL AND TO THE HOSPITAL FOR SICK
CHILDREN, GREAT ORMOND STREET.

Second Edition. Illustrated, demy 8vo., 16s. net.

' It is seldom we take up a book on dietetics which is at the same time so readable and
so scientific as this is. It is the author's intimate touch with the actualities of life which
gives to this book much of its vivacity, and lightens the load of the scientific facts which
are found on every page.'—*Hospital.*

'The most valuable work of the kind which has yet appeared. The arrangement of the
work is admirably systematic.'—*Manchester Guardian.*

'A well-written and complete treatise on that most important of all daily questions,
what to eat and drink, and can be heartily recommended to all those for whom it has been
written—medical men and the general public alike.'—*Literature.*

ANIMAL BEHAVIOUR.

By C. LLOYD MORGAN, F.R.S.,

AUTHOR OF 'ANIMAL LIFE AND INTELLIGENCE,' 'HABIT AND INSTINCT,' ETC.

Large crown 8vo., with nearly thirty Illustrations, 10s. 6d.

'Mr. Lloyd Morgan has always plenty to say that is novel in his books, and he says it
in a way to be understood, even by the least expert among his readers. This, the latest
of his works, will furnish abundant matter for thought upon one of the most important
problems of modern biology, the relation of the reasoning power of man to apparently
similar attributes in lower animals.'—*Daily Chronicle.*

'The book is full of interesting summaries of recent studies of animal habits.'—*Academy.*

' "Animal Behaviour" has all the merits of Prof. Morgan's previous works. Pleasantly
written, never exaggerated, never dogmatic, never unnecessarily technical, it can be read
by anyone with the most rudimentary knowledge of psychology, and will lead him up to
the best that is known and has been thought about the psychology of animals.'—*Manchester Guardian.*

AN ESSAY ON PERSONALITY AS A PHILOSOPHICAL PRINCIPLE.

By the Rev. WILFRID RICHMOND, M.A.

One volume, 8vo., 10s. 6d.

'A remarkably interesting work, dealing as it does with that most profound of subjects,
the "abysmal deeps of personality," and yet dealing with it in a non-technical manner, so
that readers who are repelled by philosophic jargon may follow its argument.'—*Spectator.*

MEMORIES OF THE MONTHS.
(SECOND SERIES.)

By the Right Hon. SIR HERBERT MAXWELL, BART., F.R.S.

One vol., large crown 8vo., with Illustrations in Photo-
. gravure, etc., 7s. 6d.

'Whether, indeed, to while away an idle half-hour at home, on a railway journey, or as a companion in the field, it would be difficult to find a more entertaining and instructive work of its kind. The epithet "delightful" suits it exactly.'—*Nature.*

'Sir Herbert Maxwell has written a book which has more in it of the true insight and joy in Nature than a shelf of inflated essays and tortuous poetry. It is a volume of excellent gossip, the note-book of a well-informed and high-spirited student of Nature and his fellows, where the sportsman's ardour is tempered always with the sympathy of the lover of wild things, and the naturalist's interest is leavened with the humour of a cultivated man of the world.'—*Spectator.*

'The present volume is to the full as delightful as its predecessor. These notes and reflections of a keen sportsman and a keen, often sensitive, observer of Nature, are of a kind that appeals to a larger audience than any mere sportsman can command.'—*St. James's Gazette.*

NEW NOVELS.

CASTING OF NETS. By RICHARD BAGOT. Author
of 'A Roman Mystery.' Third Impression. Crown 8vo., 6s.

'There is no preaching, no bearding of the Pope in the Vatican, no lurid picture of priestly immorality—only a careful and, to our mind, extremely interesting unfolding of conflicting motives and subtle influences which tend at last to a true religious sympathy between husband and wife. . . . Its restraint and insight, its true and unforced pathos, its picturesque touches of description, and, we may add, its admirable style, ought to win for Mr. Bagot the high place he certainly deserves.'—*Literature.*

'The courage of the author is undisputed, and the ability and force with which he has denounced the unwarranted intrusion of the priest in domestic affairs cannot be overlooked.'—*Spectator.*

'A story of excellent quality.'—*Daily Graphic.*

'A really notable book.'—*Leeds Mercury.*

'One of the cleverest and sanest of recent novels.'—*Manchester Courier.*

'Mr. Bagot's story is on all counts very well worth reading.'—*Illustrated London News.*

LORD LINLITHGOW. By MORLEY ROBERTS, Author
of 'The Colossus,' 'A Son of Empire,' etc. Second Edition, crown 8vo., 6s.

'Well imagined and well written.'—*Literature.*

'A smart political novel.'—*Leed's Mercury.*

'The tale is thoroughly up-to-date. The great merit of Mr. Roberts is that his dialogue is full of "snap," and that his narrative never halts.'—*Globe.*

'A clever, sparkling, amusing, political novel.'—*Weekly Register.*

'A brilliant book.'—*The Lady.*

THE DUKE. By J. STORER CLOUSTON, Author of 'The Lunatic at Large.' Crown 8vo., 6s.

'A most diverting novel, full of entertainment and humour.'—*Pilot.*

'A clever and readable novel.'—*Speaker.*

'Mr. Clouston's novel has quite excellent humour. The story is convincingly and very wittily told."—*Yorkshire Post.*

'A really clever and amusing novel.'—*Liverpool Post.*

'There is not a single dull page in the book.'—*Leeds Mercury.*

'A capital story.'—*Gentlewoman.*

ROSE ISLAND. By W. CLARE RUSSELL, Author of 'The Wreck of the Grosvenor,' etc. Crown 8vo., 6s.

'It is one of the best sea stories that was ever penned. It is full of good character-drawing and lively incidents, and the sea!—it carries you, terrifies you, charms you.'—*Morning Post.*

'The story has all its author's descriptive power, and more than usual in the way of novel incident. "Rose Island" is a good yarn.'—*Literature.*

'One is struck by the genuineness of the sea-lore that is woven into the very fibre of the tale.'—*Academy.*

'Probably Mr. Clark Russell's best story since "The Wreck of the Grosvenor."'—*Manchester Guardian.*

VERITY. By SIDNEY PICKERING, Author of 'Wanderers,' etc. Crown 8vo., 6s.

'"Verity" will do. The story is clever and attractive enough to please even the most jaded novel reader, and he will feel no shame to his literary sense in his pleasure, for the writing and phrasing of the book are as good as its substance.'—*Pall Mall Gazette.*

'Can be safely read by the most fastidious, and comes as a welcome relief to much of the fiction now being issued. It is a love episode, and full of human interest, and will undoubtedly add fresh laurels to a very promising author.'—*Sketch.*

JENNY OF THE VILLA. By Mrs. C. H. RADFORD. Crown 8vo., 6s.

'We have read this book with sheer delight. There is freshness and originality in it. Its outlook on life is free and frank. It has qualities that lift it high above the average novel of the day.'—*Western Daily Mercury.*

'Jenny Finsel is a charming character. Mrs. Radford is indeed a true artist. The book is natural, and that in itself is high praise. The style is graceful, quiet, and unaffected; the pathos is that of real life, and runs deep.'—*Queen.*

RED POTTAGE. By MARY CHOLMONDELEY. Forty-second Thousand. Crown 8vo., 6s.

2—2

PUBLICATIONS OF THE ESSEX HOUSE PRESS.

These books are printed at Essex House, on the presses used by the late Mr. William Morris at the Kelmscott Press, which were purchased by the Guild of Handicraft. Members of Mr. Morris's staff are also retained at the Essex House Press, and it is the hope of the Guild of Handicraft by this means to continue in some measure the tradition of good printing and fine workmanship which William Morris revived.

A new type has been designed by Mr. C. R. Ashbee, and is nearly ready ; in the meantime the books of the Essex House Press are being printed in a fine eighteenth-century Caslon fount, with specially designed ornaments and initials. It is gratifying to note that the demand for the limited editions of the books already issued is steady and persistent, and it will probably not be long before they are out of print.

Subscribers to the complete series of Essex House Publications are given priority for any new book issued, and the number of subscribers is constantly increasing.

The following volume of the Vellum Series is just ready :

Gray's Elegy written in a Country Churchyard. The third of the Vellum Series. This book will be in vellum throughout, with rubricated initials, and there will be a hand-coloured wood-block frontispiece, designed by Mr. GEORGE THOMSON, of the grave of Gray in Stoke Pogis Churchyard, Bucks. The edition is limited to 125 copies. Price £2 2s. net.

An Endeavour towards the Teaching of John Ruskin and William Morris. Being an account of the Work and Aims of the Guild of Handicraft. By C. R. ASHBEE. 250 copies. This will be the first book in the new Essex House type.

The Psalms of David, according to the text of the Anglican Prayer-Book.

Erasmus' Praise of Felly. Sir THOMAS CHALLONER'S translation (Elizabethan).

The publications already issued are:

1. **Benvenuto Cellini's Treatises on Metal Work and Sculpture.** By C. R. ASHBEE. 600 copies. A few still left. Price 35s. net.

2. **The Hymn of Bardaisan,** the first Christian Poem, rendered into English verse from the original Syriac, by F. CRAWFORD BURKITT, of Trinity College, Cambridge. 250 copies. [*Out of print.*

3. **Bunyan's Pilgrim's Progress.** Edited from the earlier editions by JANET E. ASHBEE, with a frontispiece by REGINALD SAVAGE. Vellum cover. 750 copies. Price 30s. net.

4. **The Church of Saint Mary Stratford atte Bow.** 250 copies. [*Out of print.*

5. **Shelley's Adonais.** Vellum series. 50 copies. [*Out of print.*

6. **Shakespeare's Poems.** 450 copies. [*Out of print.*

7. **The Eve of St. Agnes.** By JOHN KEATS. Vellum series. 125 copies. Price £2 2s. net. [*Out of print.*

8. **The Courtyer of Count Baldesar Castilio,** divided into Foure Bookes. Done into Englyshe by THOMAS HOBY. 200 copies. [*Out of print.*

These volumes are published on behalf of the Essex House Press by Mr. EDWARD ARNOLD, and can be ordered either from him or from any Bookseller.

SOUVENIRS FROM THE HOLY LAND.

'A souvenir of Christmas and its sacred and beautiful associations at once peculiarly appropriate and attractive has been prepared by the Rev. Harvey B. Greene, who has spent, it appears, three springs in gathering and pressing, with the aid of native helpers, wild flowers from the Holy Land. These have been tastefully and skilfully mounted in books and on cards, which should please the eyes and touch the hearts of many. The largest collection, containing seventeen specimens, bears the title of "Wild Flowers from Palestine"; a smaller set of twelve examples is embraced in "Pressed Flowers from the Holy Land"; while the single Flower from the Christ Land is an ideal Christmas Card. *Bonâ-fides* is guaranteed by printed letters from the British and American Consuls at Jerusalem, Dean Hole of Rochester has written an introduction to the Flower Volumes, and Mr. Greene has himself supplied letter-press descriptions and Scripture references. But the Syrian wild flowers speak most eloquently for themselves.'—*Scotsman*.

Mr. Harvey Greene's deeply interesting souvenirs can be obtained in the following forms :

1. WILD FLOWERS FROM PALESTINE.
· Gathered and Pressed in Palestine.
With an Introduction by the Very REV. S. REYNOLDS HOLE,
DEAN OF ROCHESTER.
Cloth elegant, 16mo., 4s. 6d.

2. PRESSED FLOWERS FROM THE HOLY LAND.
Gathered and Pressed in Palestine.
With an Introduction by DEAN HOLE.
Tastefully bound, 32mo., *paper,* 2s. 6d.

3. A FLOWER FROM THE CHRIST LAND.
A lovely Christmas Card containing a Single Pressed Flower.
Price 6d.
'Consider the lilies of the field, how they grow.'

BIOGRAPHY AND REMINISCENCES.

Adderley. FRANCIS OF ASSISI. (See page 6.)

Alexander. RECOLLECTIONS OF A HIGHLAND SUBALTERN, during the Campaigns of the 93rd Highlanders in India, under Colin Campbell, Lord Clyde, in 1857-1859. By Lieutenant-Colonel W. GORDON ALEXANDER. Illustrations and Maps. Demy 8vo., cloth, 16s.

Arnold. PASSAGES IN A WANDERING LIFE. By THOMAS ARNOLD, M.A. Demy 8vo., with Portrait, 12s. 6d.

Boyle. THE RECOLLECTIONS OF THE DEAN OF SALISBURY. By the Very Rev. G. D. BOYLE, Dean of Salisbury. With Photogravure Portrait. Second Edition. One vol., demy 8vo., cloth, 16s.

Clough. A MEMOIR OF ANNE J. CLOUGH, Principal of Newnham College, Cambridge. By her Niece, BLANCHE A. CLOUGH. With Portraits. 8vo., 12s. 6d.

De Vere. RECOLLECTIONS OF AUBREY DE VERE. Third Edition, with Portrait. Demy 8vo., 16s.

Fenton. THE JOURNAL OF MRS. FENTON. (See page 3.)

Hare. MARIA EDGEWORTH: her Life and Letters. Edited by AUGUSTUS J. C. HARE, Author of 'The Story of Two Noble Lives,' etc. With Portraits. Two vols., crown 8vo., 16s. net.

Hervey. HUBERT HERVEY, STUDENT AND IMPERIALIST. By the Right Hon. EARL GREY. Demy 8vo., Illustrated, 7s. 6d.

Hole. THE MEMORIES OF DEAN HOLE. By the Very Rev. S. REYNOLDS HOLE, Dean of Rochester. With Illustrations from Sketches by Leech and Thackeray. Popular Edition. Crown 8vo., 6s.

Hole. MORE MEMORIES : Being Thoughts about England spoken in America. By Dean HOLE. With Frontispiece. Demy 8vo., 16s.

Hole. A LITTLE TOUR IN AMERICA. By Dean HOLE. Illustrated. Demy 8vo., 16s.

Hole. A LITTLE TOUR IN IRELAND. By 'OXONIAN' (Dean HOLE). Illustrated by JOHN LEECH. Large crown 8vo., 6s.

Holmes. RECOLLECTIONS OF A LONDON POLICE COURT, By THOMAS HOLMES. (See page 8.)

Holland. LETTERS OF MARY SIBYLLA HOLLAND. Selected and edited by her Son, BERNARD HOLLAND. Second Edition. Crown 8vo., 7s. 6d. net.

Jowett. BENJAMIN JOWETT, MASTER OF BALLIOL. A Personal Memoir. By the Hon. L. A. TOLLEMACHE. Fourth Edition, with portrait. Cloth, 3s. 6d.

Le Fanu. SEVENTY YEARS OF IRISH LIFE. By the late W. R. LE FANU. Popular Edition. Crown 8vo., 6s.

Macaulay. THE LIFE AND CORRESPONDENCE OF ZACHARY MACAULAY. By Viscountess KNUTSFORD. (See page 8.)

Macdonald. THE MEMOIRS OF THE LATE SIR JOHN A. MACDONALD, G.C.B., First Prime Minister of Canada. Edited by JOSEPH POPE, his Private Secretary. With Portraits. Two vols., demy 8vo., 32s.

Merivale. THE AUTOBIOGRAPHY OF DEAN MERIVALE. With Selections from his Correspondence. With Portrait, demy 8vo., 16s.

Morley. THE LIFE OF HENRY MORLEY, LL.D., Professor of English Literature at University College, London. By the Rev. H. S. SOLLY, M.A. With two Portraits. 8vo., 12s. 6d.

Mott. A MINGLED YARN. The Autobiography of EDWARD SPENCER MOTT (NATHANIEL GUBBINS). Author of 'Cakes and Ale,' etc. Large crown 8vo., 12s. 6d.

Pasley. A MEMOIR OF ADMIRAL SIR T. S. PASLEY. (See page 7.)

Pigou. PHASES OF MY LIFE. By the Very Rev. FRANCIS PIGOU, Dean of Bristol. Sixth Edition. With Portrait. Crown 8vo., 6s.

Rochefort. THE ADVENTURES OF MY LIFE. By HENRI ROCHE-FORT. Second Edition. Two vols., large crown 8vo., 25s.

Roebuck. THE AUTOBIOGRAPHY AND LETTERS of the Right Hon. JOHN ARTHUR ROEBUCK, Q.C., M.P. Edited by ROBERT EADON LEADER. With two Portraits. Demy 8vo., 16s.

Simpson. MANY MEMORIES OF MANY PEOPLE. By Mrs. M. C. SIMPSON (née Nassau Senior). Fourth Edition. Demy 8vo., 16s.

Stevenson. ROBERT LOUIS STEVENSON. By WALTER RALEIGH, Professor of English Literature at University College, Liverpool. Second Edition. Crown 8vo., cloth, 2s. 6d.

Tollemache. TALKS WITH MR. GLADSTONE. By the Hon. L. A. TOLLEMACHE. (See page 5.)

Twining. RECOLLECTIONS OF LIFE AND WORK. Being the Autobiography of LOUISA TWINING. One vol., 8vo., cloth, 15s.

THEOLOGY.

Hole. ADDRESSES TO WORKING MEN from Pulpit and Platform. By Dean HOLE. Crown 8vo., 6s.

Hole. FAITH WHICH WORKETH BY LOVE. A Sermon preached after the funeral of the late Duchess of Teck. Vellum, 1s. net.

Holland. ESSENTIALS IN RELIGION. Sermons preached in Canterbury Cathedral. By Canon F. J. HOLLAND. Crown 8vo., 3s. 6d.

Onyx. A REPORTED CHANGE IN RELIGION. By ONYX. Crown 8vo., 3s. 6d.

HISTORY.

Belloc. PARIS : A History of the City from the Earliest Times to the Present Day. By HILAIRE BELLOC, Author of 'Danton,' etc. One vol., large crown 8vo., with Maps, 7s. 6d.

Benson and Tatham. MEN OF MIGHT. Studies of Great Characters. By A. C. BENSON, M.A., and H. F. W. TATHAM, M.A., Assistant Masters at Eton College. Third Edition. Crown 8vo., cloth, 3s. 6d.

Fisher. FINLAND AND THE TSARS. By JOSEPH R. FISHER, B.A. (See page 2.)

Gardner. FRIENDS OF THE OLDEN TIME. By ALICE GARDNER, Lecturer in History at Newnham College, Cambridge. Third Edition. Illustrated, 2s. 6d.

Gardner. ROME : THE MIDDLE OF THE WORLD. By ALICE GARDNER. Second Edition. Illustrated, 3s. 6d.

Milner. ENGLAND IN EGYPT. By Sir ALFRED MILNER, G.C.M.G., High Commissioner for South Africa. With an additional chapter by CLINTON DAWKINS. Ninth edition. Revised, with Maps. 6s.

Odysseus. TURKEY IN EUROPE. By ODYSSEUS. (See page 6.)

Oman. A HISTORY OF ENGLAND. By CHARLES OMAN, Deputy Professor (Chichele) of Modern History in the University of Oxford ; Fellow of All Souls' College, and Lecturer in History at New College, Oxford ; Author of 'Warwick the Kingmaker,' 'A History of Greece,' etc. Crown 8vo., cloth, 5s.

Also in two parts, 3s. each. Part I., to A.D. 1603 ; Part II., from 1603 to present time. And in three Divisions : Div. I., to 1307, 2s. ; Div. II., 1307-1688, 2s. ; Div. III., 1688 to present time, 2s. 6d.

Oman. ENGLAND IN THE NINETEENTH CENTURY. By CHARLES OMAN. (See p. 5.)

Price. A SHORT HISTORY OF BRITISH COMMERCE AND INDUSTRY. By L. L. PRICE. (See page 6.)

Ransome. THE BATTLES OF FREDERICK THE GREAT. Extracted from Carlyle's 'History of Frederick the Great,' and edited by the late CYRIL RANSOME, M.A., Professor of History at the Yorkshire College, Leeds. With numerous Illustrations by ADOLPH MENZEL. Square 8vo., 3s. 6d.

Rendel. NEWCASTLE-ON-TYNE : Its Municipal Origin and Growth. By the HON. DAPHNE RENDEL. Illustrated. Crown 8vo., 3s. 6d.

LITERATURE AND CRITICISM.

Bell. KLEINES HAUSTHEATER. Fifteen Little Plays in German for Children. By Mrs. HUGH BELL. Crown 8vo., cloth, 2s.

Butler. SELECT ESSAYS OF SAINTE BEUVE. Chiefly bearing on English Literature. Translated by A. J. BUTLER, Translator of 'The Memoirs of Baron Marbot.' One vol., 8vo., cloth, 3s. 6d.

Collingwood. THORSTEIN OF THE MERE : a Saga of the Northmen in Lakeland. By W. G. COLLINGWOOD, Author of 'Life of John Ruskin,' etc. With Illustrations. Price 10s. 6d.

Cook. THE DEFENSE OF POESY, otherwise known as AN APOLOGY FOR POETRY. By Sir PHILIP SIDNEY. Edited by A. S. COOK, Professor of English Literature in Yale University. Crown 8vo., cloth, 3s. 6d.

Cook. A DEFENCE OF POETRY. By PERCY BYSSHE SHELLEY. Edited, with Notes and Introduction, by Professor A. S. COOK. Crown 8vo., cloth, 2s. 6d.

Davidson. A HANDBOOK TO DANTE. By GIOVANNI A. SCARTAZZINI. Translated from the Italian, with Notes and Additions, by THOMAS DAVIDSON, M.A. Crown 8vo., cloth, 5s.

Ellacombe. THE PLANT-LORE AND GARDEN-CRAFT OF SHAKESPEARE. By HENRY N. ELLACOMBE, M.A., Vicar of Bitton. Illustrated by Major E. B. RICKETTS. Large crown 8vo., 10s. 6d.

Essex House Press Publications. (See pages 12 and 13.)

Fleming. THE ART OF READING AND SPEAKING. By the Rev. Canon FLEMING, Vicar of St. Michael's, Chester Square. Fourth Edition. Cloth, 3s. 6d.

Garnett. SELECTIONS IN ENGLISH PROSE FROM ELIZABETH TO VICTORIA. Chosen and arranged by JAMES M. GARNETT, M.A., LL.D. 700 pages, large crown 8vo., cloth, 6s. 6d.

Goschen. THE CULTIVATION AND USE OF IMAGINATION. By the Right Hon. GEORGE JOACHIM GOSCHEN. Crown 8vo., cloth, 2s. 6d.

Harrison. STUDIES IN EARLY VICTORIAN LITERATURE. By FREDERIC HARRISON, M.A., Author of 'The Choice of Books,' etc. New and Cheaper Edition. Large crown 8vo., cloth, 3s. 6d.

Hudson. THE LIFE, ART AND CHARACTERS OF SHAKE- SPEARE. By H. N. HUDSON, LL.D. 2 vols., large crown 8vo., cloth, 17s.

Hughes. DICKENS AS AN EDUCATOR. By J. L. HUGHES. (See page 2.)

Kuhns. THE TREATMENT OF NATURE IN DANTE'S 'DIVINA COMMEDIA.' By L. Oscar KUHNS, Professor in Wesleyan University, Middleton, U.S.A. Crown 8vo., cloth, 5s.

Lang. LAMB'S ADVENTURES OF ULYSSES. With an Introduction by ANDREW LANG. Square 8vo., cloth, 1s. 6d. Also the Prize Edition, gilt edges, 2s.

Maud. WAGNER'S HEROES. By CONSTANCE MAUD. Illustrated by H. GRANVILLE FELL. Third Edition, crown 8vo., 5s.

Maud. WAGNER'S HEROINES. By CONSTANCE MAUD. Illustrated by W. T. MAUD. Second Edition. Crown 8vo., 5s.

Raleigh. STYLE. By WALTER RALEIGH, Professor of English Literature at University College, Liverpool. Fourth Edition, crown 8vo., 5s.

Raleigh. MILTON. By Prof. WALTER RALEIGH. (See page 8.)

Quiller-Couch. HISTORICAL TALES FROM SHAKESPEARE. By A. T. QUILLER-COUCH ('Q'). Author of 'The Ship of Stars,' etc. Crown 8vo., 6s.

Reynolds. STUDIES ON MANY SUBJECTS. By the Rev. S. H. REYNOLDS. One vol., demy 8vo., 10s. 6d.

Rodd. THE CUSTOMS AND LORE OF MODERN GREECE. By Sir RENNEL RODD, K.C.M.G. With seven full-page Illustrations. 8vo., cloth, 8s. 6d.

Schelling. BEN JONSON'S TIMBER. Edited by Professor F. E. SCHELLING. Crown 8vo., cloth, 3s. 6d.

POETRY.

Collins. A TREASURY OF MINOR BRITISH POETRY. Selected and arranged, with Notes, by J. CHURTON COLLINS, M.A. Handsomely bound, crown 8vo., 7s. 6d.

Crabbe. POEMS OF GEORGE CRABBE. Selected and Edited by BERNARD HOLLAND, M.A. With six Photogravure Illustrations. Crown 8vo.. 6s.

Glencairn, R. J. POEMS AND SONGS OF DEGREES. By ROBERT J. GLENCAIRN. Crown 8vo., 5s. net.

Gummere. OLD ENGLISH BALLADS. Selected and Edited by FRANCIS B. GUMMERE, Professor of English in Haverford College, U.S.A. Crown 8vo., cloth, 5s. 6d.

Holland. VERSES. By MAUD HOLLAND (Maud Walpole). Crown 8vo., 3s. 6d.

Rodd. BALLADS OF THE FLEET. By Sir RENNEL RODD, K.C.M.G. Crown 8vo., cloth, 6s.

BY THE SAME AUTHOR.

FEDA, AND OTHER POEMS, CHIEFLY LYRICAL. With etched Frontispiece. Crown 8vo., cloth, 6s.

THE UNKNOWN MADONNA, AND OTHER POEMS. With Frontispiece by RICHMOND. Crown 8vo., cloth, 5s.

THE VIOLET CROWN, AND SONGS OF ENGLAND. With Photogravure Frontispiece. Crown 8vo., cloth, 5s.

FICTION.

About. TRENTE ET QUARANTE. Translated by Lord NEWTON. Crown 8vo., 3s. 6d.

'Adalet.' HADJIRA : A Turkish Love Story. By 'ADALET.' Cloth, 6s.

Adderley. STEPHEN REMARX. The Story of a Venture in Ethics. By the Hon. and Rev. JAMES ADDERLEY, formerly Head of the Oxford House and Christ Church Mission, Bethnal Green. Twenty-second Thousand. Small 8vo., elegantly bound, 3s. 6d.

Adderley. PAUL MERCER. A Tale of Repentance among Millions. By the Hon. and Rev. JAMES ADDERLEY. Third Edition. Cloth, 3s. 6d.

Bagot. CASTING OF NETS. By R. BAGOT. 6s. (See page 1.)

Bunsen. A WINTER IN BERLIN. By MARIE VON BUNSEN. Translated by A. F. D. Second Edition. Crown 8vo., 5s.

Burneside. THE DELUSION OF DIANA. By MARGARET BURNESIDE. Second Edition, crown 8vo., 6s.

Charleton. NETHERDYKE. By R. J. CHARLETON. One vol., crown 8vo., 6s.

Cherbuliez. THE TUTOR'S SECRET. (Le Secret du Précepteur.) Translated from the French of VICTOR CHERBULIEZ. Crown 8vo., cloth, 6s.

Chester. A PLAIN WOMAN'S PART. By NORLEY CHESTER. Crown 8vo., 6s.

Cholmondeley. A DEVOTEE : An Episode in the Life of a Butterfly. By MARY CHOLMONDELEY, Author of 'Diana Tempest,' 'The Danvers Jewels,' etc. Second Edition. Crown 8vo., 3s. 6d.

Cholmondeley. RED POTTAGE. By MARY CHOLMONDELEY, Author of 'Diana Tempest,' etc. Twelfth Edition. Crown 8vo., 6s.

Clark Russell. ROSE ISLAND. By W. CLARK RUSSELL. 6s. (See page 11.)

Clouston. THE DUKE. By J. STORER CLOUSTON. 6s. (See page 10.)

Coleridge. THE KING WITH TWO FACES. By M. E. COLERIDGE. Eighth Edition, crown 8vo., 6s.

Collingwood. THE BONDWOMAN. A Story of the Northmen in Lakeland. By W. G. COLLINGWOOD, Author of 'Thorstein of the Mere,' 'The Life and Work of John Ruskin,' etc. Cloth, 16mo., 3s. 6d.

Dunmore. ORMISDAL. A Novel. By the EARL OF DUNMORE, F.R.G.S., Author of 'The Pamirs.' One vol., crown 8vo., cloth, 6s.

Edwards. THE MERMAID OF INISH-UIG. By R. W. R. EDWARDS. Crown 8vo., 3s. 6d.

Falkner. MOONFLEET. By J. MEADE FALKNER. Third Edition, crown 8vo., 6s.

Ford. ON THE THRESHOLD. By ISABELLA O. FORD, Author of 'Miss Blake of Monkshalton.' One vol., crown 8vo., 3s. 6d.

Gaunt. DAVE'S SWEETHEART. By MARY GAUNT. Cloth, 3s. 6d.

Hall. FISH TAILS AND SOME TRUE ONES. Crown 8vo., 6s.

Harrison. THE FOREST OF BOURG-MARIE. By S. FRANCES HARRISON (Seranus). Crown 8vo., 6s.

Hutchinson. THAT FIDDLER FELLOW. A Tale of St. Andrews. By H. G. HUTCHINSON, Author of 'My Wife's Politics.' Cloth, 2s. 6d.

Knutsford. THE MYSTERY OF THE RUE SOLY. Translated by Lady KNUTSFORD from the French of H. DE BALZAC. Cloth, 3s. 6d.

Lighthall. THE FALSE CHEVALIER. By W. D. LIGHTHALL. Crown 8vo., 6s.

McNulty. MISTHER O'RYAN. An Incident in the History of a Nation. By EDWARD McNULTY. Small 8vo., elegantly bound, 3s. 6d.

McNulty. SON OF A PEASANT. By EDWARD McNULTY. Cloth, 6s.

Montrésor. WORTH WHILE. By F. F. MONTRÉSOR, Author of 'Into the Highways and Hedges.' Crown 8vo., cloth, 2s. 6d.

Oxenden. A REPUTATION FOR A SONG. By MAUD OXENDEN. Crown 8vo., 6s.

Oxenden. INTERLUDES. By MAUD OXENDEN. Crown 8vo., 6s.

Pickering. VERITY. By SIDNEY PICKERING. 6s. (See page 11).

Pinsent. JOB HILDRED. By ELLEN F. PINSENT, Author of 'Jenny's Case.' One vol., crown 8vo., 3s. 6d.

Podmore. A CYNIC'S CONSCIENCE. By C. T. PODMORE. Crown 8vo., 6s.

Radford. JENNY OF THE VILLA. By Mrs. H. C. RADFORD. 6s. (See page 11).

Roberts. LORD LINLITHGOW. By MORLEY ROBERTS. 6s. (See page 10.)

Roberts. THE COLOSSUS. By MORLEY ROBERTS, Author of 'A Son of Empire.' Third Edition. Crown 8vo., 6s.

Spinner. A RELUCTANT EVANGELIST, and other Stories. By ALICE SPINNER, Author of 'Lucilla,' 'A Study in Colour,' etc. Crown 8vo., 6s.

Wallace. LOTUS OR LAUREL? By HELEN WALLACE (Gordon Roy). Crown 8vo., 6s.

Williams. THE BAYONET THAT CAME HOME. By N. WYNNE WILLIAMS. Crown 8vo., 3s. 6d.

TRAVEL AND SPORT.

Bagot. SHADOWS OF THE WAR. By DOSIA BAGOT. (See page 7).

Bell. TANGWEERA : Life among Gentle Savages on the Mosquito Coast of Central America. By C. N. BELL. With numerous illustrations by the Author. Demy 8vo., 16s.

Beynon. WITH KELLY TO CHITRAL. By Lieutenant W. G. L. BEYNON, D.S.O., 3rd Ghoorkha Rifles, Staff Officer to Colonel Kelly with the Relief Force. With Maps, Plans, and Illustrations. Second Edition. Demy 8vo., 7s. 6d.

Bottome. A SUNSHINE TRIP : GLIMPSES OF THE ORIENT. Extracts from Letters written by MARGARET BOTTOME. With Portrait, elegantly bound, 4s. 6d.

Bradley. HUNTING REMINISCENCES OF FRANK GILLARD WITH THE BELVOIR HOUNDS, 1860-1896. Recorded and Illustrated by CUTHBERT BRADLEY. 8vo., 15s.

Bull. THE CRUISE OF THE 'ANTARCTIC' TO THE SOUTH POLAR REGIONS. By H. J. BULL, a member of the Expedition. With Frontispiece by W. L. WYLIE, A.R.A., and numerous full-page Illustrations by W. G. BURN-MURDOCH. Demy 8vo., 15s.

Burton. TROPICS AND SNOWS: a Record of Sport and Adventure in Many Lands. By CAPTAIN R. G. BURTON, Indian Staff Corps. Illustrated, demy 8vo., 16s.

Chapman. WILD NORWAY. By ABEL CHAPMAN, Author of 'Wild Spain.' With Illustrations by CHARLES WHYMPER. Demy 8vo., 16s.

Freshfield. THE EXPLORATION OF THE CAUCASUS. By DOUGLAS W. FRESHFIELD, F.R.G.S., lately President of the Alpine Club. Illustrated with Photogravures and Maps, 2 vols., 4to., £3 3s. net.

Gleichen. WITH THE BRITISH MISSION TO MENELIK, 1897. By Count GLEICHEN, Grenadier Guards, Intelligence Officer to the Mission. Illustrated, demy 8vo., 16s.

Gordon. PERSIA REVISITED. With Remarks on H.I.M. Mozuffer-ed-Din Shah, and the Present Situation in Persia (1896). By General Sir T. E. GORDON, K.C.I.E., C.B., C.S.I. Formerly Military Attaché and Oriental Secretary to the British Legation at Teheran, Author of 'The Roof of the World,' etc. Demy 8vo., with full-page Illustrations, 10s. 6d.

Grey. IN MOORISH CAPTIVITY. An Account of the 'Tourmaline' Expedition to Sus, 1897-98. By H. M. GREY. Illustrated, demy 8vo., 16s.

Hall. FISH TAILS AND SOME TRUE ONES. By BRADNOCK HALL, Author of 'Rough Mischance.' With an original Etching by the Author, and twelve full-page Illustrations by T. H. McLACHLAN. Crown 8vo., 6s.

Hofmeyr. THE STORY OF MY CAPTIVITY DURING THE TRANSVAAL WAR. (See page 7.)

Macdonald. SOLDIERING AND SURVEYING IN BRITISH EAST AFRICA. By Major J. R. MACDONALD, R.E. Fully Illustrated. Demy 8vo., 16s.

McNab. ON VELDT AND FARM, IN CAPE COLONY, BECHUANA-LAND, NATAL AND THE TRANSVAAL. By FRANCES McNAB. With Map. Second Edition. Crown 8vo., 300 pages, 3s. 6d.

Percy. HIGHLANDS OF ASIATIC TURKEY. By EARL PERCY. (See page 1.)

Pike. THROUGH THE SUB-ARCTIC FOREST. A Record of a Canoe Journey for 4,000 miles, from Fort Wrangel to the Pelly Lakes, and down the Yukon to the Behring Sea. By WARBURTON PIKE, Author of 'The Barren Grounds of Canada.' With Illustrations by CHARLES WHYMPER, from Photographs taken by the Author, and a Map. Demy 8vo., 16s.

Pollok. FIFTY YEARS' REMINISCENCES OF INDIA. By Lieut.-Colonel POLLOK, Author of 'Sport in Burmah.' Illustrated by A. C. CORBOULD. Demy 8vo., 16s.

Portal. THE BRITISH MISSION TO UGANDA. By the late Sir GERALD PORTAL, K.C.M.G. Edited by Sir RENNEL RODD, K.C.M.G. With an Introduction by the Right Honourable Lord CROMER, G.C.M.G. Illustrated from Photos taken during the Expedition by Colonel Rhodes. Demy 8vo., 21s.

Portal. MY MISSION TO ABYSSINIA. By the late Sir Gerald H. PORTAL, C.B. With Map and Illustrations. Demy 8vo., 15s.

Pritchett. PEN AND PENCIL SKETCHES OF SHIPPING AND CRAFT ALL ROUND THE WORLD. By R. T. PRITCHETT. With 50 full-page Illustrations. Demy 8vo., 6s.

Reid. FROM PEKING TO PETERSBURG. A Journey of Fifty Days in 1898. By ARNOT REID. With Portrait and Map. Second Edition. Large crown 8vo., 7s. 6d.

Slatin and Wingate. FIRE AND SWORD IN THE SUDAN. By Sir RUDOLF SLATIN PASHA, K.C.M.G. Translated and Edited by Sir F. R. WINGATE, K.C.M.G., Sirdar of the Egyptian Army. Fully Illustrated. Popular Edition. 6s. Also a few copies of the Original Edition. Demy 8vo., 21s. net.

Smith. THROUGH UNKNOWN AFRICAN COUNTRIES. By A. DONALDSON SMITH, M.D., F.R.G.S. With Illustrations by A. D. McCORMICK and CHARLES WHYMPER. Super royal 8vo., One Guinea net.

Stone. IN AND BEYOND THE HIMALAYAS : A RECORD OF SPORT AND TRAVEL. By S. J. STONE, late Deputy Inspector-General of the Punjab Police. With 16 full-page Illustrations by CHARLES WHYMPER. Demy 8vo., 16s.

Thompson. REMINISCENCES OF THE COURSE, THE CAMP AND THE CHASE. By Colonel R. F. MEYSEY THOMPSON. Large crown 8vo., 10s. 6d.

Warkworth. NOTES FROM A DIARY IN ASIATIC TURKEY. By EARL PERCY (then Lord Warkworth). With numerous Photogravures. Fcap. 4to., 21s. net.

THE SPORTSMAN'S LIBRARY.

Edited by the Right Hon. Sir HERBERT MAXWELL, Bart., M.P.

A Re-issue, in handsome volumes, of certain rare and entertaining books on Sport, carefully selected by the Editor, and Illustrated by the best Sporting Artists of the day, and with Reproductions of old Plates.

Library Edition, 15s. a Volume. Large-Paper Edition, limited to 200 copies, Two Guineas a volume. Also obtainable in Sets only, in fine leather bindings. Prices on application.

VOLUME I.

Smith. THE LIFE OF A FOX, AND THE DIARY OF A HUNTS-MAN. By THOMAS SMITH, Master of the Hambledon and Pytchley Hounds. With Illustrations by the Author, and Coloured Plates by G. H. JALLAND.

Sir RALPH PAYNE-GALWEY, Bart., writes : ' It is excellent and beautifully produced.'
' Is sure to appeal to everyone who has had, or is about to have, a chance of a run with the hounds, and those to whom an unkindly fate denies this boon will enjoy it for the joyous music of the hounds which it brings to relieve the winter of our discontent amid London fogs.'—*Pall Mall Gazette.*
' It will be a classic of fox-hunting till the end of time.'—*Yorkshire Post.*
' No hunting men should be without this book in their libraries.'—*World.*

VOLUME II.

Thornton. A SPORTING TOUR THROUGH THE NORTHERN PARTS OF ENGLAND AND GREAT PART OF THE HIGHLANDS OF SCOTLAND. By Colonel T. THORNTON, of Thornville Royal, in Yorkshire. With the Original Illustrations by GARRARD, and other Illustrations and Coloured Plates by G. E. LODGE.

' Sportsmen of all descriptions will gladly welcome the sumptuous new edition issued by Mr. Edward Arnold of Colonel T. Thornton's " Sporting Tour," which has long been a scarce book. —*Daily News.*
' It is excellent reading for all interested in sport.'—*Black and White.*
' A handsome volume, effectively illustrated with coloured plates by G. E. Lodge, and with portraits and selections from the original illustrations, themselves characteristic of the art and sport of the time.'—*Times.*

VOLUME III.

Cosmopolite. THE SPORTSMAN IN IRELAND. By a COSMOPOLITE. With Coloured Plates and Black and White Drawings by P. CHENEVIX TRENCH, and reproductions of the original Illustrations drawn by R. ALLEN, and engraved by W. WESTALL, A.R.A.

' This is a most readable and entertaining book.'—*Pall Mall Gazette.*
' As to the "get up" of the book we can only repeat what we said on the appearance of the first of the set, that the series consists of the most tasteful and charming volumes at present being issued by the English Press, and collectors of handsome books should find them not only an ornament to their shelves, but also a sound investment.'

VOLUME IV.

Berkeley. REMINISCENCES OF A HUNTSMAN. By the Hon. GRANTLEY F. BERKELEY. With a Coloured Frontispiece and the original Illustrations by JOHN LEECH, and several Coloured Plates and other Illustrations by G. H. JALLAND.

' The latest addition to the sumptuous "Sportsman's Library " is here reproduced with all possible aid from the printer and binder, with illustrations from the pencils of Leech and G. H. Jalland.'—*Globe.*
' The Hon. Grantley F. Berkeley had one great quality of the *raconteur.* His self-revelations and displays of vanity are delightful.'—*Times.*

VOLUME V.

Scrope. THE ART OF DEERSTALKING. By WILLIAM SCROPE. With Frontispiece by EDWIN LANDSEER, and nine Photogravure Plates of the original Illustrations.

'With the fine illustrations by the Landseers and Scrope himself, this forms a most worthy number of a splendid series.'—*Pall Mall Gazette.*

'Among the works published in connection with field sports in Scotland, none probably have been more sought after than those of William Scrope, and although published more than fifty years ago, they are still as fresh as ever, full of pleasant anecdote, and valuable for the many practical hints which they convey to inexperienced sportsmen.'—*Field.*

VOLUME VI.

Nimrod. THE CHASE, THE TURF, AND THE ROAD. By NIMROD. With a Photogravure Portrait of the Author by D. MACLISE, R.A., and with Coloured Photogravure and other Plates from the original Illustrations by ALKEN, and several reproductions of old Portraits.

'Sir Herbert Maxwell has performed a real service for all who care for sport in republishing Nimrod's admirable papers. The book is admirably printed and produced both in the matter of illustrations and of binding.'—*St. James's Gazette.*

'A thoroughly well got-up book.'—*World.*

VOLUME VII.

Scrope. DAYS AND NIGHTS OF SALMON FISHING. By WILLIAM SCROPE. With coloured Lithographic and Photogravure reproductions of the original Plates.

'This great classic of sport has been reissued by Mr. Edward Arnold in charming form.'—*Literature.*

COUNTRY HOUSE.

Brown. POULTRY-KEEPING AS AN INDUSTRY FOR FARMERS AND COTTAGERS. By EDWARD BROWN, F.L.S. (See page 5.)

BY THE SAME AUTHOR.

PLEASURABLE POULTRY-KEEPING. Fully Illustrated. One vol., crown 8vo., cloth, 2s. 6d.

INDUSTRIAL POULTRY-KEEPING. Fully Illustrated. New Edition. 1s.

POULTRY FATTENING. Fully Illustrated. New Edition. Crown 8vo., 1s. 6d.

Cunningham. THE DRAUGHTS POCKET MANUAL. By J. G. CUNNINGHAM. An introduction to the Game in all its branches. Small 8vo., with numerous diagrams, 1s. 6d.

Elliot. AMATEUR CLUBS AND ACTORS. Edited by W. G. ELLIOT. With numerous Illustrations by C. M. NEWTON. Large 8vo., 15s.

Ellacombe. IN A GLOUCESTERSHIRE GARDEN. By the Rev. H. N. ELLACOMBE, Vicar of Bitton, and Honorary Canon of Bristol. Author of 'Plant Lore and Garden Craft of Shakespeare.' With new Illustrations by Major E. B. RICKETTS. Second Edition. Crown 8vo., cloth, 6s.

Hole. A BOOK ABOUT ROSES. By the Very Rev. S. REYNOLDS HOLE, Dean of Rochester. Sixteenth Edition. Illustrated by H. G. MOON and G. S. ELGOOD, R.I. Presentation Edition, with Coloured Plates, 6s. Popular Edition, 3s. 6d.

Hole. A BOOK ABOUT THE GARDEN AND THE GARDENER. By Dean HOLE. Popular Edition, crown 8vo., 3s. 6d.

Holt. FANCY DRESSES DESCRIBED. By ARDERN HOLT. An Alphabetical Dictionary of Fancy Costumes. With full accounts of the Dresses. About 60 Illustrations by LILLIAN YOUNG. Many of them coloured. One vol., demy 8vo., 7s. 6d. net.

Holt. GENTLEMEN'S FANCY DRESS AND HOW TO CHOOSE IT. By ARDERN HOLT. New and Revised Edition. With Illustrations. Paper boards, 2s. 6d. ; cloth, 3s. 6d.

Maxwell. MEMORIES OF THE MONTHS. By SIR HERBERT MAXWELL. First Series (see page 3) ; Second Series (see page 10).

'WYVERN'S' COOKERY BOOKS.

Kenney-Herbert. COMMON-SENSE COOKERY : Based on Modern English and Continental Principles Worked out in Detail. Large crown 8vo., over 500 pages. 7s. 6d.

BY THE SAME AUTHOR.

FIFTY BREAKFASTS : containing a great variety of New and Simple Recipes for Breakfast Dishes. Small 8vo., 2s. 6d.

FIFTY DINNERS. Small 8vo., cloth, 2s. 6d.

FIFTY LUNCHES. Small 8vo., cloth, 2s. 6d.

Shorland. CYCLING FOR HEALTH AND PLEASURE. By L. H. PORTER, Author of 'Wheels and Wheeling,' etc. Revised and edited by F. W. SHORLAND, Amateur Champion 1892-93-94. With numerous Illustrations, small 8vo., 2s. 6d.

Smith. THE PRINCIPLES OF LANDED ESTATE MANAGE-MENT. By HENRY HERBERT SMITH, Fellow of the Institute of Surveyors ; Agent to the Marquess of Lansdowne, K.G., the Earl of Crewe, Lord Methuen, etc. With Plans and Illustrations. Demy 8vo., 16s.

White. PLEASURABLE BEE-KEEPING. By C. N. WHITE, Lecturer to the County Councils of Huntingdon, Cambridgeshire, etc. Fully illustrated. One vol., crown 8vo., cloth, 2s. 6d.

MISCELLANEOUS.

Bell. CONVERSATIONAL OPENINGS AND ENDINGS. By Mrs. HUGH BELL. Square 8vo., 2s. 6d.

Clouston. THE CHIPPENDALE PERIOD IN ENGLISH FURNI-TURE. By K. WARREN CLOUSTON. With 200 Illustrations by the Author. Demy 4to., handsomely bound, One Guinea net.

Fell. BRITISH MERCHANT SEAMEN IN SAN FRANCISCO. By the Rev. JAMES FELL. Crown 8vo., cloth, 3s. 6d.

GREAT PUBLIC SCHOOLS. ETON — HARROW — WINCHESTER — RUGBY — WESTMINSTER — MARLBOROUGH — CHELTENHAM — HAILEYBURY — CLIFTON — CHARTERHOUSE. With nearly 100 Illustrations by the best artists. Popular Edition. One vol., large imperial 16mo., handsomely bound, 3s. 6d.

Greene. FLOWERS FROM PALESTINE. (See page 14.)

HARROW SCHOOL. Edited by E. W. HOWSON and G. TOWNSEND WARNER. With a Preface by EARL SPENCER, K.G., D.C.L., Chairman of the Governors of Harrow School. And Contributions by Old Harrovians and Harrow Masters. Illustrated with a large number of original full-page and other Pen-and-ink Drawings by Mr. HERBERT MARSHALL. With several Photogravure Portraits and reproductions of objects of interest. One vol., crown 4to., One Guinea net. A Large-Paper Edition, limited to 150 copies, Three Guineas net.

Hartshorne. OLD ENGLISH GLASSES. An Account of Glass Drinking-Vessels in England from Early Times to the end of the Eighteenth Century. With Introductory Notices of Continental Glasses during the same period, Original Documents, etc. Dedicated by special permission to Her Majesty the Queen. By ALBERT HARTSHORNE, Fellow of the Society of Antiquaries. Illus-trated by nearly 70 full-page Tinted or Coloured Plates in the best style of Litho-graphy, and several hundred outline Illustrations in the text. Super royal 4to., Three Guineas net.

Herschell. THE BEGGARS OF PARIS. Translated from the French of M. LOUIS PAULIAN by LADY HERSCHELL. Crown 8vo., 1s.

Pilkington. IN AN ETON PLAYING FIELD. The Adventures of some old Public School Boys in East London. By E. M. S. PILKINGTON. Fcap. 8vo., handsomely bound, 2s. 6d.

ILLUSTRATED HUMOROUS BOOKS.

Ames. REALLY AND TRULY. By Mr. and Mrs. ERNEST AMES. Twenty splendidly Coloured Plates, with amusing verses, depicting the great events of the nineteenth century. 4to., 3s. 6d.

H. B. and B. T. B. MORE BEASTS FOR WORSE CHILDREN By H. B. and B. T. B. Grotesque pictures in black and white, and inimitably clever verses. 4to., with coloured cover, 3s. 6d.

BY THE SAME AUTHORS.

A MORAL ALPHABET : In words of from one to seven syllables. Fully Illustrated, 3s. 6d.

THE MODERN TRAVELLER. Fully Illustrated, with coloured cover 4to., 3s. 6d.

Lockwood. THE FRANK LOCKWOOD SKETCH-BOOK. Being a Selection of Sketches by the late Sir FRANK LOCKWOOD, Q.C., M.P. Third Edition. Oblong royal 4to., 10s. 6d.

Powles. THE KHAKI ALPHABET. (See page 2.)

Reed. TAILS WITH A TWIST. An Animal Picture-Book by E. T. REED, Author of 'Pre-Historic Peeps,' etc. With Verses by 'A BELGIAN HARE.' Oblong demy 4to., 3s. 6d.

Streamer. RUTHLESS RHYMES FOR HEARTLESS HOMES. By Colonel D. STREAMER. With Pictures by 'G. H.' Oblong 4to., 3s. 6d.

SCIENCE AND PHILOSOPHY.

Arnold-Forster. ARMY LETTERS, 1897-98. By H. O. ARNOLD-FORSTER, M.P. Crown 8vo., 3s. 6d.

Burgess. POLITICAL SCIENCE AND COMPARATIVE CONSTITUTIONAL LAW. By JOHN W. BURGESS, Ph.D., LL.D., Dean of the University Faculty of Political Science in Columbia College, U.S.A. In two vols., demy 8vo., cloth, 21s.

Graham. ENGLISH POLITICAL PHILOSOPHY: an Exposition and Criticism of the Systems of Hobbes, Locke, Burke, Bentham, Mill and Maine. By WILLIAM GRAHAM, M.A., Professor of Jurisprudence and Political Economy at Queen's College, Belfast. Octavo, 10s. 6d. net.

Hill. A MANUAL OF HUMAN PHYSIOLOGY. By LEONARD HILL, M.B. Nearly 500 pages and 170 Illustrations. Crown 8vo., 6s.

Holland. SUGGESTIONS FOR A SCHEME OF OLD AGE PENSIONS. By the Hon. LIONEL HOLLAND. Crown 8vo., 1s. 6d.

Hopkins. THE RELIGIONS OF INDIA. By E. W. HOPKINS, Ph.D. (Leipzig), Professor of Sanskrit and Comparative Philology in Bryn Mawr College. One vol., demy 8vo., 8s. 6d. net.

Hutchison. FOOD AND THE PRINCIPLES OF DIETETICS. By Dr. ROBERT HUTCHISON. (See page 9.)

Ladd. LOTZE'S PHILOSOPHICAL OUTLINES. Dictated Portions of the Latest Lectures (at Göttingen and Berlin) of Hermann Lotze. Translated and edited by GEORGE T. LADD, Professor of Philosophy in Yale College. About 180 pages in each volume. Crown 8vo., cloth, 3s. 6d. each. Vol. I. Metaphysics. Vol. II. Philosophy of Religion. Vol. III. Practical Philosophy. Vol. IV. Psychology. Vol. V. Æsthetics. Vol. VI. Logic.

Lehfeldt. A TEXT-BOOK OF PHYSICAL CHEMISTRY. By Dr. R. A. LEHFELDT, Professor of Physics at the East London Technical College. Crown 8vo., 7s. 6d.

Louis. TRAVERSE TABLES. By HENRY LOUIS and G. W. CAUNT. (See page 4.)

Morgan. ANIMAL BEHAVIOUR. By C. LLOYD MORGAN, F.R.S., Principal of University College, Bristol. (See page 9.)

BY THE SAME AUTHOR.

HABIT AND INSTINCT: A STUDY IN HEREDITY. Demy 8vo., 16s.

THE SPRINGS OF CONDUCT. Cheaper Edition. Large crown 8vo., 3s. 6d.

PSYCHOLOGY FOR TEACHERS. With a Preface by Sir JOSHUA FITCH, M.A., LL.D., late one of H.M. Chief Inspectors of Training Colleges. Fourth Edition. One vol., crown 8vo., cloth, 3s. 6d.

Paget. WASTED RECORDS OF DISEASE. By CHARLES E. PAGET, Lecturer on Public Health in Owens College, Medical Officer of Health for Salford, etc. Crown 8vo., 2s. 6d.

Pearson. THE CHANCES OF DEATH, and other Studies in Evolution. By KARL PEARSON, F.R.S., Author of 'The Ethic of Free Thought,' etc. 2 vols., demy 8vo., Illustrated, 25s. net.

Pembrey. THE PHYSIOLOGICAL ACTION OF DRUGS. By M. S. PEMBREY and C. D. F. PHILLIPS. (See page 4.)

Perry. CALCULUS FOR ENGINEERS. By Professor JOHN PERRY, F.R.S. Third Edition. Crown 8vo., 7s. 6d.

Richmond. AN ESSAY ON PERSONALITY AS A PHILOSOPHICAL PRINCIPLE. By the Rev. W. RICHMOND, M.A. (See page 9).

Shaw. A TEXT-BOOK OF NURSING FOR HOME AND HOSPITAL USE. By C. WEEKS SHAW. Revised and largely re-written by W. RADFORD, House Surgeon at the Poplar Hospital, under the supervision of Sir DYCE DUCKWORTH, M.D., F.R.C.P. Fully Illustrated, crown 8vo., 3s. 6d.

Taylor. THE ALPHABET. By ISAAC TAYLOR, M.A., LL.D., Canon of York. New Edition, 2 vols., demy 8vo., 21s.

THE JOURNAL OF MORPHOLOGY. Edited by C. O. WHITMAN, Professor of Biology in Clark University, U.S.A. Three numbers in a volume of 100 to 150 large 4to. pages, with numerous plates. Single numbers, 17s. 6d. ; subscription to the volume of three numbers, 45s. Vols. I. to XIV. can now be obtained.

Van 'T. Hoff. LECTURES ON THEORETICAL AND PHYSICAL CHEMISTRY. By Dr. J. H. VAN 'T. HOFF, Professor at the University of Berlin. Translated by Prof. R. A. LEHFELDT. 3 vols, demy 8vo. Part I.—Chemical Dynamics. 12s. net. Part II.—Chemical Statics. 8s. 6d. net. Part III.—Relations between Properties and Constitution. 7s. 6d. net.

Young. A GENERAL ASTRONOMY. By CHARLES A. YOUNG, Professor of Astronomy in the College of New Jersey, Associate of the Royal Astronomical Society, Author of 'The Sun,' etc. In one vol., 550 pages, with 250 Illustrations, and supplemented with the necessary tables. Royal 8vo., half morocco. 12s. 6d.

PRACTICAL SCIENCE MANUALS.

Dymond. CHEMISTRY FOR AGRICULTURAL STUDENTS. By T. S. DYMOND, of the County Technical Laboratories, Chelmsford. Crown 8vo., 2s. 6d.

Halliday. STEAM BOILERS. By G. HALLIDAY, late Demonstrator at the Finsbury Technical College. Fully Illustrated, crown 8vo., 5s.

Wilson. ELECTRICAL TRACTION. By ERNEST WILSON, M.I.E.E., Professor of Electrical Engineering at King's College, London. Illustrated. Crown 8vo., 5s.

THE NATIONAL REVIEW.
Edited by L. J. MAXSE.
Price Half a Crown Monthly.

The 'National Review' is the leading Unionist and Conservative Review in Great Britain. Since it passed into the control and editorship of Mr. Leo Maxse, most of the leaders of the Unionist Party have contributed to its pages, including the Marquis of Salisbury, Mr. Arthur Balfour, Mr. J. Chamberlain, and Lord George Hamilton. The episodes of the month, which give a masterly review of the important events of the preceding month, form a valuable feature of the Review, which now occupies a unique position among monthly periodicals.

BOOKS FOR THE YOUNG.

SIX SHILLINGS EACH.

FIRE AND SWORD IN THE SUDAN. By Sir RUDOLPH SLATIN and Sir F. R. WINGATE. (See page 23.)

MOONFLEET. By J. MEADE FALKNER. (See page 21.)

FIVE SHILLINGS EACH.

SNOW - SHOES AND SLEDGES. By KIRK MUNROE. Fully illustrated. Crown 8vo., cloth, 5s.

RICK DALE. By KIRK MUNROE. Fully illustrated. Crown 8vo., cloth, 5s.

THE FUR SEAL'S TOOTH. By KIRK MUNROE. Fully illustrated. Crown 8vo., cloth, 5s.

HOW DICK AND MOLLY WENT ROUND THE WORLD. By M. H. CORNWALL LEGH. With numerous Illustrations. Fcap. 4to., 5s.

HOW DICK AND MOLLY SAW ENGLAND. By M. H. CORNWALL LEGH. With numerous Illustrations. Foolscap 4to., 5s.

DR. GILBERT'S DAUGHTERS. By MARGARET HARRIET MATHEWS. Illustrated by CHRIS. HAMMOND. Crown 8vo., cloth, 5s.

ERIC THE ARCHER. By MAURICE H. HERVEY. With 8 full-page Illustrations. Handsomely bound, crown 8vo., 5s.

THE REEF OF GOLD. By MAURICE H. HERVEY. With numerous full-page Illustrations, handsomely bound, gilt edges, 5s.

BAREROCK ; or, The Island of Pearls. By HENRY NASH. With numerous Illustrations by LANCELOT SPEED. Large crown 8vo., handsomely bound, gilt edges, 5s.

WAGNER'S HEROES. By CONSTANCE MAUD. Illustrated by H. GRANVILLE FELL. Crown 8vo., 5s.

WAGNER'S HEROINES. By CONSTANCE MAUD. Illustrated by W. T. MAUD. Crown 8vo. 5s.

THREE SHILLINGS AND SIXPENCE EACH.

TALES FROM HANS ANDERSEN. With nearly 40 Original Illustrations by E. A. LEMANN. Small 4to., handsomely bound in cloth, 3s. 6d.

THE SNOW QUEEN, and other Tales. By HANS CHRISTIAN ANDERSEN. Beautifully illustrated by Miss E. A. LEMANN. Small 4to., handsomely bound, 3s. 6d.

HUNTERS THREE. By THOMAS W. KNOX, Author of 'The Boy Travellers,' etc. With numerous Illustrations. Crown 8vo., cloth, 3s. 6d.

THE SECRET OF THE DESERT. By E. D. FAWCETT. With numerous full-page Illustrations. Crown 8vo., cloth, 3s. 6d.

JOEL : A BOY OF GALILEE. By ANNIE FELLOWS JOHNSTON. With ten full-page Illustrations. Crown 8vo., cloth, 3s. 6d.

THE MUSHROOM CAVE. By EVELYN RAYMOND. With Illustrations. Crown 8vo., cloth, 3s. 6d.

THE DOUBLE EMPEROR. By W. LAIRD CLOWES, Author of 'The Great Peril,' etc. Illustrated. Crown 8vo., 3s. 6d.

SWALLOWED BY AN EARTHQUAKE. By E. D. FAWCETT. Illustrated. Crown 8vo., 3s. 6d.

HARTMANN THE ANARCHIST ; or, The Doom of the Great City. By E. DOUGLAS FAWCETT. With sixteen full-page and numerous smaller Illustrations by F T. JANE. Crown 8vo., cloth, 3s. 6d.

ANIMAL SKETCHES : a Popular Book of Natural History. By Professor C. LLOYD MORGAN, F.R.S. Crown 8vo., cloth, 3s. 6d.

ROME THE MIDDLE OF THE WORLD. By ALICE GARDNER. Illustrated. Cloth, 3s. 6d.

TWO SHILLINGS AND SIXPENCE.

FRIENDS OF THE OLDEN TIME. By ALICE GARDNER, Lecturer in History at Newnham College, Cambridge. Third Edition. Illustrated. Square 8vo., 2s. 6d.

TWO SHILLINGS EACH.

THE CHILDREN'S FAVOURITE SERIES. A Charming Series of Juvenile Books, each plentifully Illustrated, and written in simple language to please young readers. Price 2s. each ; or, gilt edges, 2s. 6d.

My Book of Wonders.
My Book of Travel Stories.
My Book of Adventures.
My Book of the Sea.
My Book of Fables.
Deeds of Gold.
My Book of Heroism.

My Book of Perils.
My Book of Fairy Tales.
My Book of History Tales.
My Story Book of Animals.
Rhymes for You and Me.
My Book of Inventions.

THE LOCAL SERIES.

The Story of Lancashire.
The Story of Yorkshire.
The Story of the Midlands.
The Story of London.

The Story of Wales.
The Story of Scotland.
The Story of the West Country.

ONE SHILLING AND SIXPENCE EACH.

THE CHILDREN'S HOUR SERIES.
All with Full-page Illustrations.

THE PALACE ON THE MOOR. By E. DAVENPORT ADAMS. 1s. 6d.

TOBY'S PROMISE. By A. M. HOPKINSON. 1s. 6d.

MASTER MAGNUS. By Mrs. E. M. Field. 1s. 6d.

MY DOG PLATO. By M. H. CORNWALL LEGH. 1s. 6d.

AN ILLUSTRATED GEOGRAPHY. By ALEXIS FRYE and A. J. HERBERTSON. Royal 4to., 7s. 6d. and 9s.

THE LONDON SCHOOL ATLAS. (See page 4.)

SD - #0039 - 100122 - C0 - 229/152/22 - PB - 9781333083243 - Gloss Lamination